# Negotiating Digital Citizenship

# Negotiating Digital Citizenship

## Control, Contest and Culture

Edited by
Anthony McCosker, Sonja Vivienne
and Amelia Johns

ROWMAN & LITTLEFIELD
INTERNATIONAL

London • New York

Published by Rowman & Littlefield International, Ltd.
Unit A, Whitacre Mews, 26-34 Stannary Street, London SE11 4AB
www.rowmaninternational.com

Rowman & Littlefield International, Ltd. is an affiliate of Rowman & Littlefield
4501 Forbes Boulevard, Suite 200, Lanham, Maryland 20706, USA
With additional offices in Boulder, New York, Toronto (Canada), and Plymouth (UK)
www.rowman.com

**British Library Cataloguing in Publication Data**
A catalogue record for this book is available from the British Library

ISBN: HB 978-1-7834-8888-9
       PB 978-1-7834-8889-6

**Library of Congress Cataloging-in-Publication Data**
ISBN 978-1-78348-888-9 (cloth : alk. paper)
ISBN 978-1-78348-889-6 (pbk. : alk. paper)
ISBN 978-1-78348-890-2 (electronic)

∞™ The paper used in this publication meets the minimum requirements of American
National Standard for Information Sciences—Permanence of Paper for Printed Library
Materials, ANSI/NISO Z39.48-1992.

Printed in the United States of America

# Contents

# List of Figures

# Acknowledgements

As with all edited collections, there are many people to thank. We have each benefited from the advice and help of colleagues. At Swinburne University of Technology, we would like to thank Rowan Wilken especially for his generous and wise guidance throughout, as well as Lisa Gye, Esther Milne, Paula Geldens, Aneta Podkalicka, Ellie Rennie and Milovan Savic. Gerard Goggin deserves special thanks for suggesting a collection during a chat about the ideas in Daegu, South Korea. At Deakin University, we would like to also warmly thank Fethi Mansouri and Michele Lobo, for allowing ideas that found their way into this collection to be fostered through generous mentorship and support, as well as Anita Harris, Paula Muraca, Sam Balaton-Chrimes, Victoria Stead, Jessica Walton and Taghreed Jamal Al-Deen, who have offered valuable counsel and feedback. Many authors also have research participants to thank, and these acknowledgements are included with each individual chapter. Thanks to Mark McLelland and Andrew Whelan for accommodating a panel discussion on the core ideas of the book early in its development.

We also wish to express our gratitude to Anna Reeve at Rowman & Littlefield International for supporting the idea in the early stages and Dhara Patel for assisting in the final stages.

Many peer reviewers have contributed to the quality of the chapters, and we thank them for their often unsung contribution. And, of course, thank you to all of the excellent contributors to the collection. Finally, we wish to acknowledge the support of our families and friends. Anthony would like to thank Leila, Lewis and Edith for their patience and encouragement. Sonja would like to thank Gill, Rosie and Ari for ongoing 'Team' support. Amelia would like to thank Lillian and Bob.

*Chapter 1*

# Digital Citizenship as Fluid Interface

*Between Control, Contest and Culture*

Sonja Vivienne, Anthony McCosker
and Amelia Johns

Digital citizenship is a highly contested notion primed for critical scrutiny. With near ubiquitous use of mobile devices and social media platforms, there is an inherent tension between the promise of new modes of civic participation, inclusion and creativity, and the threat of misuse and misappropriation, alongside the risk of harm or harassment. Expectations of young people, educators, social service providers and government authorities are framed around the 'appropriate use of technology'. We are told to strive for safe, productive and civil practices in order to counter online harassment, trolling, bigotry, identity and reputation mismanagement, intrusive personal data collection, surveillance and privacy breaches. Thus, the notion of digital citizenship is invoked negatively to address problems, with less attention to the promises of creative culture and alternative modes of participation.

This book aims to challenge the prevailing normative sense of digital citizenship by exploring digital, mobile and social media affordances that, even in their risks and failings, can point towards innovation, social change and public good. Digital citizenship, we argue, needs reframing through empirical research and critical scholarship so it can better reflect the diverse experiences that constitute a life integrated with digital and networked technologies. *Negotiating Digital Citizenship* does this work by probing restrictions and opportunities for social action through new forms of *control*, possibilities for *contest* and the capacity for creative *cultures* of practice. Our definition of digital citizenship encompasses these three overlapping elements and is articulated through iterative processes, tested and contested through multiple forms of activism and reconfigured through creative expressions of identity and cultural action. Digital citizenship is not simply a set of rights and responsibilities or appropriate behaviours, but emerges as a fluid interface that connects control mechanisms with people and practices within even the most intimate of cultural contexts. Each of the chapters in this collection corresponds to one or more of these overlapping elements; but each builds and deepens our understanding of what digital citizenship is becoming.

Broadly speaking, understandings of citizenship have revolved around national identity and a list of material and philosophical expectations framed as the rights and responsibilities of a citizen subject. Some scholars lean more to measures of political or economic participation, while others consider distinct rhetorical stances (Young, 1997; 2011) spanning from deliberative (aimed at consensus) to communicative (aimed at mutual understanding). Other scholars such as Dahlgren (2006) argue for cultural citizenship that is inclusive of less formal definitions of civic agency and complexities of 'meaning, practices, communication and identities' (Dahlgren, 2006).

Meanwhile, back in 2007, Mossberger, Tolbert and McNeal defined digital citizens as those who use the internet 'effectively' and every day (Mossberger et al., 2007). Their approach emphasises participation in society through digital infrastructures and the internet. This entails three aspects of online participation—inclusion in social discourses through digital literacy, facilitation of democratic participation and equal opportunity in the marketplace. Their focus builds on the dominant US conception of citizenship through civic and economic participation, with the 'digital' as a form of arbiter or mediating adjunct. Similarly, Couldry et al. (2014) consider 'digitally supported' activity but extend the parameters wider to canvas 'storytelling, narrative, story archiving and commentary'. They also call for 'recognition' as a defining trait of digital citizenship, although this is a measure that is complicated by asking, recognised *by whom*? This question corresponds with broader citizenship debates, in which citizenship is often regarded as a tool for integrating subjects into the nation state (Marshall, 1977; Schudson, 1999). Under policies for managing cultural diversity, this has involved formal minority recognition whilst maintaining the core values of the hegemonic culture. Critics of this approach have argued that this does not meet the needs of various marginalised groups including, for example, disabled people, diverse gender and sexualities, and migrant, ethnic and cultural minority youth, who have a strong desire for increased agency and social participation beyond the bounded forms of recognition on offer (Noble, 2011; Harris, 2013).

Throughout the history of citizenship debates there is a through line to do with being 'a part of' something bigger than oneself (society, nation state, republic, city-based community), or alternatively being 'apart from' that thing (indigenous subjects, asylum seekers, temporary migrants). In the context of ubiquitous media technology, we argue that the digital is now a part of, rather than apart from, citizenship and an implicit component of new claims to cultural rights, inclusion and participation. Following calls for an end to digital dualisms that somewhat arbitrarily distinguish between 'virtual' and 'real' lives, we consider the possibility that emergent digital norms—including literacies, surveillance, resistance and creativity—are intrinsically intertwined with the fluid acts of being and meaning making that constitute citizenship. Now, more than ever, these acts traverse spaces, times and durations, creating new local and global 'scenes' in which individuals and groups can 'act and react with others', assert rights and make claims that produce them as citizens (Isin & Neilsen, 2008, p. 39).

However, if all citizenship has become inherently digitally mediated, what purpose does the qualifier serve? We consider the complete conflation of these two domains in modern life as constitutive components of a new realm of concerns for cultural inclusion and exclusion. As nation states increasingly offer public services such as welfare, medical care and identity registration via 'digital-by-default' platforms, opportunities for citizenship that explicitly rebuff the digital are dwindling. For example, elderly pensioners and welfare recipients in an increasing number of countries must engage with digital platforms to receive benefits. Similarly, a person with a passport but no digital trace of that identity will likely not be granted access to crossing borders. Children who are educated 'without screens' (as per the broad interpretation of Steiner and Mormon philosophies) must nevertheless encounter technology as they simultaneously encounter adulthood and formal citizenship. Even the rare abdication from Facebook or other forms of 'digital disconnection' from media must arrive at their decision with knowledge of what they are leaving behind. They are therefore, somewhat ironically, imbricated in the digital even after departure.

Rethinking the 'digital' in citizenship is imperative if we are to understand the complex implications for policy, governance and social and cultural participation. It is worth noting that the concept of digital citizenship, in addressing the *appropriate* use of technology, can produce caricatures of participation and damaging norms. We see this in current digital citizenship policies that are framed by often inchoate opportunities for civic participation and social inclusion, in parallel with increased monitoring and surveillance of young people's internet usage. This in turn has given rise to alternative modes of resistance as citizen users engage networked publics to renegotiate their identities and civic commitments, in the process subverting and transforming existing political and legal orders and structures. In these ways, digital citizenship creates a new interface for advocating diversity, equity of access, inclusion and the development of new literacies.

Thus, the field worthy of consideration is vast, expansive beyond already problematic boundaries. We therefore delimit our analysis in this book by categorising thematically similar case studies or approaches in three sections—control, contest and culture. *Control* considers modes of regulating or exploiting digital citizenship and the drawing of lines between inclusion and exclusion, and appropriate or inappropriate technology use. *Contest* considers cases that challenge the role of governing bodies (nation states, platform operators) and regulatory codes, often by marginalised groups. *Culture* considers performances of digital citizenship where neat boundaries are made messy and in which participants themselves may regard their contributions as having nothing to do with nationhood or rights. They nevertheless contribute to the slow erosion of social norms, which, in turn, can shift expectations of relationships between the individual and the state.

## CONTROL

As a starting point, the first section of this book explores attempts to govern digital environments or govern people through them. Digital citizenship has been co-opted by organisations, interest groups, individuals and state regulators, often in response to perceived or identified risks and perhaps in recognition of the importance of the digital for social participation more broadly. Understanding these incarcerating aspects of digital citizenship might help to prise open a space for productive critique. The aim is to uncover the term's parameters and limitations, in order to underpin critical research beyond the tenets of political and civic participation (Lutz, Hoffmann & Meckel, 2014).

We can start by pointing to the hazy idea of the digital citizen subject. Isin and Ruppert caution that 'we cannot simply assume that being a digital citizen online already means something (whether it is the ability to participate or the ability to stay safe) and then look for those whose conduct conforms to this meaning' (2015, p. 19). However, that is what we are so often charged to do once the notion of digital citizenship is invoked. More precisely, the digital citizen can be understood critically as a subject *of* power and constraints wielded by states and institutions, or even platform registration that first offers and then demands online participation while establishing the means to closely monitor that participation. The digital citizen can also be considered from a technological perspective as subject *to* the subtle or explicit forms of control built into our digital media platforms and devices. But importantly, with Isin and Ruppert (2015), we maintain that the digital citizen does not already exist but comes into being through digital acts and rights claims and through the varied and often resistant responses to the restrictions and allowances of participation. However, this potential remains difficult to realise under the often-competing pressures of platforms, states, corporations, organisations and interest groups that have very specific perspectives on what 'good' digital citizenship should look like.

To make headway in reframing digital citizenship, we need to break out of several conceptual and practical traps. The first involves a critical tradition that takes aim at the governance of society through internet technologies. The diffusion of computer code and internet protocol has long raised concerns about the new modes by which human affairs are governed (e.g. Lessig, 1999; Galloway, 2004; Chun, 2006; 2011). A strong tradition of critical internet and social media studies has followed (e.g. Andrejevic, 2007; Pasquale, 2015). A key point of this literature has been that the functional codes, algorithms or protocols shaping the internet, software, apps and devices are less obvious than parliamentary legislation but have an increasing role in shaping social interactions and digital environments (e.g. Bucher, 2012; Gerlitz & Helmond, 2013; Gillespie, 2014).

One of the unintended effects of some critical accounts of control is their tendency to abstract internet activity and social media use in order to trace its various exploits. The focus is often on surveillance or the commodification of personal data. Those perspectives do not always accommodate the tactics of the multitudes who continue to live, work and socialise digitally, and who benefit from relinquishing their data and offering up a digital trace. For instance, while we repeatedly see vocal rejection of government data collection programmes and a persistent fear of uses of personal data by governments, health marketers or social researchers, there is also willingness to self-track and give up swathes of intimate personal data through new apps and commercial social media, or through search or health-tracking platforms (Isin & Ruppert, 2015, p. 90). Likewise, open data projects do not usually seek to restrict the collection of intrusive personal data but rather put it to use for the public good, even if people remain uneasy about transparency and longevity of such projects (e.g. US Project Open Data, project-open-data.cio. gov). In response to these governmental aspects of digital citizenship, critical debate often hinges on an unhelpful dichotomy between freedom and control. While our aim is to move beyond this dichotomy, the first section of the book probes some tenets of its reach and impact, and the stranglehold it places on the notion of digital citizenship.

Elements of control also reveal themselves in the normative or commercial interests of governments, corporations, groups and individuals striving to shape social activities and behaviours within digital environments. The norms of digital society are far from settled; and the mechanisms for governance are in their infancy. The continuous manoeuvres of social media services adjusting privacy settings and terms of service agreements can leave users unaware and vulnerable when their rights and responsibilities change. This is nowhere more evident than in the plight of young people acting online, or for those with disabilities managing technical systems mostly designed for able or normal bodies, and in the intersection of bodies, health, personal data and digital participation. Chapters in the first part of the book address the currents of control that have come to circumscribe digital citizenry and the environments within which people might act together online.

In chapter 2, Anthony McCosker focuses on the regulatory, technical and educational controls created to combat 'cyberbullying' and other forms of online harassment in the name of cybersafety, where digital citizenship is problematically positioned as the *appropriate* use of technology. McCosker argues that this dominant sense of digital citizenship as appropriate use has brought into being three interconnected layers of control operating through state laws and offices, platform controls such as algorithms, protocols and flagging tools, and through educational organisations and cybersafety or security programmes. These modes of regulation frame digital citizenship as an interface involving global (platformed), national and local negotiations. In chapter 3, Amanda Third and Philippa Collin rethink citizenship as it is experienced by young people. They examine programmes and policies aimed at managing young people's use of technology, but point to the possibilities for 'digital dialogue' through an analysis of a 'Living Lab' experiment that disrupts intergenerational attitudes towards social media use and cybersafety. Crucial to any understanding of the 'process' of becoming a citizen, Third and Collin argue, is the 'time-space of the everyday'. Rather than positioning the everyday as oppositional to 'formal politics' or the real time of public events, Third and Collin follow Isin (2008), along with cultural theorists Henri Lefebvre and Michel de Certeau, in emphasising the acts through which young people assert themselves as 'claim-making subjects'.

Gerard Goggin, in chapter 4, reminds us that to properly consider digital citizenship as the ability to participate in society through the internet and digital technologies, we must properly account for disability. We create exclusions within the 'digital forms and architectures of social life', and so access(ability) remains essential to any framework that pairs the digital with citizenship. For Goggin, rights mechanisms like the 2006 UN Convention on the Rights of Persons with Disabilities 'prompt us to reconceive how we imagine and do participation and, by implication, citizenship'. In chapter 5, Deborah Lupton highlights the means by which personal technologies and intimate bodily data interpolate women directly into the realm of governance as an effect of what she refers to as the 'digitised reproductive citizen'. Digital technologies, smartphone apps and wearable self-tracking devices multiply the forms of public scrutiny in the monitoring of women's health and well-being, particularly during pregnancy. Lupton canvases both the potential overreach, but also the value that this kind of health data might have. Public commentary on our emerging techno-society continues to weave itself around these issues of risk, access and surveillance. The chapters we have grouped together around the concept of control each take as their focus the policy orientations and implications of delimiting digital citizenship. However, each also implicates those forms of disruption, resistance or subversion that mark digital citizenship as a highly contested and fluid interface.

## CONTEST

With the integration of digital technologies into all aspects of our lives, how we understand ourselves as political subjects and citizens with rights and responsibilities has undergone transformation. The growth of literature on convergent and networked publics, cyber-activism, digital citizenship and governance has seen analysis shift from viewing digital technologies as mediators that mobilise and sustain 'offline' political struggles and actions—to being the site and cultural generator of contest and claims making (Isin & Ruppert, 2015).

In terms of how these shifts have been imagined, much has been made of the materiality and metaphor of the network. Castells (1998) argues that digital networks have transformed human experience and political geographies, making questions of access and control over global networks of data and information flow, the central political conflict of our times. This has led to the emergence of new political subjectivities (i.e. Wikileaks, Anonymous) and techniques (hacktivism, use of platform APIs to contest, interrupt or work around government systems of surveillance and platform controls) and a radicalisation of democracy (Dahlgren & Siapera, 2007). Interrogating more normative conceptions of democratic participation, boyd (2010), Couldry (2010) and Papacharissi (2009) explore how our understandings of *the public sphere*, so central to representative democracy and associated issues of voice, recognition, inclusion and participation, are restructured by the affordances of networked technologies, opening up new possibilities for minority voices, narratives and representations to gain visibility and contest their marginalisation within national frames (Georgiou, 2013; Siapera, 2010).

For studies of social movements and digital activism (Bennett & Segerberg, 2013), globally networked media has destabilised and transformed how we think of *collective identity* and *agency*, enabling new battlegrounds that transgress national boundaries, and neat categorisations of state and citizen. The emergence of global movements such as the Arab spring, Indignados, Occupy Wall Street, Anonymous and Wikileaks has subverted normative understandings of the *'we'* of collective political action in a spectacular and arresting fashion. Here, it is argued that networked participation challenges hierarchical and bounded forms of political organisation (i.e. embedded in the nation state or other political organisations such as trade unions etc.) instigating movement towards transnational connection, self-organisation and horizontality (McDonald, 2015). This has been understood to provoke leaderless and transparent forms of social and political organisation, and new radical democratic imaginaries (Dahlberg & Siapera, 2007).

However, digital technologies have not just transformed the underlying architectures of political communication and mobilisation. Rather, other developments such as open source software and tools (Juris, 2005; Leurs & Ponzanesi, 2011) have reordered power relations at the everyday level, leading to a broadening of our understanding of digital cultures and agency beyond the network metaphor and opening a space for consideration of how people engage and participate with media. This puts the focus on the practices of users, who are able to resist and contest the encroachment of corporate and state-based forms of 'control' by using digital media tools to block, subvert and shape new sociopolitical imaginaries. This can be considered through actions that seek, through a range of digital expressions, to maintain the democratic possibilities of the internet or 'net neutrality'.

And yet, despite instances where digital media empowers and mobilises citizens to contest unequal arrangements of power, increased corporate, government and platform control remains a pressing concern, challenging the view that the internet has the potential to deepen and enhance democracy. Media theorists have critically examined how technical affordances shape user experiences and also interact with pre-existing socially ordering practices and norms (i.e. reinforcing gender and racial inequality, heteronormativity etc.) In particular, this has led some theorists to conclude that digital sociality maintains rather than overcomes, in most instances, pre-existing arrangements of power. This is specifically the case where 'value laden algorithms' (Leurs & Ponzanesi, 2011) and digital identifications that mark users as raced or gendered and so on continue to 'pre-structure' online interactions and the decisions of platform operators and moderators. Critical scholarship has highlighted that, most often, 'technologically determined spaces are exclusionary, white by default, masculine-oriented, and heteronormative' (Leurs & Ponzanesi, 2011). Nonetheless, this continuation of expressions of power and inequality through digital affordances and sociality has also triggered new battlegrounds and 'culture wars'.

These examples reveal digital media environments as spaces of contestation and struggle where digital affordances and tools democratise civic and political participation and facilitate social inclusion, whilst also simultaneously shaping user experiences in ways that limit users' agency and capacity to shape decisions that govern their lives. This in turn has opened up new vistas of struggle and claims to digital rights and practices. These issues are addressed in the 'Contest' section of the book via chapters that explore digital modes of resistance and assertion of individual and collective political rights and voice vis-à-vis forms of state control, legal regulation and platform governance and moderation.

In chapter 6, Eugenia Siapera traces the emergence of XNet, a citizen-led movement mobilised in Spain to contest austerity measures introduced in the wake of the Global Financial Crisis (GFC). XNet is characterised as a collective of digital activists and citizens who use a range of digital strategies to reoccupy and reclaim the political field. Strategies include Wikileaks-type tactics that expose injustice and hold governments accountable, as well as tactics drawn from ideas of hacktivism, hacklabs and makerspaces, whereby citizens reclaim power lost in the 'post-democratic' moment of austerity politics, by 'doing' and acting together. This radicalises digital citizenship and opens up a space where dominant sociopolitical imaginaries can be subverted and challenged 'from below'.

Bronwyn Carlson and Ryan Frazer, in chapter 7, focus on the capacities of Facebook and Twitter to amplify and connect indigenous voices and struggles across local, national and global boundaries. In the case study that the authors examine in this chapter—the mobilisation of a grass-roots campaign to contest the planned closure of indigenous communities in Western Australia via use of the hashtag moniker #SOBLAKAUSTRALIA—digital organising is viewed as an extension of earlier struggles of Australian indigenous peoples, firstly to be legally recognised and granted rights as citizens vis-à-vis colonial and racist laws and governing structures, and then to refuse recognition and citizenship rights that do not afford full recognition of aboriginal sovereignty.

In chapter 8, Andrew Quodling shifts the focus away from the domain of what Siapera refers to as 'politics proper', to identify social media platforms, particularly giants such as Facebook and Twitter, as entities who themselves have user bases that exceed the populations of some nation states and, therefore, whose governing strategies and regulations provoke new types of political and cultural struggle and claims to citizenship. Quodling uses the cases of 'Gamergate' and other instances where the social and technical affordances of platforms like Facebook and Twitter, which enable gender-based harassment and abuse, mobilise campaigns and actions to make platforms more accountable to user-citizen demands.

In the last chapter of the section, Sonja Vivienne outlines a case for Intimate Citizenship 3.0. When Ken Plummer coined the term 'Intimate Citizenship' in 2003—to encapsulate rights to choose what we do with 'our bodies, our feelings, our identities, our relationships, our genders, our eroticisms and our representations'—he could not have anticipated the complications invoked by the convergence of networked publics (boyd, 2014). The revised conceptual framework of Intimate Citizenship 3.0 affords examination of some constitutive networked practices that intersect across intimacy, privacy, publicness and social difference to complicate normative understandings of what citizenship means for those who enact and perform 'intimate' rights of citizenship (i.e. asserting control over embodied gender representation, birth choices and the choice of whether to live or die). This chapter foreshadows the fluid negotiations of culture that will be broached in the last section of the book.

## CULTURE

The first two sections of this book emphasise that multiple understandings of 'citizenship', as a mode of active and meaningful belonging, and the 'digital', as something all pervasive and either utopian or dystopian, making it difficult to lock down clear definitions of the emergent state of *digital citizenship*. This section of the book explores digital citizenship in practice, manifest among diverse communities in daily life, and we describe these case studies shortly. First, however, we briefly explore some of the scholarship on voice, and the constitution of collective and individual identities online, in order to offer context for cultural interpretations of citizenship.

It is now commonly accepted that web 2.0 has provided user-citizens of globally connected digital media with the tools to share, learn and create together in a manner that has dramatically shifted techno-social arrangements of power (Isin & Ruppert, 2015). This is highlighted by the fragmentation of monolithic public spheres and the emergence of micro-public spheres where ordinary citizens, and particularly marginalised citizens, can narrate their own lives and stories in the face of dominant, hostile and wounding forms of misrecognition. In this media environment, Papacharissi (2009) and Dahlgren (2006) claim that assessing modes of digital participation against traditional ideas of the public sphere misses the point; and that self-organised, do-it-yourself (DIY) forms of digital culture and community (Ratto & Boler, 2014) are significant, not because they expand modes of democratic participation, but because they enable members to experiment with alternative forms of community, representation, deliberation and understanding of moral obliga-tions and rights of the ethical citizen. For some theorists the development of shared norms and rules of participation in digital cultures and communities, even when not directly related to political discussion or activities, produce specific understandings of moral rights and responsibilities by 'investing identities through narrative; creating social worlds and communities of sup-port; and creating a culture of common problems' (Couldry et al., 2014, p. 617; see also Plummer, 2003 & Dahlgren, 2006).

Amplified by social media, networked affinity groups form publics that can attain sufficient collective voice to sustain social movements. And yet, as Plummer claims, with the fragmentation of a singular public sphere into multiple publics and counter-publics, the myth of political deliberation of equal citizens towards a 'consensus' or 'common good' is permanently undermined. Under these conditions, Plummer claims that conflict, pas-sions, emotion and intimate forms of communication are being reclaimed as vital expressions of democratic participation and citizenship. Papacharissi (2009), van Zoonen et al. (2010) and McCosker and Johns (2014) identify the emotion-filled and passionate forms of disagreement and contest that often characterise social media and digital participation as a performance that links citizenship to 'agonistic pluralism' (Mouffe, 2013). In Mouffe's theory of radical democracy, the aim of democracy is not to eradicate passions and hostilities from the public sphere—but instead various media and other institutions of democracy should allow 'collective passions . . . to express themselves over issues which, while allowing enough possibility for identification, will not construct the opponent as an enemy but as an adversary' (Mouffe, 2000, p. 103). Feelings of belonging and exclusion are central both to expression of a passionate voice and to building affinity with a collective. Thus, the negotiation of boundaries and consensus is an inherent and fluid characteristic of digital citizenship. In communities that are historically excluded from, or oppressed by, dominant public discourse, 'belonging' has higher stakes than among ambivalent or disparate groups and these minority voices are often inflected with heightened emotion. While young people are by no means a minority, their voices are nevertheless often set aside or diminished in public discourses pertinent to citizenship. Consequently, it is perhaps unsurprising that social networking sites have become popular spaces in which young people can 'write themselves and their communities into being' (boyd, 2007, p. 14), once again illuminating a collective dimension to citizen making. Even where the interactions occurring on these sites are not directly politically motivated, boyd considers the possibility that experimentation with forms of public self-making and community building respond to the call of citizenship, while subverting normative expectations and scripts for these activities.

Putting aside questions of collectives momentarily, when digital self-representation affirms self-making and individual identity formation, the inherent dimensions of online fluidity and fragmentation can become somewhat problematic. Pre-World-Wide-Web, introduced to the public in 1991, Giddens pointed out that 'the individual's biography . . . must continually integrate events which occur in the external world, and sort them into the ongoing "story" about the self' (Giddens, 1991, p. 54). However, far from popular understandings of a singular inner truth or 'story', social media makes our many inconsistencies visible. While it must be acknowledged that identity construction is an ongoing process, and singular or 'consistent' identity is accreted through cumulation of layered performances, digital technologies complicate possibilities for 'inconsistent' performances by archiving (and making searchable) a digital trace. A further clue to the postmodern puzzle of identity can be found in Giddens's caveat: 'The reflexive project of the self, which consists in the sustaining of coherent, yet continuously revised, biographical narratives, takes place in the context of multiple choices as filtered through abstract systems' (Giddens, 1991, p. 5). The 'abstract systems' Giddens refers to are largely institutional, and he acknowledges their oppressive and normative potential. An updated 'post-internet' understanding of these abstract systems might also include the mediating influence of platforms, devices, Instagram filters etc.

Giddens also attributes differential access to self-actualisation (via class, gender, ethnicity etc.) as central to empowerment and/or marginalisation. As an aside, these questions of access and the influence of 'abstract systems' are just as pertinent to collective community making as self-making. Giddens highlights the role of commodification as a standardising influence on identity construction 'since capitalistic production and distribution form core components of modernity's institutions' (1991, p. 5). This analysis demonstrates astute foresight in the context of Facebook (among other social media platforms) that are founded on market segmentation and advertising revenue. Gillespie (2010) regards Facebook as an exemplar of 'platform politics' as it conflates data commodification and negotiations with corporate interests in service of rhetoric that emphasises platforms of 'opportunity' for self-expression. Meanwhile, Facebook CEO, Mark Zuckerberg, is often cited for his assertion that 'having two identities for yourself is an example of a lack of integrity' (Kirkpatrick, 2010). The backlash against Facebook's real-name policy also illustrates the dynamic ways in which new understandings of privacy, integrity and personal coherence take shape, influenced simultaneously by institutional and infrastructural mediation and popular resistance.

Central to emergent notions of digital citizenship is the right of citizens to 'give an account of themselves' (Butler, 2005). While many scholars acknowledge the correlations between 'voice' and both collective and individual storytelling as political acts (Couldry, 2010), widespread distribution, searchability and longevity (boyd, 2010) of these narratives also make them prone to critiques of inconsistency and/or incoherence. The internet and digital citizenship forces pre- and postmodern conceptualisations of self 'out of the closet' so to speak. Queer identities have long been illustrative of problematic notions of coherence or consistency because, by virtue of heteronormativity, individuals are invariably assumed heterosexual unless otherwise defined. Similarly, gender is assumed to be binary and aligned with genitalia, chromosomes and a gender identity assigned at birth. However, for many people, lived experience accumulates to a point where these incorrect assumptions must be addressed publicly, otherwise known as 'coming out'. Queer and gender-diverse people are not alone in claiming fluid, emergent identities. When it comes down to the realities of transitioning from childhood to adulthood, inconsistencies or experiments in self-presentation are widely endorsed. Continuity is only maintained by proximity of one performance to another, or alternately, by affinity that allows an intimate audience to perceive a continual through line between differential presentations. However, while transitions from childhood to adulthood are socially sanctioned and normalised, other forms of transgression, for example, across boundaries of gender, sexual identity, faith and class, are not so widely endorsed, and online visibility substantially increases the risks of being 'called out' and further stigmatised. In alignment with some queer theory, who is looking and how they are 'oriented' must also be taken into account when making meaning out of digital representations of individuals and communities. Cultural analyses that take account of the implicit tensions between static and finite representations versus continually emergent and fluid iterations of identity over time and space, and multiple perspectives, are thus crucial to understandings of digital citizenship.

In this third section—the intersections of digital citizenship with culture—the chapters explore creative cultural citizenship as practices and processes that are amorphous, emergent and defined by a multiplicity of meanings. While many of the participants in these case studies may not regard themselves as digital citizens, they are nevertheless actively involved in reshaping digital cultures, civic participation and voice in a variety of ways. They employ a variety of 'everyday activisms' mediated by digital platforms and tools. Vivienne (2016) argues that everyday activism can be understood as the many sophisticated negotiations with disparate networks that take place in affirming otherwise stigmatised identities. Through nuanced digital self-representation and the sharing of deeply personal aspects of self in public online spaces, everyday activists can also be regarded as digital citizens, engaged in challenging deep-seated social norms. In this section of the book, scholars explore diverse sites of activism, spanning Muslim youth, young people's use of mobiles for expressing intimacy, birth rites, the right to die, non-binary gender and sexuality, maker culture and localised urban communities that curate memories of place and belonging. These chapters canvas intimate concerns and creative experimentation among passionate communities of affinity, affirming foundational work from Berlant on intimate publics (1997) and Warner on counter-publics (2005).

In the first chapter, 'Somewhere in America', Amelia Johns and Abbas Rattani draw on the case study of 'Mipsterz', an online US-based community of young Muslim 'hipsters'. They gained popular attention in 2013 when a YouTube music video of Jay Z's 'Somewhere in America', which depicted fashionable headscarf-clad young women riding skateboards, hanging out and taking selfies, went viral. Johns and Rattani consider mechanisms established by community leaders for accommodating discord within the parameters of so-called 'safe space' online. In 'Holding a Space', Sonja Vivienne, Brady Robards and Sian Lincoln, consider how young queer and gender-diverse people analyse and curate their networked digital lives and broaden the discussion to consider how researchers also contribute to the curation of their participants' identities. They call for greater use of research methodologies

and creative interventions that centre (and thereby make visible) what has previously been peripheral—selective and 'stenographed' self-representations
(boyd, 2014). Continuing a theme of digitally mediated sexuality and young
people's self-representation, Albury explores how the practices of sexting
have been framed in contrasting, media, educational and governmental discourses. Her research privileges a youth perspective and has, in recent years,
influenced reframes of youth sexuality and digital technology at policy and
education levels.

In 'Civic Practices, Design, and Makerspaces', Pip Shea builds on theories
of DIY citizenship by analysing two makerspaces in Northern Ireland and
their roles in shaping civic practices. Shea argues that tensions between individual and collective needs and notions of inclusion are crucial in grass-roots
makerspaces if they are to serve emergent understandings of cultural citizenship across a broad spectrum of social contexts. In the final chapter, Mike
de Kreek and Liesbet van Zoonen expand on theories of cultural citizenship
through close analysis of two local memory websites in Amsterdam. They
explore the ways that organisational characteristics shape online dynamics and consider how distinct modes of engagement (e.g. 'do it yourself'
and 'do it together') influence feelings of social inclusion and collective
empowerment.

As a cross section of current cultural digital citizenship, this section of
the book speaks back to regulation and surveillance and extends contest into
creative practice. A central tenet of the digital citizenship that emerges is
everyday activism, reflected in negotiations over privacy, intimacy and public
space. This activism supports emergence of another defining feature, the formation of collective communities of affinity.

## CONCLUSION

To intervene in contemporary debates threaded throughout the normative
frame of digital citizenship, this book brings together new scholarship that
explores a movement from normative frameworks and governance, through
activism and alternative models of digital participation, towards cultures of
creativity. The three parts of the collection delineate its contribution to this
interdisciplinary field: (a) control—explores norms and emerging modes of
internet (and civic) governance to critically reframe digital citizenship as
centred in popular discourse and ideas of meaningful belonging; (b) contest—
examines and underscores the thresholds of political engagement, conflict,
resistance and activism; (c) culture—highlights innovative digital methodologies and case studies that facilitate creative and productive engagement with
civil society, among participants who may not regard themselves as activist

citizens. We conclude that definitions of digital citizenship are always already under negotiation, embedded in a multi-dimensional web of power, discourse and emergent meanings. If anything, it is this fluidity and multiplicity that defines digital citizenship—the fact that it is indeed many things to many people and is unlikely ever to settle into a stable status quo.


## REFERENCES

Andrejevic, M. (2007). *Ispy: Surveillance and power in the interactive era.* Lawrence, Kansas: University Press of Kansas.

Bennett, W. L., & Segerberg, A. (2013). *The logic of connective action: Digital media and the personalization of contentious politics.* Cambridge: Cambridge University Press.

Berlant, L. (1997). *The queen of America goes to Washington City: Essays on sex and citizenship.* Durham: Duke University Press.

Bucher, T. (2012). Want to be on the top? Algorithmic power and the threat of invisibility on Facebook. *New Media & Society, 14,* 1164–1180.

Butler, J. (2005). Giving an account of one self. New York: Fordham University. Press.

boyd, d. (2007). 'Why youth (heart) social network sites: The role of networked public in teenage social life.' In Buckingham, D. (ed.) Youth, Identity, and Digital Media Volume. Cambridge, MA: MIT Press.

boyd, d. (2010). Social network sites as networked publics: Affordances, dynamics, and implications. In Z. Papacharissi (Ed.), *Networked self: Identity, community, and culture on social network sites* (pp. 39–58). New York: Routledge.

boyd, d. (2014). *It's complicated: The social lives of networked teens.* New Haven, CT: Yale University Press.

Castells, M. (1998). *Networks of outrage and hope: Social movements in the internet age.* Cambridge, UK; Malden, MA Polity Press.

Chun, W. H. K. (2008). *Control and freedom: Power and paranoia in the age of fiber optics.* Cambridge, MA: MIT Press.

Chun, W. H. K. (2011). *Programmed visions: Software and memory.* Cambridge, MA: MIT Press.

Couldry, N., Stephansen, H., Fotopoulou, A., MacDonald, R., Clark, W., & Dickens, L. (2014). Digital citizenship? Narrative exchange and the changing terms of civic culture. *Citizenship Studies, 18*(6–7), 615–629.

Couldry, N. (2010). *Why voice matters: Culture and politics after neoliberalism.* Los Angeles: SAGE.

Dahlberg, L., & Eugenia S. (2007). *Radical Democracy and the Internet: Interrogating Theory and Practice.* Basingstoke, Hampshire; Palgrave Macmillan.

Dahlgren, P. (2006). Doing citizenship: The cultural origins of civic agency in the public sphere. *European Journal of Cultural Studies, 9*(3), 267–286.

Galloway, A. R. (2004). *Protocol: How control exists after decentralization.* Cambridge, MA: MIT press.

Georgiou, M. (2013). Diaspora in the digital era. *Journal on Ethnopolitics and Minority Issues in Europe,* (12), 80–99.

Gerlitz, C., & Helmond, A. (2013). The like economy: social buttons and the data intensive web. *New Media and Society, 15*(8), 1348–1365.

Giddens, A. (1991). *Modernity and self–identity: Self and society in the late modern age.* Cambridge: Polity.

Gillespie, T. (2014). The relevance of algorithms. In T. Gillespie, P. J. Boczkowski, & K. A. Foot (Eds.), *Media technologies: Essays on communication, materiality, and society* (pp. 167–193). Cambridge, MA: MIT Press.

Gillespie, T. (2010). The politics of 'platforms'. New Media of Society, *12*(3): 347–364.

Harris, Anita. (2013). *Young people and everyday multiculturalism.* New York: Routledge.

Juris, J. (2005). New digital media and activist networking within anti-corporate globalisation movements. *Annals of the American Academy of Political and Social Science, 597,* 189–208.

Kirkpatrick, D. (2010). The facebook effect. New York: Simon and Schuster.

Isin, E., & Ruppert, E. (2015). *Being digital citizens.* London: Rowman & Littlefield International.

Isin, E. F., & Nielsen (Eds.). (2008). Acts of citizenship. London: Zed Books.

Isin, E. F. (2008). Theorizing acts of citizenship. In E. F. Isin & G. M. Nielsen (Eds.), *Acts of citizenship* (pp. 15–43). London: Zed Books.

Lessig, L. (1999). *Code and other laws of cyberspace.* New York: Basic books.

Leurs, K., & Ponzanesi, S. (2010). Mediated crossroads: Youthful digital diasporas. *M/C Journal, 14*(2).

Lutz, C., Hoffmann, & Meckel, M. (2014). Beyond just politics: A systematic literature review of online participation. *First Monday, 19*(7).

Marshall, T. H. (1977). *Class, citizenship and social development: Essays by TH Marshall.* Chicago: University of Chicago Press.

McDonald, K. (2015). From Indymedia to Anonymous: Rethinking action and identity in digital cultures. *Information, Communication and Society, 18*(8): 968–982.

McCosker, A., & Johns, A. (2014). Contested publics: Racist rants, bystander action and social media acts of citizenship. *Media International Australia,* (151), 66–72.

Mossberger, K., Tolbert, C. J., & McNeal, R. S. (2007). *Digital citizenship: The internet, society, and participation.* Cambridge, MA: MIT Press.

Mouffe, C. (2013). *Agonistics: Thinking the world politically.* London: Verso.

Mouffe, C. (2000). *The democratic paradox.* London: Verso.

Noble, G. (2011). 'Bumping into alterity': Transacting cultural complexities. *Continuum: Journal of Media & Cultural Studies, 25*(6), 827–40.

Papacharissi, Z. (2009). The virtual sphere 2.0: The internet, the public sphere, and beyond. In A. Chadwick & P. N. Howard (Eds.), *Routledge handbook of internet politics* (pp. 230–245). London: Routledge.

Pasquale, F. (2015). *The black box society: The secret algorithms that control money and information.* Cambridge, MA: Harvard University Press.

Plummer, K. (2003). *Intimate citizenship: Private decisions and public dialogues.* Seattle: University of Washington Press.

Ratto, M., & Boler, M. (Eds.). (2014). *DIY citizenship: Critical making and social media.* Cambridge, MA: MIT Press.

Siapera, E. (2010). *Cultural diversity and global media: The mediation of difference.* Malden, MA: Wiley-Blackwell.

Schudson, M. (1999). *The good citizen: a history of American civic life,* Cambridge, MA: Harvard University Press.

Young, I. M. (1997). *Intersecting voices: Dilemmas of gender, political philosophy, and policy.* Princeton: Princeton University Press.

Young, I. M. (2011). *Justice and the Politics of Difference.* Princeton: Princeton University Press.

van Zoonen, L., Vis, F., & Mihelj, S. (2010). Performing citizenship on YouTube: Activism, satire and online debate around the anti-Islam video Fitna. *Critical Discourse Studies, 7*(4), 249–262.

Vivienne, S. (2016). *Digital identity and everyday activism: Sharing private stories with networked publics.* London: Palgrave Macmillan.

Warner, M. (2005). *Publics and counterpublics.* New York: Zone Books.

*Part I*

# CONTROL

*Chapter 2*

# Managing Cyberbullying

## *The Three Layers of Control in Digital Citizenship*

### Anthony McCosker

In recent years, cyberbullying, online abuse and harassment and related 'misuses' of social media have generated new laws and platform controls, and stimulated the development of countless cybersafety educational programmes. Where harms like youth suicide can be identified, strong reactions follow. One prominent example in the United States is the case of Megan Meier, who in October 2006 committed suicide after weeks of coordinated and sustained online harassment. This incident led to tougher anti-cyberbullying laws in Missouri and sparked national debate about the harms of online harassment.[1] As a result of cases like this, a range of cybersafety measures have emerged around the world to curb what are seen as the ultimate dangers of social media use. The story of cybersafety is intimately bound to the idea of digital citizenship as the ability to participate in society online, but also to norms and assumptions regarding the 'appropriate' use of networked technologies. In the name of security and safety, young people, families and educational institutions have been allocated a growing role in regulating digital environments. At stake in these developments is the openness of the internet, its productive potential, and the utility of social media platforms. Behind the public concerns lies a certain ideal regarding what digital citizenship might be.

In this chapter, I look at how digital citizenship has predominantly (but not irreversibly) come to function as a concept of appropriate internet use. Enthusiasm in the concept often follows attempts to manage online activity through emerging laws of *state regulation*, alongside *platform controls* in the form of technical codes and monitoring and flagging tools, and the application of social norms through *educational programs*. These three layers of control are difficult to map as they operate globally, transnationally, nationally and locally. Each layer wavers between governance by code (whether law or software, algorithm and protocol) and governance by design (including norms and social codes of practice). Mapping these layers of control can help to clarify the digital and geopolitical ecologies through which negotiations of digital citizenship are taking place.

I begin this mapping work by comparing national cybersafety regulation targeting young people's well-being through issues of harassment and cyberbullying. Recent Australian regulation, with the establishment of an office of the Children's eSafety Commissioner, applies national law in an attempt to govern local uses of global social media services. To understand the role of social media platforms and internet corporations such as Facebook, Twitter, Microsoft or Google, I point to the control delivered through algorithms and code and through tools like flags that help to police platform usage. In the final section, I review US- and UK-based digital citizenship and cybersafety programmes, in addition to the eSmart cybersafety programmes run in many Australian schools, by the Alannah and Madeline Foundation. The examples point to the varied ways digital citizenship continues to be negotiated across three complex, interconnected layers of control that work together to constitute, shape and manage our social media ecologies.

In a significant US report on *Child Safety and Online Technologies*, safety is parsed into several key areas of public concern (Palfrey, boyd & Sacco, 2010). As the report was commissioned by a joint State Attorney Generals' Multi-State Working Group on Social Networking, it foregrounded three familiar spheres of law, order and governance: the 'dangers of sexual solicitation, online harassment, bullying, and exposure to problematic and illegal content' (Palfrey, boyd & Sacco, 2010, p. 4). Because the specific aim was to 'determine the extent to which today's technologies could help to address these online safety risks', the taskforce included a long list of internet service providers, social media companies and other technology corporations (p. 4). The report provided many insights through a review of research and user statistics and mirrored popular public concerns emerging at that time around the growing ubiquity of social media and connected mobile devices. One of its salient assertions was that 'too little is known about the interplay among risks and the role that minors themselves play in contributing to unsafe environments' (p. 5).

While there has been a long history of research targeting young people's 'exposure' to various 'risks' of 'problematic' media content in many media contexts, reaching back to the introduction of comics, cinema, television and video and digital games, the shift comes with the distributed and interactional base of online media. Young people themselves are considered part of the problem as content contributors. As a response, the tech-influenced task force cautioned 'against overreliance on technology in isolation or on a single technological approach', placing emphasis on the responsibilities of young people, parents and schools rather than the platforms and systems engineers or new state laws (Palfrey, boyd & Sacco, 2010, p. 6). For the *Child Safety* report, the Attorney Generals sought technological solutions, but the task force fell back on 'multi-faceted measures' that rely heavily on individual responsibilities and education. Whether explicitly or implicitly, the *Child Safety* report and similar 'safety' reviews around the world call into being what has come to be known as the digital citizen.

Research examining young people and mobile, networked and social media use has often followed suit, and to varying degrees emphasises risk, vulnerability and safety, but also offers a more positive focus on the promises of stronger, empowered civic engagement and political participation alongside new modes of digital literacy. Though variously labelled 'young networked citizen', 'wired youth' or 'mediated youth participation' (Livingstone, 2002; Livingstone et al., 2011; Mesch & Talmud, 2010; Loader, Vromen & Xenos, 2014; Collin, 2015), there is a sense that young people bear the weight of negotiations over emerging forms and ideals of digital citizenship. This is because of the holistic and integrated play of identity, social relations, cultural contexts, media devices and social media platforms that have come to be associated with young people's digital cultures.

Recent empirical studies have sought to define the prevalence of online harassment. In the United States, Pew research has shown that the majority of internet users (73%) have witnessed forms of online harassment, and 40% of all internet users report experiencing at least one form of harassment, ranging from insults to stalking and sexual abuse (Pew Research Centre, 2015). Attempts to define and conceptualise online hate and harassment have a long detailed history that follows changing media forms and evolving nomenclature, reaching at least as far back as Dery's 1994 collection of essays on the culture of *Flamewars* (Dery, 1994; see also McCosker, 2014). But concepts and definitions have a 'slipperiness' that makes consistency of analysis difficult. As Miltner notes, 'Being a hater is definitely not the same thing as being a troll, and while bullies and trolls are frequently collapsed into the same category, they have different definitions and are largely carried out by different groups of people' (Shepherd et al., 2015, p. 4). Meanwhile, beyond these problematic attempts to give flesh and bones (or profiles) to these imagined 'figures of hate', certain digitally mediated *acts* have given rise to a trajectory of regulation and social intervention in the name of safety or security.[2] Defined generally as 'sending or posting harmful or cruel text or images using the Internet or other digital communication devices', cyberbullying has thus driven the development of cybersafety programmes and new forms of hard or soft government control (Li, Cross & Smith, 2012, p. 6). A more precise definition, which extends traditional or offline bullying research, emphasises repetition and power imbalance: 'An aggressive act or behaviour that is carried out using electronic means by a group or an individual repeatedly and over time against a victim who cannot easily defend him or herself' (Smith et al., 2008, p. 378; Smith, Steffgen & Sittichai, 2013).

In the last ten years, cybersafety has emerged as a point of intervention bound up with educational initiatives and public policy around child safety and at least to some extent health and well-being, targeting young people's digital media use as a way of redressing risks and harms (Swist et al., 2015). In this context, cyberbullying persists as a dominant category of digitally mediated violence or harm and designates a particular set of actions and interactions that make an explicit call for the need to protect young people, and hence to regulate online environments. In many ways, young people have been positioned through cybersafety and cyberbullying as a kind of interface for governmental processes aimed at producing and maintaining good society and compliant citizenship. A deficit or not-yet-citizen status is assumed of young internet users. Following White and Wyn (2004), Philippa Collin characterises 'adolescence as a "project of modernity", fundamentally oriented towards the production of good, rational, productive citizens', a project that is underpinned by a 'deficit approach to youth citizenship whereby young people are situated as "citizens-in-the-making"' (Owen, 1996; Collin, 2015, p. 7; these issues are taken up critically and in greater detail in the next chapter). Even in programmes and policies aimed at fostering cybersafety, we see the prescription of a social good oriented around desirable behaviours and sanctioned uses of digital communication technologies. This is accompanied by a persistent idea that 'the social' should be rational, conflict and risk free.

The ideal of citizenship can be both limiting and liberating. Drawing on Arendt, and reflecting a growing body of critical citizenship scholarship, Azoulay talks of the 'civil condition' and citizenship as an *interface* rather than as a thing, an ideal or an essence (2015, p. 105). Azoulay's context concerns national, cultural and religious conflicts in the Middle East, but the idea of citizenship as interface also applies to the boundaries that young people and children traverse as (digital) citizens-in-the-making. While citizenship generally denotes fixed borders, inclusions and exclusions and the impositions of a sovereign nation state, to conceive of citizenship as an interface highlights the liminal, uncertain and contested identities many experience. This means moving away from those strictly legal meanings to include the cultural negotiations of citizenship (Hartley, 2012). And we should not underestimate the role of subversion, of 'acting up' or the 'silly citizenship' of digitally mediated cultures and practices (Hartley, 2012). Digital domains are inherently agonistic, never free of antagonism, conflict and cultural negotiations (Van Zoonen, Vis & Mihelji, 2011; McCosker, 2014). How that conflict is managed remains highly contested but also central to emerging notions of digital citizenship and the technical codes, laws and educational programmes staged in its name.

Attending to 'acts of citizenship' (Isin & Nielsen, 2008) is vital for considering the role of the digital in negotiations of citizenship, and for understanding the sites at which those negotiations take place. Isin and Ruppert (2015) have sought to disrupt the concept of digital citizenship by looking to the digital acts that are 'refashioning, inventing, and making up citizen *subjects* through the play of obedience, submission, and subversion' (p. 77). We also have to define the material contexts, the national, platformed and local sites in or across which these acts take place.

The management of digital acts takes place through the constantly evolving features, tools and affordances at play within social media platforms and operating systems. But it also involves organisations charged with developing digital literacy or promoting strategies for digital well-being and self-care in local social contexts like workplaces, schools or families. Before I examine those sites of control and management, I will look at the move from security and safety towards governmental frameworks for digital citizenship. Nation states are showing an increasing willingness to intervene by applying legislative forms of control. The triggers for such control have traditionally concerned security and sovereignty, along with safety, but are also now associated with more 'productive' governance measures in the name of health and well-being, particularly for children and young people.

## GOVERNING DIGITAL CITIZENSHIP AS APPROPRIATE TECHNOLOGY USE

In the name of security—in the sense of national sovereignty and civil law and order—governments and technology corporations wield significant power over internet infrastructure and applications, in the management of broadband access, data surveillance, internet filtering and censorship, and increasing controls on social media activity, rights and freedoms. As Cuiker and Mayer-Shönberger (2013) point out, successive historical developments in information and media technologies reaching back to the printing press have brought about massive changes to the way we govern ourselves. At the broad level of internet governance, the movement between cybersecurity and cybersafety tells us something about the emergence of the concept of digital citizenship and its specific social concerns. Concerns with security have a longer history that parallels historical moments of computer and internet innovation (Parikka, 2007).

The connection between security and safety is not always obvious, but illustrates the role of nation states in managing internet and social media use as digital citizenship. Cybersecurity refers to potential damage or misuse of infrastructure, hardware and software, or theft of information and data, network disruptions and misdirection, DDoS attacks, identity-information theft or breech (especially financial), spam, malware and so on. Around cybersecurity, governments have for many years devised strict regulation. Cybersecurity addresses harm in relation to national sovereignty or transnational law, construing particular kinds of *bad* digital citizenship tied to the nation state's sovereign power, global commerce and international trade. Whereas cyber-*safety* deals with the potential harms associated with internet, social media and technology use that take in a broader set of social behaviours and norms, usually targeting children and young people. As Livingstone points out, the harms and risks associated with cybersafety are tied to 'societal conceptions of childhood—particularly in relation to the place of sexuality and violence in childhood', and are far more difficult to define (Livingstone, 2013). In the name of safety, cyberbullying laws and programmes call for law, order and control over internet use, but do so by shifting responsibility from states to schools, families and young people as citizens.

In the United States, the *Children's Internet Protection Act, 2000*, provides an early example of the way safety has been regulated. This law targets learning institutions: US state schools are only eligible for 'E-Rate' programme funding if internet safety programmes have been put in place alongside technical measures for filtering 'obscene or harmful content'.[3] Nearly all US states have passed laws addressing online harassment and cyberbullying, often responding to high-profile cases of suicide (Hinduja & Patchin, 2016). Seeking to extend controls nationally, the *SAFE Internet Act 2009* was introduced to US Congress but, like many such bills, was not enacted. The bill sought to sanction online harassment and stalking by making individual citizens more directly responsible for 'any communication, with the intent to coerce, intimidate, harass, or cause substantial emotional distress to a person, using electronic means to support severe, repeated, and hostile behavior'; and the bill proposed $175 million in funding for cybersafety education programmes.[4] Not surprisingly, this was a proposal that Google publicly supported, no doubt seeing a chance for access to public funds to provide educational material.

Unlike children's specific internet protection laws in the United States, in the United Kingdom there are no designated laws. Rather, harassment and stalking are sanctioned by parts of the *Malicious Communications Act 1988*, the *Communications Act 2003*, the *Protection from Harassment Act 1997* and the *Crime and Disorder Act 1998* (European Commission, 2015; The Cybersmile Foundation, 2015).[5] This approach brings concerns with safety into cybersecurity instruments or established criminal law and makes specific reference to the use of online communication in acts of harassment and stalking.

Recent Australian legislation attempts to find a middle ground by addressing cybersafety through the newly created Office of the Children's eSafety Commissioner, created by the *Enhancing Online Safety for Children Act 2015* (the Act).[6] The remit of the office is to provide information, education and resources covering typical aspects of cybersafety, positioning digital citizenship as a set of activities, behaviours and associated 'risks': balancing online time, cyberbullying, online gaming, sharing of personal images, protecting personal information, sexting, digital reputation, offensive or illegal content, trolling and unwanted contact. But further to this, in addition to existing harassment and stalking laws under Section 474.15 and 474.17 of the *Criminal Code Act 1995*, and a range of state laws, the office establishes a process whereby Australian children under 18 (or parent/guardian of a child) can report cyberbullying and Australian residents can make a complaint about offensive online content. The office and the commissioner act to intervene on behalf of Australian citizens under 18 where a valid complaint is made and not acted on by platforms or individuals within 48 hours.

The Act regulates cyberbullying actions where an ordinary person would conclude that 'the material would be likely to have the effect on the Australian child of seriously threatening, seriously intimidating, seriously harassing or seriously humiliating the Australian child' (s 5). As a key part of the office's strategy, the Act establishes a two-tier scheme into which social media services are placed.[7] Any social media service can apply to be categorised as a Tier 1 partner indicating greater trust and collaboration with the office. Current Tier 1 partners include Ask.fm, Flickr, Twitter, Yahoo7 Answers, Yahoo7 Groups, presumably for their moderation practices or explicit commitment to safety. Tier 2 social media services include Facebook, Google+, Instagram and YouTube; 'Tier 2 is a civil enforcement scheme that can attract legally binding notices and penalties' (Office of the Children's eSafety Commissioner, 2016). For individuals who do not comply with end-user takedown notices (e.g. for offensive material), civil penalties can be applied. However, under Section 40 of the Act, for non-compliant social media service providers, the commissioner can only 'draft and publish a notice on the Office's website to that effect'.

The Act aims for cooperation through a partnership system rather than applying penalties and sanctions. The lack of teeth in dealing with social media corporations, and structure of sanctions, means that this regulatory move continues to place responsibility mainly with young people and their guardians to self-manage their social media use, with some light pressure on platforms to enforce their own community standards. However, this initiative accelerates the push for *national* avenues for imposing legal constraints and remedies for activities taking place within social media sites and platforms based in other jurisdictions.

## PLATFORMED CONTROL: SEARCHING
## FOR TECHNICAL SOLUTIONS

The global character of social media platforms and content flows challenges the whole basis of the governance of digital acts and platforms through state regulation. Many online safety advocates thus look to the dominant social media corporations and platforms to find technical solutions, while those corporations' interests are often bound to notions of 'openness' and so they resist intervention. Like other platforms, Facebook operates almost seamlessly across national borders, with notable restrictions such as its ban in China; hence, it creates new geographies for social action and interaction. Notions of digital citizenship push against the internet corporations' desire to become global social utilities. Google's privacy battles in Europe, or Facebook's struggle to implement Free Basics in India circumventing net neutrality principles, are reminders that national borders still matter. Nonetheless, social media corporations deliberately evoke the language and politics of *platforms* to represent themselves as social utilities that provide a public good, by operating with objective, value-free principles of neutrality (Gillespie, 2010).

Major internet corporations do have a stake in publicly articulating notions of digital citizenship and literacy; but ironically, they are heavily invested in advocating behavioural and social responses rather than technical ones. Microsoft and Google offer good examples. In its 2011 whitepaper *Fostering Digital Citizenship*, Microsoft offers a definition of digital citizenship framed around 'the norms of behaviour with regard to technology' (Ribble, Bailey & Ross, 2004; Microsoft, 2011). The two key elements of digital citizenship for Microsoft are 'digital literacy' and 'digital ethics and etiquette'. The whitepaper outlines risks of 'content, conduct and contact' and ultimately urges a hands-off or light-touch approach to its management by government and law enforcement agencies, while setting out parameters for user, parental and educational responsibilities and behavioural norms. Under the heading 'What Governments Can Do', the document warns against legislation that includes 'excessive restrictions or mandates on technology': 'While it is tempting to try to protect young people by passing technology mandates, the reality is that 'tech mandates' have generally proven ineffective, given the global reach and scale of the internet' (Microsoft, 2011, p. 12).

Making similar public gestures towards digital citizenship and safety, Google has also staked out an ambiguous position. Through its partnership with iKeepSafe, Google paints its own picture of responsibilities and actions constituting good digital citizenship. iKeepSafe provides online resources and online learning programmes dealing with topics like digital reputation, cyberbullying, 'responsible downloading, and balancing screen time with real life'.[8] While publicly supporting the push towards federally funded educational programmes in the United States, Google also lobbies actively against stricter personal data and privacy laws in the European Union (Holt & Malčić, 2015), and simultaneously seeks favourable conditions in the newly ratified Trans Pacific Partnership (TPP) (Lawrence, 2015).

Despite the public outreach around digital citizenship, it is at the platform layer, at the layer of systems engineering and design, protocol, algorithm, application and software, that the conditions for digital citizenship are most comprehensively delineated or jeopardised. Twitter can, for example, make a simple decision to delete 125,000 accounts 'promoting or threatening terrorism', using algorithmic selection processes, even while the company has been slow to develop measures for curbing abuse and harassment (Frier, 2016; Twitter Blog, Feb 8, 2016; see Quodling in this volume). What might be grating about Microsoft and Google's educational approach to digital citizenship is the sense of rational and ideal sociality embedded in their intended outcomes. The platforms they have designed and engineered should not be 'mistakenly understood as bloodless spaces of rational determination', as Crawford puts it (2016).

The issue with algorithms and protocols as mechanisms of digital control is that the work they do is usually not publicly visible. A strong tradition of media and legal scholarship has examined the subtle, less visible forms of digital media control, exploring the ways users are subject to power through the 'black box' workings of code, protocol and algorithm (Lessig, 1999; Galloway, 2004; Chun, 2006; Pasquale, 2015). As William J. Mitchell asked in 1995, 'Who shall write the software that increasingly structures our daily lives? What shall that software allow and proscribe? Who shall be privileged by it and who marginalized?' (Mitchell, 1995, cited in Longford, 2005, p. 68). In this line of research and critical thought and in so many ways we are still yet to discover, control can be understood as the sum of the limits and possibilities for acting online and living a digitally mediated life. Longford, for instance, points to the ways 'citizenship norms, rights, obligations and practices are encoded in the design and structure of our increasingly digital surroundings' (2005, p. 68). A social network site's affordances, features and restrictions and its data collection and monetisation techniques are themselves measures that shape and often adversely affect the rights of digital citizens.

Ironically, it is through code, algorithm and other technical measures that the potential chaos or dangers of the internet and digital activity is managed. For Chun, 'Computational codes are increasingly privileged as *the* means to guarantee "safe living" because they seem to enforce automatically what they prescribe' (Chun, 2015, p. 139). Protocol, as Galloway reminds us, 'is not a new word. Prior to its usage in computing, protocol referred to any type of correct or proper behavior within a specific system of conventions' (Galloway, 2004, p. 7). Even as they indicate objective, value-free global agreements on standards, protocols are negotiated socially, institutionally and politically. 'Thus, protocol is a technique for achieving voluntary regulation within a contingent environment' (Galloway, 2004, p. 8). These regulations bring into being new media forms and modes of communication and connection; they are thus an important part of the mix in determining the conditions for digital citizenship.

Algorithms select information for us, organise social media timelines and interactions and determine recommendations (Gillespie, 2014). Tufekci points to certain 'algorithmic harms' in their lack of visibility, information asymmetry and hidden influence (Tufekci, 2015, p. 208). The criteria by which algorithms act, and the decisions through which they automatically intervene in internet use, are political—for instance, in simply preferencing some material over others and hence shaping knowledge and visibility in social media contexts. Even at this level of code and computational decision-making, there is conflict and antagonism. Crawford notes the 'tensions and contests of life in calculated publics' in the 'human and algorithmic operators in spaces like Reddit, Amazon, 4chan, and Facebook' (Crawford, 2016, p.79). She argues, 'Algorithms may be rule-based mechanisms that fulfil requests, but they are also governing agents that are choosing between competing, and sometimes conflicting, data objects' (2016, p. 85). They can themselves become 'antagonistic agents, at odds with each other' (Crawford, 2016, p. 86). For Crawford, 'this is the stuff of governance' (2016, p. 79), hidden and automated forms of governance.

Like algorithms, flags are socio-technical and political measures that play a central role in moderating or regulating online activity and content. Flags, however, are those features of a social media site's design that nominally places control over content and interaction with users. In flagging systems, both social practices and technical mechanisms interact and evolve over time (Crawford & Gillespie, 2014). Flagging offers a simple input tool for reporting offensive content or inappropriate use on a social media platform, and in this sense 'flagging mechanisms allow users to express their concerns within the predetermined rubric of a platform's "community guidelines"' (Crawford & Gillespie, 2014, p. 2). But they are not as straightforward as they might seem, working as a 'complex interplay between users and platforms, humans and algorithms, and the social norms and regulatory structures of social media' (2014, p. 2). Crawford and Gillespie make the point that 'the obligation to police is sometimes a legal one, but social media platforms generally go well beyond what is legally required, forging their own space of responsibility' (2014, p. 2; see also Verhulst, 2005). As with Microsoft's stated preference to maintain platforms' self-regulation of misuse and abuse, flags offer a rhetorical device that suggests that this is possible even among Facebook's billion-plus users.

As one example, Ask.fm is a social media platform where people create profiles and ask one another questions. It also highlights the role played by platform features, algorithms and flagging functions in managing 'appropriate use'. Founded in Latvia in 2010, the site has been popular amongst young school-aged people, but soon developed a strong reputation for fostering abuse and bullying, particularly as it enabled anonymous public communication and direct messaging. Originally, the site had no reporting or tracking systems or control settings that might curb abuse. After it was acquired by InterActiveCorp (IAC) in 2013 and relocated to Dublin, Ask.fm invested heavily in relatively nuanced site safety measures and a suite of safety tools for users to manage settings and flag or block instances of inappropriate use. Users can allow or block anonymous questions, block specific users from asking questions, control public visibility, control which questions appear on their profile and report abuse.[9] Ask.fm has developed partnerships with cyber-safety organisations such as Childnet International and, as noted above, has been included as a Tier 1 partner with the Office for the Children's eSafety Commissioner in Australia. Despite these measures, in a recent study of young people's perceptions of cyberbullying, the particular affordances and features of Ask.fm the site was still understood to enable forms of humiliation and bullying (Nilan et al., 2015). Platform features and the ways they are negotiated are, for this reason, crucial to how cybersafety, and digital literacy should be conceived and addressed.

Under the broad concept of digital citizenship, any attempt to govern or affect good cybersafety must account for this 'platformed' socio-technical, political and economic context that is itself far from neutral or value and conflict free. The design decisions, security features and user settings for the products and services of Microsoft, Apple, Google, Facebook, Twitter and others *matter*. And yet these are often brushed over on the way to examining user behaviours, social use patterns and in the search for state regulation. All of this illustrates unevenness and conflict in the ways social media operators and platforms curate communication and public discourse, and enable social connections and interactions, but also fashion them (Gillespie, 2010, p. 347; van Dijck, 2013). When non-profit organisations and educational institutions take a 'behaviour change' approach to cybersafety in localised contexts like school programmes, or when state regulators apply superficial pressure for platforms to takedown content, the active role of platforms and technology (whether positive or negative) can become further obscured.

## THE INTERVENTIONS OF SCHOOL-BASED
## DIGITAL CITIZENSHIP PROGRAMMES

As one of the most visible edges of digital citizenship, non-profit or entrepreneurial cybersafety organisations offer a potentially problematic but also
productive point of intervention into these questions of internet governance
and platformed sociality. There is a strong need for further research, review
and evaluation of cybersafety programmes and the specialist organisations
or entrepreneurs providing interventions across global, national and local
contexts (Cross et al., 2013). As demonstrated above, this also involves the
different interventions of state regulation, but also must take into consideration the role of internet and social media platforms in affecting their own
kinds of 'behaviour change' and modulation through technical affordances
and measures.

One prominent and active player in the United States, Cyberwise, illustrates
the goal of targeting parents and, through them, children in establishing safe
online environments. Founded by Diana Graber and Cynthia Lieberman, and
with connections to Verizon Wireless, Google and iKeepSafe, Cyberwise
promises that no 'grownup' will be left behind, with its online safety education
targeting parents and teachers. In addition to learning resources around topics like 'Being a Responsible Citizen of the Digital World', Cyberwise offers
online and face-to-face workshops on 'cyber civics' in California, emphasising
critical thinking, ethical discussion and decision-making about digital media
issues.[10] Providing similar online and localised services, the UK-based non-
profit organisation Childnet International, which delivers the Digizen online
resources and Kid Smart programmes, draws funding from the European Commission's Digital Agenda for Europe, and 2012 European strategy for a Better
Internet for Children, and Safer Internet programmes (European Commission,
2015).

Often opaque connections to parent organisations, government funding and
private enterprise are not necessarily problematic, but often obscure a range
of agendas. As well as partnering with major technology corporations such
as Google as noted above, iKeepSafe was established in 2005 as a 'nonprofit
international alliance of more than 100 policy leaders, educators, law enforcement members, technology experts, public health experts and advocates'.[11]
But more than this: 'iKeepSafe assists countries worldwide in implementing
digital citizenship and safety strategies by informing their departments of
public health, ministries of communication and law enforcement agencies
in these initiatives'. i-SAFE Ventures, founded in 1998 to address 'a growing threat to America's youth as more and more young people ventured onto
the internet', operates as a hybrid non-profit and for-profit entity (i-SAFE
Ventures).[12] Across these kinds of programmes and organisations, there is a

less visible sense of both synergy and tension with technology companies and platforms, as well as government regulators. It is clear that funding flows between these three layers. Less clear are the often competing interests of technology companies seeking light-touch regulation and reputation management. And while states often partner with non-governmental organisations to deliver governance programmes, there are a growing number of entrepreneurs and consultants profiting from this area of public concern.

Alongside the increasingly consistent language of citizenship and safety deployed across these sites and programmes, there are also significant local processes, interests and concerns at play. One useful case study involves a range of cybersafety tools and programmes developed by Melbourne-based non-profit organisation, the Alannah and Madeline Foundation (AMF), in collaboration with RMIT University (amf.org.au). Through its suite of eSmart cybersafety programmes, the AMF targets cyberbullying with the aim of delivering a civil environment for digital media use within and around schools and other settings such as libraries and family homes. The particular locations or spheres of digital media use are important for achieving a 'whole of community approach' to cybersafety. The programmes are designed to audit and identify benefits and risks of digital and networked technologies in a specific local setting, and develop a common language around cybersafety and online behaviours along with appropriate responses to problems. Within the school programmes, the targets for intervention are further broken down around six domains: effective school organisation; school plans, policies and procedures; a respectful and caring school community; effective teacher practices; an eSmart curriculum; partnerships with parents and local communities.[13]

Interconnections with internet corporations and both state and federal government departments, regulation and policy are strong and point to the interplay of interests and stakeholders. Like iKeepSafe, the AMF has partnered and been co-funded by Google, and has a multi-year $8 million partnership with Australian Telecommunications and Internet Service Provider Telstra through the Telstra Foundation.[14] In addition, the AMF is funded directly by the federal Department of Education and Training, and pilot phase schools received a financial incentive. The Victorian (state) government also provided early support to make eSmart available in all Victorian public schools and has explored cybersafety as part of a 2010 Parliamentary Inquiry into the Potential for Developing Opportunities for Schools to Become a Focus for Promoting Healthy Community Living.[15] Clearly, governments see organisations like the AMF as an opportunity to implement programmes that align with its policy frameworks particularly around public health and child safety.

Independent evaluation of eSmart Schools surveyed more than 6000 individuals across two states over a two-year period. According to the AMF's eSmart Schools Evaluation Summary, 'the great majority (80%) of principals said eSmart Schools has changed school-wide culture and behaviour with regard to cybersafety, technology and bullying, prompted action that would not have otherwise be undertaken and improved the management of issues' (Alannah & Madeline Foundation, 2015). Within the programme evaluation, again, links are explicitly drawn with approaches applied in public health campaigns to affect behaviour change 'guiding communities of students, teachers and parents to adopt a values-led approach to on and offline behaviour' (2015, p. 3). The evaluation document cites the EU approach to digital competence as a foundational principle for the eSmart programmes, grounded in basic ICT skills and attitudes alongside digital literacy as 'the core skill of critical thinking' involving 'the integration of listening, speaking, reading, and writing', 'cultural knowledge' and 'practical competencies for playing, learning and working in a knowledge economy' (2015, p. 6). They also emphasise critical digital literacy, 'which involves the ability to investigate and critically interpret the constructed nature of popular culture' (2015, p. 6). In this way, eSmart attempts to 'move away from the risk-and-fear approaches that characterise so many Government resources' in favour of a 'resilience approach' (2015, p. 7).

This kind of programme offers valuable opportunities for managing digital environments outside of direct government or platform controls *if* critical digital literacy and competencies can also take into account all three layers of control and regulation that impact on and have a stake in the idea of digital citizenship. That is, in light of the introduction of legislative measures for addressing cyberbullying and online harassment, and in relation to platforms' own 'behavioural change' or modulation measures, cybersafety programmes need to prioritise digital skills and competencies and critical digital literacy— not (just) to manage behaviours but to better understand the whole ecology in which digital acts and interactions take place. In this sense, there is an opportunity to do more to incorporate social media competencies that focus on negotiating specific platform controls, affordances, settings and cultures of use at this layer of local education.

## CONCLUSIONS

Despite the three interconnected and at times competing levels of control manifested in notions of cybersafety, as a broader framework digital citizenship can be a productive agenda setting concept that offers an entry point for improving access and literacy, successful forms of digitally enhanced sociality, political and cultural participation. Digital citizenship can be understood to operate as a locus and interface that should not be taken for granted in considering new sets of rights, experiences and social relations as they are affected by digital media and networked communication. This interface incorporates global forces, state regulation and local experiences and points of intervention.

Through programmes, policies and regulation targeting cybersafety, the management of digital citizenship takes place across three layers of governance and intervention, and these layers are not easily untangled. Organisations like the AMF and programmes that develop strong integration with federal, state and local government agencies and institutions, along with technology corporations, are uniquely placed to intervene into issues of public health and well-being in relation to technology use. This can be a positive thing if such programmes are able to negotiate the role played by regulation, lobbying by technology companies and the complicated technical control measures of social media platforms. In addition, across these three layers of control, addressing online sociality through the concept of digital citizenship, and through young people, cannot work without factoring in proper co- or participatory design (Schuler & Namioka, 1993).

One of the key challenges explored in this chapter and throughout this book is to better understand the forms of sociality that digital and networked technologies, and specific social media platforms, affect. The goal then is to reconfigure the notion of digital citizenship by more clearly accounting for those platforms' interests as they provide the channels or social media utilities through which digital citizenship can be enacted. The core question in framing digital citizenship through cybersafety is how to identify and promote critical and creative literacies while accounting for conflict, harassment and the well-being of young people without the latter dominating governance agendas. The ethics and etiquette of online life necessarily involves the interaction between individuals, groups, institutions, platforms and governments, collectively and in an integrated fashion. In this mix, there is an ongoing need to negotiate competing positions and conflicts of interest and antagonisms inherent in the environments that various governance measures are seeking to manage—rather than eliminate them under the ideal of rational consensus and technological neutrality.

## NOTES

1. NoBullying.com. 'The Top 6 Unforgettable Cyberbullying Cases Ever', last modified December 22, 2015, Retrieved from http://nobullying.com/six-unforgettable-cyber-bullying-cases/.

2. In previous research I use the concept of provocation and 'acts of citizenship' (Isin and Nielsen, 2010) to critique popular concepts of 'trolls' in favour of examining and understanding specific digital acts themselves and their material contexts (McCosker, 2014).

3. Federal Communications Commission, 'Children's Internet Protection Act', Last updated November 3, 2015. Retrieved from www.fcc.gov/consumers/guides/childrens-internet-protection-act; Implemented in 1997, the E-Rate program "provides discounted telecommunications, Internet access, and internal connections to eligible schools and libraries, funded by the Universal Service Fund (USF)": Federal Communications Commission, "Universal Service Program for Schools and Libraries (E-Rate)", Last updated November 3, 2015. Retrieved from https://www.fcc.gov/consumers/guides/universal-service-program-schools-and-libraries-e-rate.

4. Govtrack.us, "Text of the Megan Meier Cyberbullying Prevention Act", accessed February 4, 2016. Retrieved from https://www.govtrack.us/congress/bills/111/hr1966/text. Google advocated specifically in support of the Bill on its blog: Best Practices for Online Child Safety, 2009. Retrieved from http://googlepublicpolicy.blogspot.com.au/2009/07/best-practices-for-online-child-safety.html.

5. The European Union relies on a number of soft law measures to provide multistate frameworks and responses to the management of internet safety under a broad "Digital Agenda for Europe": European Commission, "Digital Agenda for Europe: A Europe 2020 Initiative", last updated July 1, 2015, http://ec.europa.eu/digital-agenda/digital-agenda-europe; The Cybersmile Foundation, "Legal Perspective", last updated, 2015, accessed February 2, 2016. Retrieved from https://www.cybersmile.org/advice-help/category/cyberbullying-and-the-law.

6. Office of the Children's eSafety Commissioner, "eSafety Information" accessed January 14, 2016. Retrieved from https://esafety.gov.au/esafety-information.

7. Office of the Children's eSafety Commissioner, "Social media service Tier scheme", accessed on January 14, 2016. Retrieved from https://esafety.gov.au/social-media-regulation/social-media-service-tier-scheme.

8. iKeepSafe, "About Us", accessed December 16, 2015. Retrieved from http://ikeepsafe.org/about-us/.

9. Ask.fm, "Safety Tools", accessed February 4, 2016. Retrieved from http://safety.ask.fm/safety-tools.

10. Cyberwise, accessed November 1, 2015. Retrieved from http://cyberwise.org.

11. iKeepSafe, "About Us", accessed November 1, 2015. Retrieved from http://ikeepsafe.org/about-us/.

12. i-SAFE Ventures, "About i-SAFE Ventures", accessed February 7, 2016. Retrieved from http://www.isafeventures.com/about/.

13. eSmart Schools, "Welcome to eSmart Schools", accessed February 3, 2016. Retrieved from www.esmartschools.org.au.

14. The Alannah and Madeline Foundation, (2016) "Corporate Partners", accessed February 2, 2016. Retrieved from http://www.amf.org.au/corporatepartners/.

15. Parliament of Victoria, "Inquiry into the Potential for Developing Opportunities for Schools to Become a Focus for Promoting Healthy Community Living", accessed January 17, 2016. Retrieved from http://www.parliament.vic.gov.au/57th-parliament/etc/inquiry/36.

# REFERENCES

Alannah & Madeline Foundation (AMF) (2015). *eSmart schools evaluation summary*. Melbourne. Retrieved from http://esmart.org.au/wp-content/uploads/2015/09/eSmart-Evaulation-Results-2015.pdf.

Azoulay, A. (2015). *Civil imagination: A political ontology of photography*. London: Verso Books.

Chun, W. H. K. (2008). *Control and freedom: Power and paranoia in the age of fiber optics*. Cambridge, MA: MIT Press.

Chun, W. H. K. (2015). Crisis, crisis, crisis; or, the temporality of networks. In R. A. Grusin (Ed.), *The nonhuman turn* (pp. 139–166). Minneapolis: University of Minnesota Press.

Collin, P. (2015). *Young citizens and political participation in a digital society: Addressing the democratic disconnect*. Basingstoke, U.K.: Palgrave McMillan.

Crawford, K. (2015). Can an Algorithm be agonistic? Ten scenes from life in calculated publics. *Science, Technology & Human Values, 41*(1), 77–92.

Crawford, K., & Gillespie, T. (2014). What is a flag for? Social media reporting tools and the vocabulary of complaint. *New Media & Society, Online first*, 1461444814543163. Retrieved from http://nms.sagepub.com/content/early/2014/07/15/1461444814543163.abstract.

Cross, D., Campbell, M., Slee, P., Spears, B., & Barnes, A. (2013). Australian research to encourage school students' positive use of technology to reduce cyberbullying. In P. K. Smith & G. Steffgen (Eds.), *Cyberbullying through the new media: Findings from an international network* (pp. 222–243). New York: Psychology Press.

Cukier, K., & Mayer-Schönberger, V. (2013). *Big data: A revolution that will transform how we live, work, and think*. New York: Houghton Mifflin Harcourt.

Dery, M. (1994). *Flame wars: The discourse of cyberculture*. Durham: Duke University Press.

European Commission (2012). *European strategy for a better internet for children*, Brussels. Retrieved from http://eur-lex.europa.eu/LexUriServ/LexUriServ.do?uri=COM:2012:0196:FIN:EN:PDF.

Galloway, A. R. (2004). *Protocol: How control exists after decentralization*. Cambridge, MA: MIT press.

Gillespie, T. (2010). The politics of 'platforms.' *New Media & Society, 12*(3), 347–364.

Hinduja, S., & Patchin, J. W. (2011). *State cyberbullying laws: A brief review of state cyberbullying laws and policies*: Cyberbullying Research Center. Retrieved from http://cyberbullying.org/state-cyberbullying-laws-a-brief-review-of-state-cyberbullying-laws-and-policies.

Holt, J., & Malčić, S. (2015). The privacy ecosystem: Regulating digital identity in the United States and European Union. *Journal of Information Policy 5*, 155–178.

Isin, E. F. (2008). Theorizing acts of citizenship. In E. F. Isin & G. M. Nielsen (Eds.), *Acts of citizenship* (pp. 15–43). London: Zed Books.

Isin, E., & Ruppert, E. (2015). *Being digital citizens*. London: Rowman & Littlefield International.

Lessig, L. (1999). *Code and other laws of cyberspace*. New York: Basic books.

Li, Q., Cross, D., & Smith, P. K. (2011). *Cyberbullying in the global playground: Research from international perspectives*. Malden, MA: John Wiley & Sons.

Livingstone, S. (2002). *Young people and new media: Childhood and the changing media environment*. Thousand Oaks, CA: Sage.

Livingstone, S. (2013). Online risk, harm and vulnerability: Reflections on the evidence base for child Internet safety policy. *Zer: Revista de estudios de comunicación, 18*(35), 13–28.

Loader, B. D., Vromen, A., & Xenos, M. A. (2014). The networked young citizen: Social media, political participation and civic engagement. *Information, Communication and Society, 17*(2), 143–150.

Longford, G. (2005). Pedagogies of digital citizenship and the politics of code. *Techné: Research in Philosophy and Technology, 9*(1), 68–96.

McCosker, A. (2014). Trolling as provocation YouTube's agonistic publics. *Convergence, 20*(2), 201–217.

Mesch, G., & Talmud, I. (2010). *Wired youth: The social world of adolescence in the information age*. New York: Routledge.

Mitchell, W. J. (1995). *City of bits: Space, place, and the infobhan*. Cambridge MA: MIT Press.

Owen, D. (1996). Dilemmas and opportunities for the young active citizen. *Youth Studies Australia, 15*(1), 20.

Palfrey, J., Boyd, D., & Sacco, D. (2010). *Enhancing child safety and online technologies: Final report of the Internet Safety Technical Task Force*. Durham, NC: Carolina Academic Press.

Parikka, J. (2007). *Digital contagions: A media archaeology of computer viruses*. New York: Peter Lang.

Pasquale, F. (2015). *The black box society: The secret algorithms that control money and information*. Cambridge, MA: Harvard University Press.

Pew Research Centre (2015). *Online harassment*. Retrieved from http://www.pewinternet.org/2014/10/22/online-harassment/.

Ribble, M. S., Bailey, G. D., & Ross, T. W. (2004). Digital citizenship: Addressing appropriate technology behavior. *Learning & Leading with Technology, 32*(1), 6.

Schuler, D., & Namioka, A. (Eds.). (1993). *Participatory design: Principles and practices*. Hillsdale, New Jersey: Lawrence Erlbaum Associates, Inc.

Shepherd, T., Harvey, A., Jordan, T., Srauy, S., & Miltner, K. (2015). Histories of hating. *Social Media + Society, 1*(2), 1–10.

Smith, P. K., Mahdavi, J., Carvalho, M., Fisher, S., Russell, S., & Tippett, N. (2008). Cyberbullying: Its nature and impact in secondary school pupils. *Journal of child psychology and psychiatry, 49*(4), 376–385.

Swist, T., Collin, P., McCormack, J., Third, A., & Australia, W. (2015). *Social media and the wellbeing of children and young people: A literature review*. Perth: Commissioner for Children and Young People.

Tufekci, Z. (2015). Algorithmic harms beyond Facebook and Google: Emergent challenges of computational agency. *J. on Telecomm. & High Tech. L., 13*(2), 203–218.

van Dijck, J. (2013). *The culture of connectivity: A critical history of social media*. Oxford: Oxford University Press.

van Zoonen, L., Vis, F., & Mihelj, S. (2011). YouTube interactions between agonism, antagonism and dialogue: Video responses to the anti-Islam film Fitna. *New Media & Society, 13*(8), 1283–1300.

Verhulst, S. (2006). The regulation of digital content. In L. A. Lievrouw & S. Livingstone (Eds.), *The handbook of new media: Social shaping and consequences of ICTs* (pp. 329–349). London: Sage.

White, R., & Wyn, J. (2004). *Youth and society: Exploring the social dynamics of youth.* Melbourne: Oxford University Press.

Chapter 3

# Rethinking (Children's and Young People's) Citizenship through Dialogues on Digital Practice

Amanda Third and Philippa Collin

Over the last decade, the concept of 'digital citizenship' has begun to supplant 'cybersafety' as a critical pillar of policy and programmes pertaining to the use of online and networked media. We argue here that coupling 'citizenship' with 'the digital' is a move brimming with promise for *rethinking citizenship through the digital*. And yet, this potential has gone largely unnoticed and untapped.

Focusing on the Australian context, this chapter critically examines how both government and nongovernment organisations in the Western world are conceptualising digital citizenship. We argue that, by and large, digital citizenship operates as a synonym for cybersafety and that it targets those who are usually excluded from citizenship of the state: children and young people. We suggest that this emphasis misses the opportunity to take seriously the question of citizenship that is at the heart of the new terminology. To move beyond such limited framings of digital citizenship, we argue for a focus on the ways that the imbrication of the digital with the time-space of 'the everyday' (de Certeau, 1988; Lefebvre, 2000) opens up productive possibilities for disrupting and contesting citizenship, or, what Isin (2008) terms 'acts of citizenship'. We consider the potential of this reconceptualisation in relation to a novel living lab experiment set up to generate dialogues on intergenerational attitudes towards social networking and cybersafety.

## DIGITAL CITIZENSHIP: CITIZENSHIP POLICY FOR A DIGITAL GENERATION?

In Australia, the United States, the United Kingdom and New Zealand, the emergence of digital citizenship in policy and popular discourse has been profoundly shaped by the risk and safety paradigm that has dominated mainstream debate about emergent technology practices since the mid-1990s (Third, Collier & Forrest-Lawrence, 2014b). In this sense, digital citizenship policies and strategies, whilst potentially related, are distinct from those of 'e-citizenship' and 'e-government', which focus on how digital media can promote better citizen engagement and governance.

Australian digital citizenship policy and practice is a case in point and provides a useful entry point for thinking through the ways the discourse of digital citizenship articulates internationally. In the Australian context, the policy framework of the Australian Communications and Media Authority (ACMA) has played a lead role in setting the digital citizenship agenda and is a key reference point for policymakers and practitioners seeking to formulate organisation-specific policy and programmes. The ACMA's approach is grounded in 'an extensive review of existing international digital citizen programs and resources' (Office of the Children's eSafety Commissioner [OCeC][1]), its *Digital Citizens Guide* (ACMA)[2] links to both Australian and international resources and, to this extent, intersects with and exemplifies international trends.

In Australia, the embrace of digital citizenship is self-consciously framed as an evolution or maturation of cybersafety strategies. As a 2009 ACMA policy document asserts, the turn towards digital citizenship marks 'a subtle but discernible shift in attention from online safety to the promotion of appropriate use of [digital] media or "digital citizenry"' (ACMA, 2009, p. 52). Operating within a risk and safety paradigm, traditionally Australian cybersafety strategies have focused narrowly on the risks and necessary protective measures associated with the use of digital media. This focus has established cybersafety as a key issue affecting the Australian public and raised awareness within the community. However, recent research internationally suggests that maximising the benefits of participating online can support users to mitigate the risks (de Haan, 2009; Online Safety and Technology Working Group [OSTWG], 2010; Collin, Rahilly, Richardson & Third, 2011; Third, Bellerose, Dawkins, Keltie & Pihl, 2014a). Moreover, the overarching focus on risk and safety may be impeding users in realising the full range of benefits of engaging online. As de Haan expresses it, 'Safety initiatives to reduce risk tend also to reduce opportunities' (2009, p. 189). As a consequence, there has been a shift—albeit partial—within cybersafety policy and practice in Australia and many other parts of the world[3] towards more holistic and strengths-based approaches to supporting digital practices that recognise the importance of skilling users to engage safely and to maximise the full potential of connectivity.

It is in this context that 'digital citizenship' has gained traction within technology-oriented policy and practice. Its emergence represents a concerted effort to broaden the focus of conventional cybersafety discourse; to account for (digital) media literacy and community connectedness; and to enable users to leverage the contexts, relationships and practices associated with digital media to capitalise on the benefits of being online. The evolution of ACMA's digital citizenship framework evidences this shift. Whereas the 2009 digital citizenship resources emphasised 'safe and secure participation online' (ACMA, 2009), the 2013 *Digital Citizens Guide* foregrounds 'positive engagement' and resilience alongside 'being cybersmart'[4] (OCeC, 'Digital Citizenship').[5] Nonetheless, digital citizenship is frequently anchored in anxieties about users' vulnerability online, and the primary policy and practice objective remains that of securing their safety and security. Indeed, this is evident in the fact that some policies and programmes have used the terms 'digital citizenship' and 'cybersafety' interchangeably (see ACMA, 2009).[6]

Another striking and paradoxical feature of digital citizenship discourse is that it targets those who are, at best, configured as partial citizens or citizens-to-be (White & Wyn, 2004; Collin, 2008) or, at worst, not considered citizens at all, namely children and young people. Whilst digital citizenship policies and programmes assert that 'everyone online is . . . a digital citizen' (Britnell, 2015) and ostensibly address 'adults and children alike' (ACMA, 2009, p. 4), children and young people are implicitly—and often overtly—the key targets. For example, the case studies and strategies outlined in the ACMA's policies (2009; n.d., *Digital Citizens Guide*) primarily relate to children and young people, as do the images that are used to promote them. Tellingly, when the Australian Federal Government restructured the ACMA in 2015 and established the OCeC, responsibility for the curation of the ACMA's digital citizenship resources was transferred to the new entity. Given the commissioner's office supports children's safety and is mandated to 'educate and help prevent harmful behaviour online' (OCeC, 'Role of the Office'), the relocation of the ACMA's digital citizenship portfolio reproduces the idea that digital citizenship is primarily about promoting behavioural change in children and young people to secure their online safety. Configured in these ways, digital citizenship tends to recognise children and young people as social actors, and even consumers, but not as political actors already utilising online and networked media to shape the kind of society they wish to live in (Vromen, 2003). Adults, by contrast, are situated primarily as the educators or parents of children and young people—in effect, as the full citizen guardians of apprentice citizens.

In policy and practitioner discourses, digital citizenship centres on either the *protection rights* of children and young people or their *responsibilities* towards others as members of a community. For example, the ACMA's digital citizenship lesson plans for school students state, '[as] digital citizens . . .

students should come to recognise the importance of protecting their private information online, the value of taking responsibility for themselves and their actions, and the necessity of treating others with an appropriate standard of behaviour online' (OCeC, 'Role of the Office' 2016).

A moral economy drives the discourse, constructing digital citizenship in terms of 'duties' to exhibit 'appropriate behaviours' and promote 'good digital practices'. The ACMA's 2013 *Digital Citizens Guide* promotes 'positive digital citizenship', mobilising the concept of citizenship to refer to access and use of digital media in a normatively 'good' way via the acquisition of skills and literacies and—where necessary—behavioural change. Technology is framed in instrumental and reductive terms as a tool for accessing information, sharing content and connecting with others: 'A digital citizen is a person with the skills and knowledge to effectively use digital technologies to participate in society, communicate with others and create and consume digital content' (ACMA). This kind of digital citizenship targets a narrow suite of activities and behaviours in a manner that reproduces the emphases—and, therefore, the limitations—of mainstream cybersafety strategies.

Digital citizenship discourse operates at the nexus of two distinct but mutually constitutive framings of children and young people and their digital practices. On the one hand, children and young people are positioned within the discourse as vulnerable—and often passive—subjects requiring protection from a range of nefarious threats and influences. That is, digital media is viewed as fostering an anarchic space in which young people are potentially vulnerable to a range of exploitative acts including misinformation and misdirection (Coleman, 2008, p. 191). Indeed, a white paper entitled *Citizens and the ACMA* places young people in a special category for 'vulnerable citizens' (ACMA, 2010, p. 6), reproducing mainstream ideas about the innocence and malleability of children and young people. Thus, when digital citizenship discourse foregrounds children's and young people's rights, it is their right to protection from harm that is privileged—and not their rights to provision, much less participation (Livingstone & O'Neil, 2015).

On the other hand, youth is constructed in agentic terms as a period of experimentation, and children's and young people's digital participation is framed as a playground of (both wilful and inadvertent) rule breaking and risk taking and the contestation of adult-centred social norms. In this configuration, mainstream concerns about securing the 'proper' socialisation of children and young people overlay fears about the juggernaut quality of technological development and the rapid uptake of digital media by children and young people. As Ito and colleagues have noted, underpinning these concerns is the idea that 'as users at the forefront of experimentation with new media forms', youth digital practices are unfolding outside adult authority and producing citizens who mobilise digital media to 'push back at existing structures of power and authority' (Ito et al., 2008, p. ix). As Harris has observed, mainstream anxieties about the subversive or disruptive potential implicit in children's and young people's digital practices have intensified in the wake of the emergence of social media, which enable online social interactions over which adults perceive themselves to have very little control (Harris, 2008). Here, it is digital media's and, specifically, social media's facilitation of expansive networks of social connection, its imbrication with the potentially counter-hegemonic impulses of user-generated content production, and its 'viral' capacities in particular, that are posited as potentially undermining adult authority. In this context, children's and young people's digital media practices present as needing to be 'appropriately' channelled, contained and/or disciplined. The dystopian social order of the *Lord of the Flies* haunts the edges of these formulations. As such, the thrust of digital citizenship policy and practice is directed at *encouraging* children—or, in more didactic manifestations, *educating* them—to perform personal responsibility, restraint and self-management in the exercise of what might be described as a 'minimal' (Evans, 1995) or 'thin' (Marsh, O'Toole & Jones, 2007) form of citizenship.

Either way, in the same manner that children and young people are constructed within mainstream society as 'not-yet-adult', digital citizenship discourse positions them as 'not-yet-citizens' who are in need of both protection and socialisation strategies to become '*good* digital citizens'. Digital citizenship policy is thus 'top-down' and symptomatic of what Coleman has described as 'managed citizenship' (Coleman, 2008), which constructs children and young people as apprentice citizens who need to learn 'politeness, consensus-seeking, [and] due respect for authority and rationality' (Coleman, 2008, p. 197). Managed approaches to digital citizenship constitute citizenship in terms of rights and duties and focus on regulating and modifying young people's online behaviour. In this way, digital citizenship strategies foreclose the meanings of citizenship, reinscribing children and young people as 'citizens in the making' and reinforcing adult practices and institutions as the measure of legitimate 'citizenship'. Or, in Isin's terms, digital citizenship strategies foster young citizens who 'follow scripts and participate in scenes that are already created' (2008, p. 38).

As such, the majority of digital citizenship policy and practice fails to take on the challenge of citizenship. What would it mean to take seriously the concept of citizenship that lies at the heart of the new terminology? Beyond fostering the benefits of children's and young people's online engagements, we argue that the emergence of digital citizenship represents a unique opportunity to *reinvigorate the meanings and practices of citizenship more broadly*. This requires thinking critically about citizenship.

## DIGITAL CONTESTATIONS

Coleman has argued that 'cyberspace' operates as a 'locus for the contestation of claims about citizenship' (2008, p. 202). We might understand him as gesturing towards the characteristics of digital media that problematise conventional framings of citizenship as grounded in the (nation-) state; in particular, digital media's capacity to catalyse 'networked publics' (boyd, 2008; boyd, 2014). Such publics extend beyond and/or cross-cut the geographical boundaries of states, 'producing new, if not paradoxical, subjects of law and action, new subjectivities and identities, new sites of struggle and new scales of identification' (Isin, 2008, p. 16). The backdrop to Coleman's claim is his argument that dialogue about the terms of citizenship is a precondition for democratic citizenship. He posits that democratic citizenship must be underwritten by a dual purpose. On the one hand, it enables a process whereby normative democratic values and practices are fostered. On the other, it creates the space and the opportunity for the very terms of citizenship to be contested. Importantly, implicit in Coleman's argument is the idea that citizenship is not primarily a status but is, rather, fundamentally dynamic and processual.

Hartley further argues that citizenship theory 'has focused too much on citizenship as a static or definable condition, frequently understood as universal, when in fact it should be understood as . . . relational, . . . inconstant, dynamic, and evolving' (2010, p. 4). For Hartley, who focuses on citizenship in the era of digital mediation, citizenship is as much 'performative as it is deliberative' (Hartley, 2010, pp. 22–23). As such, he is concerned with the processes through which citizenship is constituted; or, the processes through which 'claim-making subjects' are called into being 'in and through various sites and scales' (Isin, 2008, p. 16). Whilst citizenship conceived of as a legal status of membership in the (nation-)state excludes children and young people, framing citizenship in terms of performativity opens up possibilities for thinking about children and young people as citizen-subjects, albeit in ways that are qualitatively different from adult citizen-subjectivity. Indeed, for Hartley, children are perhaps the most productive figure through which to (re)think the forms and meanings of citizenship precisely because of their ambivalent positioning as citizens/non-citizens: 'Children are . . . at one and the same time the least important component of institutionalised citizenship, since they remain non-citizens, and its most important 'subjects', since they necessarily and continuously constitute the practice of citizenship formation' (Hartley, 2010, p. 3). Discursively positioned, both individually and collectively, at the forefront of processes of 'citizen-formation', children's 'actions, forms of association, and . . . identities' are both a litmus test of and a new model for the processes that underpin citizenship in the digital age. In a similar vein, Third argues that the 'digitally enabled child' problematises legal definitions of citizenship as status and asserts alternative possibilities for thinking the category of both 'child' and citizen-subject:

> The digitally enabled child . . . problematizes the place-based boundaries that define the state. If the micro-, meso- and macro-operations of the internet transcend the national borders that conventionally proscribe political rights, children's access and use of digital media confronts and contests the sovereignty of the state. (Third, forthcoming, 2016)

Children's and young people's participation in the digital thus always already troubles conventional conceptualisations of citizenship. The (digitally enabled) child resonates in relation to (digital) citizenship in terms of what Lacan has called 'the symptom' (See Third, 2014). On the one hand, the child is a representational construct that marks the limits of citizenship, through their exclusion from the (nation-)state. On the other hand, the child is also necessary to the (nation-)state inasmuch as the child's successful socialisation as citizen guarantees the future of the state. However, given the child's socialisation is incomplete and indeterminate, and given the child is positioned simultaneously 'outside' and necessary to ('within') the state, the child also represents a site of instability and potential subversion (Third, 2016). While Hartley and Third refer to children, we might also extend this observation to young people. As recent scholarship demonstrates, even once reaching the age of majority, young people tend to remain only ambivalently included as 'adult citizens' because their participation often contrasts, opposes or challenges dominant, institutional forms (Collin, 2015).

In this context, we can read mainstream digital citizenship policy and practice, with its emphases on responsibilities, duties, and 'appropriate behaviours', as an attempt to contain the challenge children's and young people's digital practices pose to dominant cultural framings of both 'childhood' and '(digital) citizenship'. Indeed, we might say that the digital citizenship strategies we critiqued earlier in this chapter, in foreclosing the meanings of citizenship, downplay the radical potential of the figure of the (digitally enabled) child by enclosing the child in a circuit of predetermined meanings that attempts—albeit never entirely successfully—to secure their place as 'non-citizens'. In this movement, it is the pre-existing category of the child (or young person) around which attendant dominant cultural concerns about their vulnerability or lack of discipline are mobilised, enabling—indeed, justifying—the clinching of the meanings of citizenship. Or, to put it in Hartley's terms, this same movement closes down the generative possibilities of the (digitally enabled) child for thinking and doing new forms of (digital) citizenship.

How might we circumvent such appropriations of the (digitally enabled) child and work at the '"generative edge" of new senses of citizenship'

(Hartley, 2010, p. 25)? We argue that a focus on the everyday, read through Isin's theorisation of 'acts of citizenship' (2008), provides a useful way of proceeding.

## ACTS OF CITIZENSHIP AND THE RUPTURE OF THE (DIGITAL) EVERYDAY

The concept of the everyday has gained recent traction within the scholarship on children's and young people's technology practices. Given digital media's pervasive presence in the quotidian of growing numbers of children and young people around the world, it has become increasingly commonplace to note the routine and ritual dimensions of their online engagements and to describe their technology practices as 'everyday'. Similarly, the idea of the 'everyday' is mobilised within the literature on young people's digitally-mediated, civic and political practices (Harris, Wyn & Younes, 2007; Harris & Wyn, 2009; Wood, 2014). Seeking to extend beyond studies of exceptional instances of the use of digital media to directly contest dominant formations of citizenship and power, some scholars draw attention to how 'ordinary' young people enact citizenship (e.g. Marsh et al., 2007; Harris, 2010) and the role of 'everyday' civic and political practices (e.g. Harris et al., 2007; Collin, 2008; Vromen & Collin, 2010; Vromen, Xenos & Loader, 2015). The idea of the everyday is used to rebut claims that assert young people's political apathy or disengagement, or which trivialise their online practices and the processes by which they formulate political views, identities and pathways of action. These scholars use the idea of the everyday to reclaim the space of 'the ordinary' and to assert its political significance (see Harris, 2008; Harris and Wyn, 2009).

Importantly, such analyses tend to use the term 'everyday' adjectivally. For example, Harris et al. analyse 'young people's "everyday" engagement with social and political issues' (2007, p. 22); Wood seeks to unpack 'the everyday ways [young people] define and understand civic participation' (2014, p. 215); and Marsh et al. claim that an 'everyday focus' enables a window on the relationship between young people's lived experiences and their interest and participation in formal politics (2007, p. 212). Whilst these perspectives all contribute vital insights to ongoing debates, nonetheless, the very category of 'the everyday' tends to escape theoretical interrogation, presenting as a 'discursive enigma' (Drotner, 1994, p. 341).

In using the everyday in the attributive, these discussions implicitly or explicitly align the everyday with informality, 'family, friends, media and everyday activities' and 'more subtle kinds of engagement' (Harris et al., 2007, p. 22). The result is that the everyday is constructed as oppositional to 'formal politics'; it is defined 'against the formal structures and visible laws dominating for example school, work and politics' (Drotner, 1994, p. 347). For instance, Harris and Wyn argue that 'young people's exclusion from the formal public sphere where politics conventionally takes place has resulted in them constructing informal and familiar spaces to try out political discussions and learn about political and social issues' (2009, p. 329). Much of the ensuing debate thus focuses on the opportunities to bridge this binary, on creating 'links between everyday and formal political spheres' (Harris et al., 2007, p. 24). Further, in this literature, the everyday signals the domain of routine and ordering repetitions; the concern is with habits and 'familiar spaces' (Harris & Wyn, 2009, p. 329). Whilst it has been important to assert the value of children's and young people's everyday practices, the question this raises is that surfaced by Isin (2008): Can a focus on order, routine and habit illuminate new possibilities for thinking citizenship?

In Isin's analysis, the majority of modern social and political thought privileges 'routine over rupture, order over disorder, and habit over deviation' (2008, p. 20) and, as such, is not well equipped to account for the complex processes by which individuals and groups of people previously excluded from citizenship assert themselves as 'claim-making subjects'. Amidst a vast literature that charts the subaltern 'practices through which [citizenship] claims are articulated and subjectivities are formed', the emphasis, he argues, lies on routines, rituals, customs, norms and habits, and the 'question of how subjects become claimants under surprising conditions or within a relatively short period of time has remained unexplored' (Isin, 2008, p. 17). Isin thus argues that there is a need to break new ground in citizenship studies by centring 'acts of citizenship as the object of investigation' (2008, p. 16).

For Isin, acts of citizenship are related to but distinct from actions and actors. In the first instance, the distinction is temporal in that acts *precede* both actors and actions. Indeed, acts, he argues, call actors into being as *consciously claim-making subjects*. If citizenship requires *habitus*—'ways of thought and conduct that are internalised over a relatively long period of time' (Isin, 2008, p. 15)—acts of citizenship resonate as decisive and creative breaks with and, as such, are qualitatively different from the *habitus* of citizenship. As Isin states, 'The essence of an act . . . is that [it] is *a rupture in the given*' (2008, p. 25, emphasis added). Acts are fundamentally dialogical in that they are an expression of the need to be heard *by others*. They may be intentional or accidental but, either way, they assume the quality of *surprise*; they are the setting in motion of 'the unexpected, the unpredictable, and the unknowable' (Isin, 2008, p. 27). In disrupting habitus, they create a *scene* that opens up a space for reconfiguring the boundaries of citizenship and constituting new subjectivities ('beginning oneself anew'). In this sense, to act 'is neither arriving on a scene nor fleeing it, but actually engaging in its creation' (Isin, 2008, p. 27). The significance of the scene is precisely *as a moment of encounter* that produces the possibility of the political. Acts forge a 'stumbling across' others that compels an unfolding of subjects and objects in relation to each other *at the scene*. Acts responsibilise the actor inasmuch as, in producing the scene, they also produce the necessity of embracing discomfort and sticking around at the scene to deal with the fallout.

We are now in a position to understand the limitations of deploying the term 'everyday' adjectivally. Describing children's and young people's (digital) citizenship as everyday focuses attention on 'actors' and 'practices' and, as such, misses the opportunity to go beyond the study of the habitus through which citizenship is (re)produced. It means we 'arrive too late on the scene' (Isin, 2008, p. 37) and reproduce precisely the same terrain across which the fixed and binarised categories of 'active' and 'failed' young citizens (Harris, 2010), or 'dutiful' and 'actualising' citizens (Bennett, 2008), can continue to flourish. In an effort, therefore, to 'arrive a little earlier', we argue that the everyday must be mobilised in the nominal, as a *setting* for the enactment of potential 'scenes'. To make this argument, we turn to theorists of the everyday, Lefebvre and de Certeau.

## (RE)TURNING TO THE EVERYDAY

Coming out of the Situationist tradition, Lefebvre and de Certeau, are concerned with the possibilities inherent in consumer culture for forms of political resistance that can elicit social change. For Lefebvre (2000, p. 24), 'the everyday' is

> what is humble and solid, what is taken for granted and that of which all the parts follow each other in such a regular, unvarying succession that those concerned have no call to question their sequence; thus it is undated and (apparently) insignificant; though it occupies and preoccupies it is practically untellable, and it is the ethics underlying routine and the aesthetics of familiar settings.

Lefebvre notes that the everyday is an effect of modernity—'the modern'. He describes it as that which remains after all that is extraordinary has been removed from quotidian experience; it is the set of routines we perform, the spaces we inhabit and the routes we traverse. Its temporal expression is that of repetition. The routine of time supplements and sustains the ordering of space. That is, the everyday is a spatial and temporal template that governs the ways individuals perform the rituals of daily life, locking subjects into particular modes of operating and ensuring their compliance with the laws of social order. The everyday has its own momentum. It propels us forward; it guides us through the performance of life in ways that safeguard and perpetuate the stability of dominant order, implicating us in the modern project of progress, and binding us in modern time.

The everyday is naturalised, evading detection and, as such, critique. Not just a set of practices, it is also the sets of ideas and social relations that legitimise the routinised organisation of time and space. Importantly, the everyday is totalising in reach, consisting of 'pressures and repressions at all levels, at all times and in every sphere of experience including sexual and emotional experience, private and family life, childhood, adolescence and maturity' (Lefebvre, 2000, p. 145). Lefebvre might appear at first glance to simply reproduce the preoccupation with order, routine and habit that Isin critiques as characteristic of modern social and political thought. However, he theorises the everyday as simultaneously a mechanism of dominant order—a tool of repression—and a site for the transgression and deconstruction of that order. For Lefebvre, the everyday is both 'the point of delicate balance and that where imbalance threatens' (2000, p. 32).

To a greater extent than Lefebvre, de Certeau emphasises the subversive possibilities of the everyday, contrasting 'tactics' with 'strategy'. 'Strategy' is the organisational force of the everyday, which operates in alignment with the priorities of dominant order. Strategy occupies the terrain of the spatial—'it postulates a place that can be delimited as its own' (de Certeau, 1988, pp. 35–36)—and this dominance of place enables the assertion of quotidian routine and order. The temporal expression of strategy is that of repetition and regularity or, in Isin's terms, *habitus*. Against the totalising organisational impulse of strategy, political opposition assumes the form of 'tactics'. Tactics are distinguished from strategy by their relationship to both space and time. Unlike strategy, tactics have no enduring claim to the spatial realm of dominant order. Rather, tactics borrow the spaces of the other and use or, rather, reuse them to momentarily subvert that same order. They operate on the principle of speed, seizing opportunities and, like Isin's acts of citizenship, *surprising*. Whilst the tactic itself disappears, it nonetheless has lasting effects. Indeed, like acts of citizenship, tactics 'create a scene' with generative potential. By radically intervening in the temporal order of modernity that is held in place by the routine of the everyday, tactics momentarily expose the assumptions on which modern order is based. In the moment of disruption, tactics open up the space for thinking the world otherwise.

Drawing together this reading of the everyday and the concept of acts of citizenship, we thus might understand Isin's acts as tactical interventions into the time-space of the everyday that open up unprecedented possibilities for doing citizenship differently. It is across the settings of the everyday—at the nexus of the trajectories of repression and disruption—that children's and young people's lives, like those of adults, play out. But what are the implications of this for a notion of (digital) citizenship?

The digital is, by now, a key component of the infrastructured (Star and Bowker, 2006) ecology of the everyday in many parts of the world; indeed, to the extent that, in the same way we have been talking about (digital) citizenship to gesture the imbrication of the digital with forms of citizenship, we might also talk about the (digital) everyday. Within the time-space of the (digital) everyday, technologies articulate as artefacts or devices, but they are also implicated in activities and practices, as well as social arrangements and organisational forms (Lievrouw & Livingstone, 2006, p. 2). In this respect, thinking specifically about children and young people and remembering that they don't readily distinguish between the online and the offline (Third et al., 2014a) in the ways that adult-centred discourses—like that of 'digital citizenship'—often demand, the digital has implications for their 'time spent online' but also for their broader social and political lives. The multifarious appropriations of the digital thus operate *strategically*, according to the dictates of repetition and habit, to organise us and guide us through daily rituals and routines. However, it is precisely in the totalising reach of its strategic impulses that the (digital) everyday is exposed to the potentiality of *tactical* disruption, to acts of (digital) citizenship that can create scenes through which to reconfigure dominant framings of the political. While not *every* instance of the (digital) everyday can give rise to an 'act of citizenship', *any* instance of the (digital) everyday offers up the opportunity to break 'from everyday habits as well as broader institutional practices in official and non-official ways' (Morrison, 2008, p. 289).[7] It is thus in accordance with this sense of the everyday that we might turn our attention to better understanding acts of (digital) citizenship that reconfigure—suddenly and unexpectedly—children's and young people's relationship to citizenship.

Isin suggests that 'acts of citizenship' can be studied through the 'orientations (intentions, motives, purposes), strategies (reasons, manoeuvres, programmes) and technologies (tactics, techniques, methods)' that constitute forms of 'solidaristic, agonistic and alienating modes of being with each other' (2008, p. 37). With this in mind, we now turn to the analysis of a small-scale living lab 'experiment' set up to examine intergenerational attitudes towards social networking and cybersafety (Third et al., 2011). We argue that, through the tactical disruption of the everyday, this project created a scene through which participants could rethink children's and young people's (digital) citizenship.

## INTERGENERATIONAL DIGITAL DIALOGUES:
## A LIVING LAB CASE STUDY

Research shows that many parents remain concerned about their children being online and sometimes feel ill-equipped to guide their children to participate safely (Third et al., 2011). In this context, parents are frequently advised that the best way to support their children's online safety is to 'remain vigilant and seek help from external experts' (Long, 2005, p. 129). These external experts are typically adults who have established careers in parental cybersafety education that are supported by an expanding market of software, programmes and strategies. However, very few of these 'solutions' have been evaluated for their efficacy, and even fewer take a child-centred approach that centres parents' need to better understand how and why children go online.[8]

Our Young and Well Cooperative Research Centre project investigated the intergenerational dynamics shaping attitudes towards and use of social networking services (SNS) and safety online through a small-scale 'living lab' process whereby four young people designed, delivered and evaluated a three-hour experiential learning workshop for eight parents of children aged 6 to 18.[9] In doing so, the living lab deliberately sought to disrupt the usual power relations that structure the everyday of formal cybersafety learning experiences to assess to what extent this might generate new conversations between young people and parents about their (safe) online engagement. Researchers observed the living lab in process, documenting and analysing the intergenerational exchanges that ensued.

The living lab drew on user-centred, participatory research methods. In an initial workshop, young people and researchers co-designed a learning experience that young people would later deliver to adults. In this workshop, young people brainstormed the challenges they believe parents face and then generated learning modules and accompanying teaching resources to support parents to improve their technical and navigational skills, and enhance parents' understanding of young people's motivations, online social practices, and navigation of online risks. By participating in this first workshop, young people stepped directly into subject positions—those of 'teacher' and 'expert'—from which they are normally excluded. Remembering that acts of citizenship can be either intentional or accidental, this marked the project's first *planned* moment of disruption of the everyday. For three out of the four young people,[10] this was a very uncomfortable experience, surfacing anxieties about whether or not they were 'qualified' and capable of doing a good job. The research team reassured them that they didn't have to perform their role in any predetermined way and that they should experiment with their own ways of teaching parents. The research team also reiterated that the most important thing was for young people to be guided by the adults' curiosities and concerns and to draw on their own everyday experiences to answer their questions. With this reassurance, the young people relaxed somewhat and began to play creatively with different ways of running the workshop for adults, critiquing, reworking and reinventing the meanings of the categories of 'teacher' and 'expert' from their own perspectives.

This process politicised the young people inasmuch as it facilitated a space for them to critique the adult-centred thinking and practices that underpin mainstream culture. Their critiques encompassed a critical assessment of the efficacy of the teaching practices they had experienced, particularly at school, but also extended to debates about adults' understandings of young people's technology practices. In the young people's view, parents often misunderstand how and why young people go online; they frequently overestimate the risks young people face online and downplay the benefits; and they underestimate young people's capacity to deploy strategies to stay safe online. The workshop process, that is, opened up pathways for young people to think about how existing identity categories interpolate them as subordinate, calling them into being as conscious political subjects with a desire to, as they reported, 'share their experiences' with and 'be heard by adults' in ways that might 'change adults' views' and improve how parents react to and support their children's digital media use. In other words, in this tactical disruption of the everyday, young people mobilised as 'activist citizens' (Isin, 2008).

In the second workshop with parents, young people were tasked with facilitation responsibilities. One young participant (who, in the initial workshop, was more confident about inhabiting the role of 'teacher' and 'expert') led a whole of group discussion—which he entitled 'Social Networking 101'—to get adults thinking about how both they and their children use social media in their daily lives. Then, each young person paired with an adult and a set of digital devices (computer, tablet, smart phone) and invited the parents to work through a set of scenarios the young people had developed in the previous workshop. The scenarios focused on common parental concerns including cyberbullying, sexting, access to inappropriate content and internet 'addiction'. Finally, young people conducted 'vox pop' interviews with the adult participants to capture their reflections on what they had learned, and to what extent their pre-existing views had been confirmed or challenged.

Positioning young people as the 'experts' was a deliberate strategy to create the second rupture in both the social order of the workshop and mainstream cybersafety discourse. Adult participants had been invited to join a workshop to learn about social networking and cybersafety and thus anticipated a standard lecture delivered by adult professionals. As they reported in the vox pop evaluation conducted at the end of the workshop, their reactions when they discovered it would be an interactive process led by young people ranged from surprise and uncertainty to incredulity. This 'act' of tactically disrupting the 'ordinary' power dynamics that structure the everyday operated to problematise the usual hierarchies of knowledge and open up new possibilities for thinking and contesting citizenship. While this did not guarantee an immediate transformation in power relations, it surfaced the *orientations* of participants and forged a space for dialogue and knowledge sharing—operating at 'generative edge' of new modes of citizenship (Hartley, 2010, p. 25).

While young people aimed for parents to gain a better appreciation of the meanings of social media in their lives through the workshop, in the initial group discussion, parents expressed a desire to 'know *what* young people do online' (as opposed to *why*). Some wanted guidance on how to make decisions to keep their children safe online. Others felt worried about the pace of technological change and were looking for reassurance. In short, young people expressed a desire for change, while many of the parents initially sought an assurance of the status quo. However, this shifted noticeably when young people and parents engaged in paired discussions in front of digital media devices.

In three out of the four paired discussions, there was evidence of technical skills transfer between the young people and the adults, with parents later reporting that they felt more confident about how to navigate social media and use privacy and security settings. Further, parents reported that they benefitted from observing the young people's disposition of 'learning by discovery', that is, of experimenting with different functionalities until they found what they needed. However, more than learning specific technical skills and attitudes, parents reported that working with young people provided them with an intimate window on the myriad skills and strategies young people deploy in staying safe online. In doing so, they moved from a position of concern to one of reassurance and, importantly, respect. Michelle, a 42-year-old working mother of two young children, reported that working with Jimmy, a 20 year-old-male student, helped her understand that children do the same things she herself does online. Importantly, whilst discussions of the scenarios originally focused on technical and navigational skills, they inspired opportunities for unscripted exchange and moved very quickly towards more abstract, even philosophical, conversations about the ways digital media are (re)shaping community, family and peer relationships, and society more broadly. Disrupting the adult-child binaries that characterise the everyday enabled, that is, the unfolding of new and unexpected insights and relations; in particular, it established common ground between generations and mobilised micro-processes of opinion formation.

Whilst the living lab produced shifts, it also led to reassertions of subject positions. Whereas most adult participants were open to different ways of hearing, seeing and understanding young people and their use of digital media, Barry, a 46-year-old training designer and parent of two pre-teen boys, was highly resistant. His body language and use of the technology to assert a physical barrier between him and Lucy, a 19-year-old trainee makeup artist, betrayed a discomfort with being the 'student' in an experiential learning setting. Their discussion focused closely on the scenarios, with Barry positioning Lucy primarily as a source of information about the technology in front of him, rather than as his interlocutor. The conversation rarely moved beyond the posing of technical questions (e.g. 'how do I change the security settings on a Facebook account?'). When Lucy encouraged Barry to use the computer, he would follow her instructions and then retreat again. Barry's body language, his lack of physical interaction with the technology and the transactional conversation read as attempts to reimpose the usual power relations; to take back some control by subtly resisting the reversal that the living lab enacted. Lucy later observed that the experience reinforced that some adults just don't like the idea that 'young people might know something about something'. That is, even though Lucy found the exchange very frustrating, it still had the effect of surfacing her politics.

In the second workshop, the young participants moved from scepticism and nervousness to feeling a great sense of achievement and empowerment. They reported enjoying the opportunity to share their technical knowledge, to challenge adult's perceived negative attitudes towards 'youth' and to highlight for adults the benefits of their social networking use. Following the workshop with adults, the young people articulated a desire to teach key decision makers—such as federal politicians in Canberra—with a view to impacting digital media policy. One young person summarised their involvement in explicitly political terms: 'We'd totally do this with politicians. They totally need to know this stuff!' We can see here how the disruption of the everyday via the living lab cultivated consciously claim-making subjects.

Overall, then, the living lab's tactical disruption of the everyday produced a space for dialogue and contestation as the site of citizenship, in ways that challenged the adultist norms that both structure contemporary digital citizenship discourse and marginalise young people's experiences.

## FINDING THE 'GENERATIVE EDGE'

We began by arguing that digital citizenship policy and practice discourses, as they currently circulate in the Western world, work to foreclose the meanings of children's and young people's digital practices, proscribing a narrow, adult-centric and biopolitical form of citizenship for children and young people. Such a framing closes down the radical potential implicit in the idea of 'digital citizenship' for rethinking citizenship for and through the digital. Reading through theories of 'the everyday' and Isin's concept of 'acts of citizenship', we have argued that, in order to recover and mobilise the radical possibilities of (digital) citizenship, we must begin to extend our thinking about and incursions into the terrain of the everyday. Methodologically, this requires that we recognise research is—like citizenship—performative. That is, we must begin to understand research as *intervention* (see Third, 2016); to mobilise around the idea that, as Mike Michael observes, research does not simply reflect what is 'out there' but 'is instrumental in, and a feature of, the "making of out theres"' (2012, p. 26). Researching children's and young people's digital citizenship must thus begin to focus in earnest on generating, exposing and interrogating interruptions in the everyday of citizenship so that we may truly work at the 'generative edge' of new forms of citizenship.

## NOTES

1. Office of the Children's eSafety Commissioner [OCeC]. "Role of the Office." Retrieved from: https://www.esafety.gov.au/about-the-office/role-of-the-office.

2. ACMA. *Digital Citizens Guide,* accessed January 2, 2016. Retrieved from: http://www.cybersmart.gov.au/cybersmart-citizens/~/media/Cybersmart/Digital%20 Citizens/ACMA-Informational-PDF-Cybersmart.pdf.

3. For example, the work of EU Kids Online has consistently asserted the need to develop policies and practices that mitigate the risks whilst also fostering users' capacity to maximise the benefits online. This often takes expression as the imperative to balance protection rights with provision and participation rights. See for example, de Haan, 2009.

4. Cybersmart is a suite of online safety resources developed by the ACMA.

5. Office of the Children's eSafety Commissioner [OCeC]. "Digital Citizenship." accessed January 10, 2016. Retrieved from: https://www.esafety.gov.au/ education-resources/classroom-resources/digital-citizenship.

6. ChildNet International. "What is digital citizenship?: Digital citizenship from Childnet's point of view", accessed Febraury 4, 2016. Retrieved from: http://www. digizen.org/digicentral/digital-citizenship.aspx?video=s.

7. In distinguishing between 'every' scene and 'any' scene, we take our inspiration from Thomas Keenan's lectures, 'Claiming Human Rights', delivered for the *Thinking Out Loud* lecture series in 2016.

8. One exception to this is the Australian 'youth-driven movement against cyberbullying', Project Rockit. See http://projectrockit.com.au.

9. Given that intra-family dynamics might compromise the efficacy of this strategy, the young participants did not teach their own parents.

10. The fourth young person readily embraced the idea of being the 'expert'. His approach was much more conventionally didactic and thus resonated as a form of 'mimicry' (Bhahbha, 1994), which problematised adult-centred discourses and pre-existing subject positions differently from the other three young participants.

## REFERENCES

Australian Communication and Media Authority (ACMA) (2009). *Developments in internet filtering technologies and other measures for promoting online safety: Second annual report to the Minister for Broadband, Communications and the Digital Economy.* Retrieved from http://www.acma.gov.au/webwr/_assets/main/ lib310554/developments_in_internet_filters_2ndreport.pdf.

Australian Communication and Media Authority (ACMA) (2010). *Citizens and the ACMA: Exploring the concepts within Australian media and communications regulation: Occasional Paper.* Retrieved from http://www.acma.gov.au/theACMA/About/Corporate/Authority/citizens-and-the-acma.

Bennett, W. L. (Ed.). (2008). *Civic life online: Learning how digital media can engage youth.* Cambridge, MA: MIT Press.

boyd, d. (2008). *Taken out of context: American teen sociality in networked publics.* (PHD in Information Management and Systems), University of California, Berkeley.

boyd, d. (2014). *It's complicated: The social lives of networked teens.* New Haven, CT: Yale University Press.

Coleman, S. (2008). Doing IT for themselves: Management versus autonomy in youth e-citizenship. In W. L. Bennett (Ed.), *Civic life online: Learning how digital media can engage youth* (pp. 189–206). Cambridge, MA: MIT Press.

Collin, P. (2008). The internet, youth participation policies, and the development of young people's political identities in Australia. *Journal of Youth Studies, 11*(5), 527–542.

Collin, P. (2015). *Young citizens and political participation in a digital society: Addressing the democratic disconnect.* Basingstoke, U.K.: Palgrave McMillan.

Collin, P., Rahilly, K., Richardson, I., & Third, A. (2011). *The benefits of social networking services.* Retrieved from https://www.youngandwellcrc.org.au/knowledge-hub/publications/benefits-social-networking-services-literature-review/.

de Certau, M. (1988). *The practice of everyday life.* (S. Rendall, Trans.). Berkeley: University of California Press.

de Haan, J. (2009). *Maximising opportunities and minimising risks for children online.* Bristol: The Policy Press.

Drotner, K. (1994). Ethnographic enigmas: 'The everyday' in recent media studies. *Cultural Studies, 8*(2), 341–357.

Evans, K. (1995). Competence and citizenship: Towards a complementary model for times of critical social change. *British Journal of Education and Work, 8*(2), 14–27.

Harris, A. (2008). Young women, late modern politics, and the participatory possibilities of online cultures. *Journal of Youth Studies, 11*(5), 481–495.

Harris, A. (2010). Young people, everyday civic life and the limits of social cohesion, *Journal of Intercultural Studies, 31*(5), 573–589.

Harris, A., & Wyn, J. (2009). Young people's politics and the micro-territories of the local. *Australian Journal of Political Science, 44*(2), 327–344.

Harris, A., Wyn, J., & Younes, S. (2007). Young people and citizenship: An everyday perspective. *Youth Studies Australia, 6*(3), 19–27.

Hartley, J. (2010). Silly citizenship. *Critical Discourse Studies, 7*(4), 1–39.

Isin, E. F. (2008). Theorizing acts of citizenship. In E. F. Isin & G. M. Nielsen (Eds.), *Acts of Citizenship* (pp. 15–43). London: Zed Books.

Ito, M., Davidson, C., Jenkins, H., Lee, C., Eisenberg, M., & Weiss, J. (2008). Foreword. In D. Buckingham (Ed.), *Youth, identity, digital media* (pp. vii–ix). Cambridge, MA: MIT Press.

Lefebvre, H. (2000). *Everyday life in the modern world.* London: Athlone.

Long, J. (2005). Be [net] alert, but not alarmed?: Regulating the parents of generation MSN. *Media International Australia, 114*(1), 122–134.

Marsh, D., O'Toole, T., & Jones, S. (2007). *Young people and politics in the UK: Apathy or alienation?* Basingstoke, UK: Palgrave.

Marsh, D., O'Toole, T., & Jones, S. (2007). *Young people and politics in the UK: Apathy or alienation?* Basingstoke, UK: Palgrave.

Michael, M. (2012). Anecdote. In C. Lury and N. Wakeford (Eds), *Inventive methods: The happening of the social* (pp. 25–35). London: Routledge.

Morrison, I. (2008). Act 11 acts of commemoration. In E. F. Isin & G. M. Nielsen (Eds.), *Acts of citizenship* (pp. 289–291). London: Zed Books.

Online Safety and Technology Working Group (OSTWG) (2010). *Youth safety on a living internet: Report of the online safety and technology working group.* Retrieved from https://www.ntia.doc.gov/legacy/reports/2010/OSTWG_Final_Report_060410.pdf.

Third, A. (2014). *Gender and the political: Deconstructing the female terrorist.* New York: Palgrave.

Third, A. (2016). Children's rights in the digital age: Thinking human rights beyond citizenship and the nation-state. *Global Studies of Childhood.*

Third, A. (2016). The tactical researcher: Cultural studies research as pedagogy. In A. Hickey (Ed.), *The pedagogies of cultural studies.* New York: Routledge.

Third, A., Bellerose, D., Dawkins, U., Keltie, E., & Pihl, K. (2014). *Children's rights in the digital age: A download from children around the world.* Retrieved from: http://www.unicef.org/publications/index_76268.html.

Third, A., Bellerose, D., Dawkins, U., Keltie, E., & Pihl, K. (2014a). *Children's rights in the digital age: A download from children around the world.* Retrieved from: www.youngandwellcrc.org.au/knowledge-hub/publications/intergenerational-attitudes-towards-social-networking-cybersafety/.

Third, A., Collier, A., & Forrest-Lawrence, P. (2014b). *Addressing the cybersafety challenge: From risk to resilience.* Retrieved from: http://www.telstra.com.au/uberprod/groups/webcontent/@corporate/@aboutus/documents/document/uber-staging_279130.pdf.

Vromen A. (2003). 'People try to put us down…': Participatory citizenship of 'generation x'. *Australian Journal of Political Science, 38*(1), 79–99.

Vromen, A., & Collin, P. (2010). Everyday youth participation? Contrasting views from Australian policymakers and young people. *Young, 18*(1), 97–112.

Vromen, A., Xenos, M. A., & Loader, B. (2015). Young people, social media and connective action: From organisational maintenance to everyday political talk. *Journal of Youth Studies, 18*(1), 80–100.

Wood, B. E. (2014). Researching the everyday: Young people's experiences and expressions of citizenship. *International Journal of Qualitative Studies in Education, 27*(2), 214–232.

*Chapter 4*

# Reimagining Digital Citizenship via Disability

Gerard Goggin[1]

Human dignity needs a new guarantee which can be found only in a new political principle, in a new law on earth, whose validity this time must comprehend the whole of humanity.

—Hannah Arendt (1948[1973], p. xi)

Democracy is what makes the institution of citizenship problematic.

—Étienne Balibar (2015, p.2)

It might be a very good idea for us to expand the possibilities of democracy precisely because democracy offers us unfinished and infinitely revisable forms of political organization that stand the best chance, in the long run, of responding adequately to the human rights of the unpredictable creatures we human are.

—Michael Berubé (2003, p. 53)

A February 2016 protest by disability activists in Bolivia, featuring wheel-chair users suspended from the country's bridges, is widely shared across the world, via photos, videos, manifestos and writings, circulating on Facebook, Twitter and other social media platforms. Operating from Malta, the online platform *Global Disability Watch: Powering Advocacy* assembles and reports 'timely, accessible and usable ground driven information on disability, disability rights violations and development policy and practice from a range of global contexts, prioritising the global South'.[2] In December 2015, Alice Wong, founder of the US-based *Disability Visibility Project*,[3] kicked off a Twitter-based campaign #crippingthemighty, critiquing the well-resourced website, *The Mighty*, that publishes personal essays about disability (often drawing freely, and without payment, on the disability blogosphere).[4] In the United Kingdom, in 2011–2012, availability of videos, online reports, circulated by digital platforms, were used as a key tool to coordinate, publicise and amplify disability protests, when mainstream media were slow to provide coverage (Pearson & Trevisan, 2015). In Canada, in 2013–2015, arts-based approaches to digital storytelling and drama are used to create an 'archive of over 100 digital stories from women and people of all genders living with disabilities/differences and healthcare providers' (Rice et al., 2015). These vignettes are but a few instances that illustrate the burgeoning practices of digital citizenship engaging communities, publics and individuals concerned with disability.

If we tackle the topic squarely, we find that digital citizenship is a concept that's tricky to pin down. In 2007, the first book on the topic opened with a deceptively simple formulation: 'Digital citizenship' is the ability to participate in society online' (Mossberger, Tolbert & McNeal, 2007, p. 1; see also, Mossberger, 2009). However, this neat assurance turns out to be a complicated proposition, as the next sentence suggests: 'What, however, does it mean to invoke the notion of citizenship in relation to the use of a technology?' The 2007 *Digital Citizenship* book contained two mentions of disability, including the notion that the 'individual benefits of broadband use' would be 'reducing the impact of distance and disability': 'Some of the most promising applications for broadband are in telemedicine, distance learning, and Internet accessibility for people with disabilities' (p. 1).

In the intervening decade, a particular version of digital citizenship has been established as the default approach across various settings, especially in schools. Mike Ribble's *Digital Citizenship in Schools*, also appeared in 2007, published by the International Society for Technology in Education. In its third edition (2015, p. 1), Ribble's *Digital Citizenship* sums up it this way:

> What are the appropriate behaviours in a digital society? How can an individual learn what is appropriate and what isn't? These are core questions . . . The goal of digital citizenship is to provide a consistent message to students and educational professionals so that they can become productive and responsible users of digital technologies.

Digital access is the first of the nine elements of digital citizenship outlined by Ribble, and the book includes significant acknowledgement of disability and accessibility as integral to digital citizenship. This kind of incorporation of disability in discussions of digital citizenship is encouraging. However, we have a long way to go, not just in incorporating disability, but in acknowledging the deep ways in which it challenges citizenship itself, especially digital citizenship.

The topic of disability, digital technology and accessibility has grown slowly across practice, policy, and research over at least a thirty-year period, and is finally gaining critical mass and influence—and many people, especially those engaged in digital technology, would have a sense of this. What has received much less attention is the radical way in which disability stands to recast our understanding of digital technologies, society, power and participation.

With our opening vignettes in mind, we could suggest that the coordinates of a new account of digital citizenship can be found in the 2006 UN *Convention on the Rights of Persons with Disabilities* (CRPD). The CRPD resembles a Arendtian 'new law on earth', aiming to 'promote, protect and ensure the full and equal enjoyment of all human rights and fundamental freedoms by all persons with disabilities, and to promote respect for their inherent dignity' (CRPD, Article 1). Equal access to technology is a concept that straddles many articles of the CRPD, and forms part of its general obligations upon states-parties, for example: 'to undertake or promote research and development of and to promote the availability and use of new technologies, including information and communications technologies, mobility aids, devices and assistive technologies, suitable for persons with disabilities' (clause g., Article 4). Article 21 ('Freedom of Expression and Opinion, and Access to Information'), Article 29 ('Participation in Political and Public Life') and Article 30 ('Participation in Cultural Life, Recreation, Leisure and Sport'), in particular, include extended reference to accessible and alternative formats, information, cultural material, media content, digital technologies as well as material being available in sign languages. While its implementation may be slow and uneven, the CRPD is being widely used and debated as a reference point for discussions on the adequacy of digital participation, as it is across all other realms of social life. At a deeper level, the CRPD prompts us to reconceive how we imagine and do participation and, by implication, citizenship, so we do justice to (1) the new digital forms and architectures of social life and (2) emergent understandings of disability. Before we explore this further, it is important to understand the issues faced in rethinking and enlarging citizenship to embrace disability.

## RETHINKING CITIZENSHIP WITH DISABILITY

Citizenship is a rich area of political thought and struggle, comprising different conceptualisations and traditions. Disability is still a relatively new and little understood way to approach citizenship, let alone digital citizenship. Whether one works in liberal traditions of citizenship (Nussbaum, 2006; Silvers & Pickering Francis, 2009; Badano, 2014; Donaldson & Kymlicak, 2016), social citizenship and rights traditions (represented by the influential work of Davis, 1999; T. H. Marshall; Dwyer, 2010; Roulstone & Prideaux, 2012)[5] or critical traditions (relied upon here), disability problematises concepts of citizenship and how such concepts of citizenship are operationalised.

Hence, the contention of North American scholar Michael Berubé that 'disability issues are—or should be—central to theories of social justice in a much broader sense' (Berubé, 2003, p. 53). As Berubé (2003, p. 43) encapsulates it:

> Disability is not the only area of social life in which the politics of recognition are inseparable from the politics of redistribution: other areas central to citizenship, such as immigration, reproductive rights, and criminal justice, are every bit as complex.

What Berubé points out is that disability very often underpins or plays a crucial role in the mix of factors that the shape the technologies of policy, power and governance exercised in society, especially by states (p. 54). Digital life remains a form of technology too, because it is part of these things. The burden of these powerful dynamics of the representation, constitution and marshalling of disability, including in new digital forms, fall heavily and consequentially on people with disabilities, especially as they seek to articulate, realise and vouchsafe their rights through citizenship. As a way of redressing this, and expanding notions of citizenship, Canadian scholars Richard Devlin and Dianne Pothier have suggested that 'the landscape of citizenship discourse needs to be expanded to respond to the particular experiential circumstances of persons with disabilities' (2006, p. 18).

Various disability scholars have explored the ways that disability is pivotal to how power, control, and the distribution of resources operates in contemporary societies. Germane is Karen Soldatic and Helen Meekosha's account of disability as a strategically crucial category in the neo-liberal conditions of the current phase of capitalism (made all the more acute with the politics of austerity and precarity). Soldatic and Meekosha (2012, p. 206) note that 'work', 'care' and eligibility for social and state support, among other things, all require marshalling of flexible, and changing definitions of disability:

> We learn from the neoliberal turn the 'ambiguity' of disability, as a class of citizenship. While medical science wishes us to imagine that disability is predicated on a concrete and stable measuring of the body, in fact, the historical specificity of disability and its meaning as a class of citizenship is continually moving.

This is a point also made by the US-based scholar Julie Avril Minich (2013, p. 15) in her study of disability and citizenship in 'Greater Mexico':

The racializing logic of citizenship is deeply intertwined with a logic of able-bodied supremacy. . . . Neoliberalism . . . exacerbates the racializing and disabling effects of dominant constructions of citizenship.

For our consideration of digital citizenship and disability, the implications of this are important to register in relation to the cardinal and much-debated institution of the state. Soldatic and Meekhosha (2012, p. 206) therefore contend:

> Thus the state plays a central role in creating social, moral and political understandings of disability, and therefore we need to 'bring the state back in' (Jessop 2001) to our analysis. . . . Regulatory practices that enable the state to legitimate its power and control are integral to understanding how disabled people experience not only their daily lives but also their lived experience of discrimination, marginalization and stigmatization.

In relation to digital technology and disability, we might think of the rise of e-government and digital government (Herman, 2010; Martin & Goggin, 2016), which is increasingly being relied on for disability social support as well as a range of other ways in which the state touches upon and shapes the lives of people with disabilities.

This brief discussion of disability and citizenship hopefully points towards some of the reasons why it has proven difficult to imagine people with disabilities as citizens. There are simply deeply embedded assumptions, values and emotions that disability challenges and disrupts. The idea, for instance, that people with cognitive disabilities have the right to participate on equal terms with others in terms of democracy, political participation, governance and management, sexuality, culture and leisure continues to be troubling for many and difficult for many societies to enact (Goodey, 2011; Brooke Warren, 2015). By precluding and excluding many people with disabilities from full citizenship—including a fair stake in the very definition of what citizenship might mean—normalcy is able to be 'enforced' (Davis, 1995).

These confining versions of citizenship are implicated in the narrow ways that disability is still often imagined in relation to digital technology. In the first place, we might recall that digital technology, as it has emerged in the period of 1970s to 2010s, is closely associated with neo-liberalism. Although its complexity lies outside the scope of this essay, digital technology involves shifts in markets, the state, governance and regulation (for instance, privatisation, deregulation, trade and competition regimes), as well as it does technical and social innovation. Digital technology also offers new 'affordances' (or capabilities) for exercising power and control, as much as social progress, democracy, justice and other goals.

These overarching conditions of digital technology bear upon disability. In particular, digital technology is framed as salvational, wholly transformative and a great boon for the challenges people with disabilities face. Many scholars and commentators have critiqued this myth of technology as salvation for the 'problem' of disability for a couple of decades, to little avail (Goggin & Newell, 2003; Ellis & Kent, 2011; Mills, 2016; Roulstone, 2016). In the case of schools, it is commonplace to find smartphones and tablet computers, especially the iPad, represented as a 'revolution' for people with disabilities, as in this article on Brisbane schools: 'A learning revolution is under way in special schools, with the lives of disabled students profoundly changed with the introduction of iPads' (Chilcott, 2011). It is certainly true that many forms of digital technologies have been sources of benefit for people with disabilities, who have used and shaped them in very interesting, typically understudied and little recognised ways. Yet, many of the myths of disability and technology that frame news stories, policy and everyday conversations have a strong undercurrent that technology will finally 'solve' the problems that people with disabilities face, and that societies struggle with. In their study of such representations, Haller et al. (2016) put it this way:

> Liberation. Revolution. Cure. Miracle. Even magic. These are just a few of the words the news media use to describe the growth of tablet, smartphone and iTechnology used by people with communication disabilities, particularly children. . . . Such words also represent the social construction of disability as a problem needing a solution by denying people with disabilities a role in employing iDevices meaningfully in their respective environments.

Haller et al. find that while 'some new narratives about technology are informing some stories about people with communication disabilities, the news media tended to give credit to the technology as enabling people to communicate rather than credit being given to people with disabilities who make the technology work' (2016).

The enduring and oppressive power of the great myth of disability and technology came home to me in late 2015, when I attended a big Australian conference on disability, entitled 'New World Conference: Disability in the 21st Century'. For the purposes of the conference, this new world of disability revolved around technology: 'Our conference will showcase innovative technology designed to enhance the lives of people with disability and enable choice and control and full participation in life'.[6] Much of the discussion was excellent, led by and engaging many experts and other participants with disability, and with high levels of accessibility and participation. Yet, the framing assumptions were highly problematic, especially as this conference was the flagship event for the new Australian National Disability Insurance Scheme (NDIS).

In principle, the NDIS scheme offers person-centred and directed disability support for any citizen who requires it. In many ways, it is a scheme responding to the vision of social citizenship, extending the welfare state. In reality, there are many challenges and notable exclusions that go well beyond existing critiques made of social citizenship and welfare. In particular, the role of digital technology in delivering the scheme has been presented as a breakthrough; yet the social and power relations of such technology as it unfolds in this, and other new arenas, of disability support are very problematic. For all its great promise, the NDIS is very consistent with, and in many ways, delivered on market-based, neo-liberal principles, enabled and co-eval with digital technologies. So, we may heed Soldatic and Meekosha's warning here—to trace, interrogate and challenge the ways in which the state, and broader regulation and governmentality (Lynn Tremain, 2005), works through digital technology to exert insidious, new forms of control in our lives. There is the danger, for instance, of ongoing digital surveillance of individualised budgets to ensure that disabled people are spending their funds 'responsibly', a theme of welfare elsewhere. There are also the many ways in which internet and mobile-enabled surveillance technologies are being used in disability and health contexts (including homes), ostensibly for beneficial purposes but also with significant issues for rights.

In order to explore these challenges, let us take up the setting of schools— which is a recurrent location and theme in digital citizenship.

## TOO COOL (OR TROUBLING) FOR SCHOOL?

How digital citizenship is actually conceived and implemented in schools in relation to disability and accessibility varies greatly, despite some acknowledgement in various places and discussion in the research literature (such as Ribble's *Digital Citizenship* text discussed earlier). If we examine digital citizenship 'on the ground' more closely, what we find raises disturbing questions concerning disability.

Recently, my 12-year-old son started high school in Sydney, and commenced a class on 'digital citizenship' (faintly amused that I'm writing an essay on the topic). In the state of New South Wales (NSW), the government provides a suite of curriculum and information on the topic to underpin teaching in schools: 'Digital Citizenship: Essential information for students, teachers and parents about digital citizenship and being safe, positive and responsible online'.[7] High school students are asked the following:

> Do you use the internet to share information about yourself or others, communicate with friends, comment on what you see online, play games, get material

for an assignment or buy stuff online? If you answered YES to any of these, you
are a digital citizen.[8]

To explain why digital citizenship is important, the education department
goes on to say:

> Do you want to get the best out of using the internet and keep yourself and
> others safe and healthy in an online world? Use these materials to learn what it
> takes to become a positive digital citizen.

The resources include a range of reasonably up-to-date information, learning
activities, videos and games on cybersafety, cybersecurity, consumer protection, content creating and sharing, online community participation and other
issues.

In reviewing this material, I found nothing relating to disability and accessibility. Nor is there any material on digital inequalities or access broadly
construed. There is some basic effort to prompt consideration of inter- and
cross-cultural issues—notably, in the 'Global Citizenship' activity module.
If this was improved, this is one place in school curriculum where disability
could be introduced and integrated—as a stepping stone to a contemporary
account of online cultural dynamics.

So, what's wrong with this picture? Certainly, this is only one provincial
education system, but—with variations—this kind of material would be
familiar in many parts of the world, something evident in the circulation of
approaches and resources across jurisdictions. Clearly, there is some effort
among proponents of digital citizenship in schools to include broader treat-
ments—as represented by Ribble's *Digital Citizenship*. Yet, the version of
digital citizenship that often appears instead, and dominates public discourse
also, typically resembles the version found in NSW schools' curriculum. The
crucial effort to teach students to reflect upon and critically use digital technologies does not appear to connect with crucial dimensions of citizenship
that disability entails. Whereas, if we take seriously disability as indivisible
to digital citizenship, this would mean a much larger and richer account of
digital citizenship—and indeed of citizenship itself.

Elsewhere in schools, and other educational settings, some effort is under
way to improve digital accessibility for all students (Alper, 2014; Edyburn,
2014; Goggin, 2016). So, it's likely that in pioneering or good-practice settings, disability, accessibility and technology are being taught alongside, or as
part of, digital technology education, which might even extend to digital citizenship notions. However, I suspect this is not widespread, which is a serious
problem for digital citizenship. Following Graham Longford, for instance,
it could be argued that inaccessible digital technologies represent a 'politics

of code'—'technical features' and narrow design assumptions that amount to 'hidden pedagogies of citizenship', teaching students a powerful message that disabling technologies are 'normal' (Longford, 2005). The exposure and analysis of such taken-for-granted things that digital technologies 'teach' us would be an excellent, critical mission for digital citizenship.

To understand why digital citizenship is not really grappling with disability, it is necessary to step back and look at the big picture on disability in schools. Many school students with disability, especially high school students, face very difficult barriers to education that often result in exclusion. A stark illustration of this can be found in a 2015 case in a government school in Canberra, Australia. A ten-year-old student with autism was confined in a small cage: a two metre by two metre fenced enclosure made of pool fencing (Mosley, 2015). As the revelation of this shocking incident made news around the world, Diane Joseph, the director general of the Education and Training Directorate in the Australian Capital Territory (ACT), explained:

'The structure has been in the classroom from 10 March until 27 March', she [Joseph, the director general] said. 'It was built for a particular student to help manage his behaviour and to provide a space for that student to withdraw.' (in Hurst, 2015)

The ACT education minister, Joy Burch, did not mince her words, declaring she was 'quite frankly, disgusted that this structure was allowed in our school. . . . It is absolutely unacceptable' (in Hurst, 2015). After a formal investigation of the incident, the school principal was sacked (Davey, 2015). These are welcome responses, however Minister Burch also expressed her view that this was a 'one-off incident' (in Hurst, 2015). In relation to this school, this view was immediately contradicted by the action of an unknown person, who pinned up a photo of the cage, with the ten-year-old boy sleeping in it, under the caption 'Sanctuary':

A source told the ABC [Australian Broadcasting Corporation] their understanding was the sign was put up to try to 'normalise the fact that there was a cage in the classroom, to the other children, and to the boy himself'. 'Let's label it a sanctuary, stick up a photo and it won't look and feel so bad', the source said. (Mosely, 2015)

Disability and human rights advocates have pointed out that people with disabilities, not only in institutional settings (Rosenthal & Ahern, 2012) but also in households, schools and elsewhere, are subject to confinement and treatment that would in relation to other groups be immediately regarded as torture (Wadiwel, 2017). In relation to school education, as well as university education, children and young people with disabilities are still subjected to behaviour management and other policies and practices that deny them their human rights to education.[9] A challenging aspect of this oppressive situation is that schools vary widely on how they educate and support students with disabilities.

Learning, intellectual, cognitive and developmental disabilities especially experience variable, inadequate and often unjust treatment by schools (Sleeter, 1987; Connor & Ferri, 2010; Barker, 2010, 2007; Schwartzenberg, 2005). There are various factors that contribute to this denial of rights by many schools and their communities, while others do better. One problem across an educational system is that a student can have a good experience in one school, and then proceed to another school and find themselves effectively excluded because of poor practice there. If this occurs at a key transition point—from primary school to high school, for instance—the negative impact on a young person's education and life prospects can be all the more disabling. Further, if schools actively reproduce—rather than challenge—cultural attitudes of stigmatization, these can be normalised at such an early age for all children.

Returning to our topic of digital citizenship, we can see that the contexts and sites of citizenship are crucially important. Schools are an important site for citizenship, especially for children and young people with disability. Yet, when it comes to schools especially, the links with broader ideas of citizenship, including social equality, political participation and rights, are unclear. Also hazy are the links between digital citizenship and disability. There is a 'disconnect' which emerges from the ACT case, if we notice a parallel development.

In August 2015, Joy Burch, the very minister for education and training who was involved in the 'cage' scandal discussed above, established a six-month topic-specific advisory committee on digital citizenship. The advisory committee included representatives from bodies such as the Youth Coalition, Aboriginal and Torres Strait Islander Elected Body and a 'community representative' (from the Young Women's Christian Association)—but no representative from a disability organisation. Charged with advising on '[o]pportunities to strengthen the partnership between parents and schools to enable the setting of consistent and high expectations for the use of ICT by students and teachers', the 'Digital Citizenship Advisory Committee was scheduled to only meet twice, discussing cybersafety and digital literacy'.[10] Again, we find a foreclosure of digital citizenship, where, in relation to disability in schools in this state especially, an expansion of citizenship, in all its forms, was sorely needed.

Of course, it could be rightly objected that the dominant version of digital citizenship we find in various places internationally, but especially in relation to children and young people in schools, is widely regarded as too narrow, and only a small part of a large framework needed to understand and address the realities of digital citizenship. In the context of this volume, and the broader digital citizenship debates, conceptualisation and research, we have the opportunity, of course, to consider and advocate for more expansive, accurate and fit-for-purpose conceptions of digital citizenship. In this context, disability is very promising as a productive way of approaching, reimagining and refining digital citizenship, as I will now discuss.

## DISABILITY AND DIGITAL CITIZENSHIP: RIGHTS AND REALITIES

Contemporary social relations rely upon digital technology, often as a precondition of effective citizenship. This especially applies to the transformational project of delivering disability justice—that is, the now acknowledged goal of reforming societies to genuinely incorporate and enable everyone, especially people with disabilities, as spelt out in the UN (often in tension with the systems of work, welfare and disability social support being reconfigured globally). What, for instance, are the distinctive dimensions of digital citizenship that come into sharp relief, once we take seriously the uses, social practices, claims and desires of people with disabilities in relation to digital technology? To sketch some possibilities here for how to reimagine digital citizenship via disability, I discuss three leading areas: accessibility, disability activism and intimate, everyday citizenship.

### Accessibility

Accessibility is the liminal issue for disability and digital citizenship. If people cannot access or use digital technology because its design, implementation or affordances pose barriers, then they are potentially excluded from the spaces and arena of digital citizenship. The most well-known example here is web accessibility, the subject of considerable design, standards work, compliance and debate. A landmark human rights and anti-discrimination case in web accessibility occurred when a blind man, Bruce Maguire, took a complaint against the Sydney Olympics Organizing Committee (SOCOG) for its inaccessible website.[11] The outcome of this case, and the growing recognition of the importance of the web for public information and participation, especially modern concepts of government, services and citizenship, led to web accessibility being mandated for government websites in many countries.

This 'struggle for web accessibility' continues and has many more dimensions than is typically understood (Blanck, 2014). The web now is used on mobile devices, and this area of accessibility is underdeveloped (Goggin, 2015). Further, digital accessibility encompasses a broader terrain of digital technologies than simply by web. Accounts of effective and fair citizenship have often assumed access to, literacy in and mastery of traditional media (print media, such as newspapers, magazines and books), information and advertising, and radio and television broadcasting. As we know, these traditional media are being reconfigured with digital technologies, formats and social practices. So, to what extent do today's—or tomorrow's—citizens with disabilities enjoy access to digital books or newspapers? The lack of such access to books and printed materials led to the Marrakesh Treaty on intellectual property and extension of copyright extensions so that people with vision impairments and print disabilities can gain access to digital material (Harpur & Suzor, 2013). Similarly, there are pressing issues with access for people with disabilities to television and radio—two forms of media pivotal for providing resources and opportunities for the formation and exercise of citizenship.

So, the issues in accessibility for digital citizenship are wide ranging—and a long way from being addressed. If we explore them in greater depth, we also find that there is profound complexity to accessibility, that helps us to reflect upon citizenship itself (Titchkovsky, 2011; Ellcessor, 2016).

## Digital Citizenship and Disability Activism

The dominant ways that societies have conceived and constructed their public spheres exclude and diminish many from participating on equal terms, especially many people with disabilities. The resurgent movements of people with disabilities and their allies have seen assertion of citizenship, political participation and agency. A visible manifestation of this has been the use of digital tools by people with disabilities and allies, often in creative ways to express ideas and to organise and contest policies, power and authority in a wide variety of domains (Trevisan, 2016). This is often associated with new and emergent domains and cross-category forms of politics—for instance, the politics of care or the cross-category politics of health and disability; the resistance of disability activists on the front line of contests over austerity politics; and the rise of disability culture as a rich repository for ideas, practices and critique in contemporary culture in general (Ellis, Goggin & Kent, 2015). A much-cited example is the aforementioned use of social media by disability activists confronting the welfare reforms in the United Kingdom, coinciding with protests over the London Paralympics.

Particular social media platforms have become generative for disability culture, activism and conversation. Facebook is notable in many places and across many strands and communities of disability for its amenability to distributing information on disability—especially in a relatively easy-to-share, multimedia form. Twitter is another obvious platform that has become used with force and precision in fomenting and directing controversies in public culture. In a number of cases, a problematic, biased or negative thing has happened in public culture relating to disability. The matter or event has met with an immediate, fast-growing response on Twitter, among those who follow disability issues. In turn, the reaction has been registered back in the public culture, puncturing the ableist consensus and providing an entry point for disability activists, academics and commentators to express their views. In terms of theories of 'listening' (Dobson, 2014), we could suggest that Twitter has the potential to become an echo chamber by which listeners can speak back, thread together new dialogues and amplify these (via retweeting and by posting and recirculating across social media and other kinds of media platforms). This eruption into the public culture—and mainstream public spheres—demands attention, as it did in the case of #crippingthemighty mentioned at the opening of this chapter. It might be countered that such attention is still not often 'mainstream', and rather is desultory and temporary. Still, at the least it qualifies as an important practice in disability digital citizenship—pointing to the need for a recasting of the general terms of digital citizenship.

## Intimate, Everyday Disability and Digital Citizenship

Perhaps, the central area where citizenship has been debated and rethought in recent decades has revolved around the division between public and private spheres and the argument, from different standpoints and traditions, that citizenship does not simply take place in the traditional, high ground of public, political life. The critique has been well made concerning the need to acknowledge and remake the gendered, sexed and racially constructed nature of citizenship and its grounds. One of the very interesting and widely debate characteristics of contemporary digital media is their troubling of the boundaries between public and private, official and intimate, work and leisure, exceptional and everyday (Berlant, 1997; Olesky, 2009; Papacharissi, 2010). This poses challenges for most users, in terms of understanding, negotiating and controlling these new modes and possibilities for enacting and exercising citizenship. For social media users with disabilities, however, this can offer possibilities to present other versions of themselves and other representations of disability, for different audiences. These new architectures of cultural representation have considerable political implications for how we understand and reconfigure public spheres (Siebers, 2001; Clifford, 2012; Hirschmann, 2015).

There are many instances in which digital platforms have been associated with shifts in disability and representation. Blogs were taken up by people with disabilities to discuss a wide range of quotidian, apparently personal topics that, by dint of being chronicled, circulated and commented upon, brought them into public spheres in ways they have not been previously (Goggin & Noonan, 2006; Ellis & Kent, 2011). As well as collective blogs or blogs associated with disability media, individuals were able to blog about aspects of their experiences and daily lives. Particularly interesting strands of the blogosphere were developed, taking advantage of multimedia capabilities of the internet. An excellent example of this is the growth of sign language deaf stories in vlogs (video-based blogs) and interwoven platforms such as You-Tube. Such sign language vlogs offer a way for the deaf to telecommunicate, which was simply not possible before, effectively creating deaf ecologies of networked television. Such vlogs, and the affordances of YouTube, also provided an infrastructure and audiences for deaf people and communities to address their hearing counterparts, as, for instance in the 'Deaf Vloggers: 5 Reasons I Like Being Deaf' production, with sign language and captioning, produced by the National Deaf Children's Society in the United Kingdom.[12]

The uses of digital platforms have been expanded with the growth of Facebook use by people with disabilities. For instance, people with intellectual disabilities have finally received long overdue acknowledgement as users of Facebook, which they commonly use also to connect with family and friends (Shpigelman & Gill, 2014). In other subtle ways, in the everyday processes of resistance, appropriation and domestication of digital technology by people with disabilities, we can see the operations of citizenship occurring. This is something that arises from Arseli Dokumaci notion of the 'micro-affordances of disability', which she suggests are 'non-normative ways of moving, sensing, and being in the everyday . . . potentially transformative actions in the world' (Dokumaci, 2015, p. 80). Holding that participation has always been a socio-technological process, Dokumaci draws attention to how disability ruptures our assumptions about bodies and environments, and thus 'disabled individuals . . . are forced to seek new niches to occupy and create new affordances within which their corporeal difference would be accommodated' (Dokumaci, 2015, p. 80).

These intimate versions and everyday representations of disability are not readily, or usually, available in dominant media or popular culture (Ellis, 2015). In many ways, this kind of example, of which there are very many instances now available, over at least three decades of digital technology and cultures, offer a base of social practices concerning digital technology and culture—as a ground to consider how to expand our ideas of what digital citizenship might look like.


## CONCLUSION

In recent times, disability has gained prominence as an important arena of social justice, politics and citizenship. This applies also to digital technologies and cultures where 'acts of citizenship' are increasingly generated (Isin & Nielsen, 2008). Slowly, disability has become recognised as integral and generative part of social life and relations, especially in digital societies. As

I have argued in this essay, there are various ways in which disability could be explicitly recognised as core to digital citizenship. However, to do this, we need to confront significant cultural baggage.

The expansion of digital citizenship to 'include' disability is a good first step. Also helpful is the use of digital tools to tackle the many instances of exclusion, discrimination, abuse and violence that people with disabilities daily face. We need to go much further, still, to challenge the foundational exclusion of disability from citizenship, especially as it is unfolding in digital societies.

Despite over a decade, where we have had an international treaty articulating the human rights of people with disabilities, including the right to education, the realities of how life proceeds and how citizenship is experienced are often dramatically different—as we see in the case of the child with disability in a Canberra school. There are many instances of this occurring in the digital technologies, where poor web and mobile accessibility prevent or degrade equal access to government services; new (and old) forms of television are not accessible to viewers who are blind due to lack of audio description; online video cannot be consumed by deaf consumers due to lack of captioning; interfaces and technologies are not designed with the requirements, patterns of use or expectations of a wide range of users with diverse disabilities. In the settings and institutions of education, especially schools, such exclusions and narrow imaginings of digital society and technology are all the more troubling, given education is key to citizenship.

Thus, especially when it comes to the remaking of society with technology, citizenship is an ongoing process, with real flexibility as well as potentially new forms of oppression. As Minich reminds us: 'Citizenship . . . functions as a way of making the distribution of rights more equitable, not as a fixed relationship to a nation-state' (Minch, 2013, p. 18). People with disabilities have long had a fraught relation to states and nations, so there are positive developments with the emergence of cosmopolitan forms of disability, which see solidarity, exchange and communication occur across different global, regional and local settings. The role of digital technologies is woven into this new, transnational fabric of disability, in ways we do not fully understand.

There are enough indications, however, to suggest that the altered states of citizenship via disability help us to recast digital citizenship. In the watchwords of this volume, disability can help us explore the deep *cultural* underpinning of digital citizenship; point towards emerging sources, patterns and systems of *control* as yet scarcely on the agenda for discussions of digital citizenship; and help us analyse the new kinds of *contest* this entails, especially concerning inequality, political participation and justice. In terms of a democracy yet to be fully imagined, digital citizenship, with disability, is unfinished business.

## NOTES

1. This chapter was supported by the author's Australian Research Council Future Fellowship project on *Disability and Digital Technology* (FT130100097). My thanks to Dinesh Wadiwel, Karen Solidatic, Michelle Bonati and an anonymous reviewer for their helpful and suggestive comments.
2. Global Disability Watch, http://globaldisability.org/about.
3. Disability Visibility Project, https://disabilityvisibilityproject.com/.
4. David Perry, How Did We Get Into This Mess, "Two Ethical Futures for The Mighty", accessed December 22, 2015. Retrieved from http://www.thismess.net/2015/12/two-ethical-futures-for-mighty.html.
5. Lynne Davis offers the following discussion: "Returning to Marshall, the first point to be made in relation to people with disabilities is that, in order to exercise their social rights, they need to have been able to realise their civil and political rights. The extent to which people with disabilities have been able to do this is questionable". (Davis, 1999, p. 70).
6. "New World Conference: Disability in the 21st Century", October 27–29, 2015, Brisbane, organized by the National Disability Insurance Agency (NDIA). Retrieved from http://www.ndis.gov.au/ndis-new-world-conference-2015.
7. New South Wales Department of Education and Communities (NSW DEC), *Digital Citizenship* portal, 2011, accessed February 9, 2016. Retrieved from: http://www.digitalcitizenship.nsw.edu.au/.
8. "Home", NSW DEC, *Digital Citizenship* portal, accessed February 9, 2016. Retrieved from: http://www.digitalcitizenship.nsw.edu.au/index.htm.
9. Subsequent press exposés show such practices occurring in schools elsewhere in Australia, for instance, in the state of Victoria. See Henrietta Cook, (2015).
10. Minister Joy Burch MLA, ACT Government, Digital Citizenship, School Advisory Committee, Terms of Reference, accessed August 6, 2015. Retrieved from http://www.det.act.gov.au/about_us/minister/school-education-advisory-committees.
11. *Maguire v SOCOG*, Human Rights and Equal Opportunity Commission, 99/115, Sydney, accessed October 18, 1999. Retrieved from https://www.human-rights.gov.au/maguire-v-socog.
12. National Deaf Children's Society, "Deaf Vloggers: Five Reasons I Like Being Deaf, accessed November 11, 2015. Retrieved from https://www.youtube.com/watch?v=zFTMXyL90IU.

## REFERENCES

Alper, M. (2014). *Digital youth with disabilities*. Cambridge, MA: MIT Press.
Arendt, H. (1973). *The origins of totalitarianism*. New York: Houghton Mifflin Harcourt.
Badano, G. (2014). Political liberalism and the justice claims of the disabled: a reconciliation. *Critical Review of International Social and Political Philosophy, 17*(4), 401–422.

Baker, B. (2007). The apophasis of limits: Genius, madness, and learning disability. *International Journal of Inclusive Education, 11*(1), 1–33.

Baker, B. (2010). States of exception: Learning disability and democracy in new times. *Disability Studies Quarterly, 30*(2).

Balibar, É. (2015). *Citizenship.* Cambridge, UK: Polity Press.

Berlant, L. G. (1997). *The queen of America goes to Washington City: Essays on sex and citizenship.* Durham, NC: Duke University Press.

Berubé, M. (2003). Disability and citizenship. *Dissent, 50*(2).

Blanck, P. (2014). *eQuality: The struggle for web accessibility by persons with cognitive disabilities.* Cambridge: Cambridge University Press.

Chilcott, T. (2011, Jul 19). iPads give voice to disabled kids. *Courier-Mail.* Retrieved from http://www.couriermail.com.au/ipad/ipads-give-a-voice-to-disabled-kids/story-fn6ck8la-1226097037404.

Clifford, S. (2012). Making disability public in deliberative democracy. *Contemporary Political Theory, 11*(2), 211–228.

Connor, D. J., & Ferri, B. A. (2010). 'Why is there learning disabilities?': Revisiting Christine Sleeter's socio-political construction of disability two decades on. *Disability Studies Quarterly, 30*(2).

Cook, H. (2015, Sep 08). Allegation of students in cage-like structures triggers investigation. *Age.* Retrieved from http://www.theage.com.au/victoria/allegations-of-students-in-cagelike-structures-triggers-investigation-20150921-gjrnd8.html.

Davey, M. (2015, Sep 08). Canberra School principal sacked over the caging of a boy with special needs. *Guardian.* Retrieved from http://www.theguardian.com/australia-news/2015/sep/08/canberra-school-principal-sacked-over-caging-of-special-needs-boy.

Davis, L. (1999). Riding with the man on the escalator: Citizenship and disability. In M. Jones & L. A. B. Marks (Eds.), *Disability, divers-ability and legal change* (pp. 65–79). The Hague: Martinus Nijhoff Publishers.

Davis, L. J. (1995). *Enforcing normalcy: Disability, deafness, and the body.* New York: Verso.

Dobson, A. (2014). *Listening for democracy: Recognition, representation, reconciliation.* Oxford: Oxford University Press.

Dokumaci, A. (2016). Micro-activist affordances of disability: Transformative potential of participation. In M. Denecke, A. Ganzert, I. Otto, & R. Stock (Eds.), *ReClaiming participation: Technology, Mediation, collectivity.* Bielefeld: Transcript.

Donaldson, S., & Kymlicka, W. (2016, forthcoming). Rethinking membership and participation in an inclusive democracy: Cognitive disability, children, animals. In B. Arneil & N. Hirschmann (Eds.), *Disability and political theory.* Cambridge: Cambridge University Press.

Dwyer, P. (2010). *Understanding social citizenship: Themes and perspectives for policy and practice.* Bristol: Policy press.

Edyburn, D. L. (2014). Connecting the dots: Technology trends that could significantly alter the future of special education. In J. McLeskey, N. L. Waldron,

F. Spooner, & B. Algozzine (Eds.), *Handbook of research and practice for effective inclusive schools* (pp. 451–463). New York: Routledge.

Ellcessor, E. (2016). *Restricted access: Media, disability, and the politics of participation.* New York: NYU Press.

Ellis, K. (2015). *Disability and popular culture: Focusing passion, creating community and expressing defiance.* Aldershot, UK: Ashgate Publishing, Ltd.

Ellis, K., Goggin, G., & Kent, M. (2015). Disability's digital frictions: Activism, technology and politics. *Fibreculture Journal, 26.*

Ellis, K., & Kent, M. (2011). *Disability and new media.* New York: Routledge.

Goggin, G. (2015). Disability and mobile internet. *First Monday, 20*(9).

Goggin, G. (2016). The question concerning technology and disability—and the future of education. In S. Danforth & S. Gabel, L. (Eds.), *Vital questions facing disability studies in education.* New York: Peter Lang.

Goggin, G., & Newell, C. (2003). *Digital disability: The social construction of disability in new media.* Lanham, MA: Rowman & Littlefield.

Goggin, G., & Noonan, T. (2006). Blogging disability: The interface between new cultural movements and internet technology. In A. Bruns & J. Jacobs (Eds.), *Uses of Blogs* (pp. 161–172). New York: Peter Lang.

Goodey, C. (2011). *A history of intelligence and 'intellectual disability': The shaping of psychology in early modern Europe.* Aldershot, UK: Ashgate Publishing, Ltd.

Haller, B. (2016). iTechnology as cure or iTechnology as empowerment: What do North American news media report? *Disability Studies Quarterly, 36*(1).

Harpur, P., & Suzor, N. (2013). Copyright protections and disability rights: Turning the page to a new international paradigm. *UNSWLJ, 36,* 745.

Henman, P. (2010). *Governing electronically: E-government and the reconfiguration of public administration, policy, and power.* Basingstoke, UK: Palgrave Macmillan.

Hirschmann, N. (2015). Invisible disability: Seeing, being, power. In N. J. Hirschmann & B. Linker (Eds.), *Civil disabilities: Citizenship, membership, and belonging* (pp. 204–222). Philadelphia: University of Pennsylvania Press.

Hurst, D. (2015, Apr 02). Canberra school investigated after cage-like enclosure built for special needs student. *Guardian.* Retrieved from http://www.theguardian.com/australia-news/2015/apr/02/canberra-school-investigated-after-cage-like-enclosure-built-for-special-needs-student.

Isin, E. F., & Nielsen, G. M. (Eds.). (2008). *Acts of citizenship.* London: Zed Books.

Jessop, B. (2001). Bringing the state back in (yet again): reviews, revisions, rejections, and redirections. *International Review of Sociology/Revue internationale de sociologie, 11*(2), 149–173.

Jessop, B. (2001). Bringing the state back in (yet again): Reviews, revisions, rejections, and redirections. *International Review of Sociology, 11*(2), 149–173.

Longford, G. (2005). Pedagogies of digital citizenship and the politics of code. *Techné: Research in Philosophy and Technology, 9*(1), 68–96.

Martin, F., & Goggin, G. (2016). Digital transformations?: Reconstructing the ubiquitous end-user: The new politics of gender and media policy in digital government services. *Journal of Information Policy.*

Mills, M. (2016). *On the phone: Deafness and communication engineering.* Durham, NC: Duke University Press.

Minich, J. A. (2013). *Accessible citizenships: Disability, nation, and the cultural politics of greater Mexico.* Philadelphia, PA: Temple University Press.

Mosley, L. (2015, Nov 09). Cage used to contain boy with autism described by staff as 'sanctuary' in Canberra classroom sign. *ABC News.* Retrieved from http://www.abc.net.au/news/2015-09-11/cage-used-to-contain-boy-with-autism-described-as-sanctuary/6767710.

Mossberger, K. (2009). Toward digital citizenship. Addressing inequality in the information age. In A. Chadwick & P. N. Howard (Eds.), *Routledge handbook of Internet politics* (pp. 173–185). New York: Routledge.

Mossberger, K., Tolbert, C. J., & McNeal, R. S. (2007). *Digital citizenship: The Internet, society, and participation.* Cambridge, MA: MIT Press.

Nussbaum Martha, C. (2006). Frontiers of justice: Disability, nationality, species membership. Cambridge, MA: Harvard University Press.

Oleksy, E. H. (2009). *Intimate citizenships: Gender, sexualities, politics.* London: Routledge.

Papacharissi, Z. (2010). *A private sphere: Democracy in a digital age.* Cambridge: Polity.

Pearson, C., & Trevisan, F. (2015). Disability activism in the new media ecology: Campaigning strategies in the digital era. *Disability & Society, 30*(6), 924–940.

Perry, D. M. (2015, Dec 22). Two ethical futures for the mighty. Retrieved from http://www.thismess.net/2015/12/two-ethical-futures-for-mighty.html.

Pothier, D., & Devlin, R. (2006). Introduction: Towards a critical theory of dis-citizenship. In D. Pothier & R. Devlin (Eds.), *Critical disability theory: Essays in philosophy, politics, policy, and law.* Vancouver: UBC press.

Rice, C., Chandler, E., Harrison, E., Liddiard, K., & Ferrari, M. (2015). Project re•vision: Disability at the edges of representation. *Disability & Society, 30*(4), 513–527.

Rosenthal, E., & Ahern, L. (2012). When treatment is torture: Protecting people with disabilities detained in institutions. *Human Rights Brief, 19*(2), 3.

Roulstone, A. (2016). *Disability and technology: International and interdisciplinary perspectives.* Basingstoke, UK: Palgrave Macmillan.

Roulstone, A., & Prideaux, S. (2012). *Understanding disability policy.* Bristol: Policy Press.

Schwartzenberg, S. (2005). *Becoming citizens: Family life and the politics of disability.* Seattle, WA: University of Washington Press.

Shpigelman, C.N., & Gill, C. J. (2014). How do adults with intellectual disabilities use Facebook? *Disability & Society, 29*(10), 1601–1616.

Siebers, T. (2001). Disability in theory: From social constructionism to the new realism of the body. *American literary history, 13*(4), 737–754.

Silvers, A., & Francis, L. P. (2009). Thinking about the good: Reconfiguring liberal metaphysics (or not) for people with cognitive disabilities. *Metaphilosophy, 40*(3–4), 475–498.

Sleeter, C. E. (1987). Why is there learning disabilities? A critical analysis of the birth of the field with its social context. In T. S. Popkewitz (Ed.), *The formation of school subjects: The struggle for creating an american institution* (pp. 210–237). London: Palmer Press.

Soldatic, K., & Meekosha, H. (2012). Disability and neoliberal state formations. In N. Watson, A. Roulstone, & C. Thomas (Eds.), *Routledge handbook of disability studies* (pp. 195–210). New York: Routledge.

Titchkosky, T. (2011). *The question of access: Disability, space, meaning.* Toronto: University of Toronto Press.

Tremain, S. L. (Ed.) (2010). *Foucault and the government of disability.* Ann Arbor, MI: University of Michigan Press.

Trevisan, F. (2016). *Disability rights advocacy and new media in Britain and America.* New York: Routledge.

Wadiwel, D. (2017). Black sites: Disability and torture. *Continuum.*

Warren, K. B. (2015). *Recognizing justice for citizens with cognitive disabilities.* Lanham, MA: Lexington Books.

## Chapter 5

# 'Mastering Your Fertility'

## *The Digitised Reproductive Citizen*

### Deborah Lupton

Women have been engaging in monitoring practices related to their fertility and reproductive functions for many years. Where once they may have charted their sexual activity, menstrual cycles, signs of ovulation and developments in their pregnancies using pen and paper, a plethora of digital technologies now exist to assist women in monitoring, measuring and representing these aspects of their bodies. Over the past decade, the affordances of the most recent digital technologies provide expanded opportunities for women to create online content, monitor their bodies with increasing quantitative precision and share their personal data on social media networks. These diverse practices for creating and sharing personal information about women's sexuality, fertility and reproductive capacities have far-reaching implications. These aspects of female embodiment have at least partially moved from the realm of the private to the public domain, opening women's fertility and reproductive capacities to even greater scrutiny from others, including not only friends, family members and health care workers but also commercial agencies.

In this chapter, I examine digital technologies that have been specifically developed to focus on elements of female fertility and reproduction. These applications span those on computer platforms, the apps that are available for mobile devices such as smartphones and tablet computers as well as biosensors and wearable self-tracking devices. I argue that these types of software and hardware contribute to the configuring of the subject of a specific mode of digital citizenship: that of the digitised reproductive citizen, the woman who uses digital technologies as part of devoting a high level of attention to her health, fertility, sexual behaviour and well-being. Reproductive citizenship takes concepts of healthy citizenship and applies them to ideas about the control of the female reproductive body. It incorporates neo-liberal expectations concerning responsible citizens who engage in self-regulation without requiring much intervention or assistance from the state. Digitised reproductive citizenship adds to these long-established normative precepts by contributing new expectations around how women should be using digital technologies and negotiating the digital data assemblages that are generated by these technologies.

The use of these digital technologies is intensifying an already fervid atmosphere of self-surveillance, monitoring and self-responsibility in which female reproduction (and particularly pregnancy) is experienced and performed. The deliberately created digital media content on the part of users and the by-product transactional digital data created from routine activities such as online searches enter into a digital knowledge economy in which information about human bodies and behaviour has commercial, managerial and research value. Women's personal data about their fertility and pregnancies created from such practices are circulating and being reappropriated for a range of purposes and by a range of actors and agencies. Women may be aware of and have consented to some of these uses, but they have no knowledge of others.

I adopt here a theoretical perspective that draws on sociomaterial approaches in acknowledging the entanglements of technologies with human bodies. This sociomaterial perspective views human bodies as assemblages of flesh, discourses, practices, others' bodies, material objects and spatial locations that are constantly open to reconfiguration (Coole & Frost, 2010). One of the key premises on which my analysis rests is that digital software and hardware, like any media technology, are sociocultural artefacts. They are the products of human decision-making and creative endeavour that are inevitably sited within social, cultural, political and historical contexts (Lupton, 2014; Manovich, 2013). A critical analysis of the content and affordances of digital technologies can uncover the wider discourses, practices and beliefs that are circulating about the topics they seek to address. Not only do digital technologies draw on these discourses, practices and beliefs, they also reproduce them, and, in some instances, generate new ones.

Theoretical approaches that seek to understand the ways in which female embodiment is conceptualised and experienced also contribute to my analysis in this chapter. As feminist cultural theorists have outlined, women's bodies in western societies are typically understood and represented as chaotic and volatile compared with those of men because of their apparent fluidities, leakiness and lack of containment. This is particularly the case of women who are ovulating, menstruating, pregnant, in labour or menopausal. Their bodies are considered to be more open to the world and less controlled than are men's bodies, under the influence of female hormones causing irrational or overly emotional behaviour or the generation of bodily fluids that threaten to leak from their bodies (Grosz, 1994; Shildrick, 1997; Ussher, 2006). I bring together this theorising of female embodiment with that of sociomaterialism to examine the role played by digital technologies in representing, regulating and configuring reproductive citizenship.

## DIGITISING PREGNANCY AND THE UNBORN

Human bodies have become increasingly digitised as a range of digital technologies have emerged that represent and monitor them. These include digital medical imaging and patient self-care technologies as well as images posted on social media sites and the digital data that are generated by voluntary biometric monitoring using apps and wearable devices. Through such processes and technologies, human bodies are configured as collections of digital data—digital data assemblages—that are constantly shifting and changing as new data are generated and assembled (O'Riordan, 2011; Lupton, 2016).

With the advent of mobile and ubiquitous computing, technological devices for representing and monitoring female fertility, pregnancy and the unborn have moved out of the clinic and into the domestic arena. In addition to blogs, websites and discussion boards, such media as YouTube videos, photos shared in platforms such as Instagram, specialised Facebook pages, Twitter hashtags, Google and Yahoo groups and Wikipedia now exist to give information and support related to women's reproductive health. These new media forms both reproduce and configure novel ways of representing the female reproductive body, which, as a result, has become far more visible than ever before. The unborn body has also received higher visibility: the 'public foetus' at all stages of development from the moment of fertilisation to the moment of birth is now readily available for the public gaze on websites and social media (Longhurst, 2009; Lupton, 2013a; Tiindenberg, 2015; Wilkinson, Roberts & Mort, 2015; Leaver, 2016).

There are many apps available for women to download to track their sexual activity, ovulation, menstrual cycles, associated symptoms and indicators, attempts at conception and preconception practices. Some apps remind women to take their contraceptive medications; others send notifications that their period is due or that they should check whether to change their tampon. A range of biosensor technologies is also available for fertility monitoring purposes. Women can purchase wearable sensor-embedded devices that have been specifically developed to measure their basal temperature (an indicator of ovulation) and which sync with a dedicated app or with other fertility apps. There are also digital devices on the market that measure changes in the electrolyte levels in women's saliva (placed on their tongue) or cervical mucous (using a device inserted into the vagina) caused by changes in oestrogen levels and then send these data to software that displays users' results in online charts.

Once a woman achieves conception, hundreds of pregnancy-related apps are available as well (Thomas & Lupton, 2015). Many apps for pregnancy and foetal monitoring direct and encourage pregnant women to observe and collect detailed data not only about their bodies: their diet, vitamin intake, liquid consumption, physical activity, pregnancy symptoms, moods, medical test information, body weight and body temperature. Several such apps include pregnancy countdowns so that women can see at a glance how many weeks and days along they are in the gestation timeline. Apps are available that encourage pregnant women to conduct regular foetal movement monitoring. Some work with smartphone attachments (mini-Doppler devices) to afford women the opportunity to record the foetal heart rate whenever they wish. Another group of apps facilitate progress in labour and childbirth: tracking details of contractions, for example. Many of these apps have functions that allow women to share these details on their social media outlets.

Some technologies directed at female fertility, sexuality and pregnancy enrol a range of interlinked software and hardware as part of their offerings. Platform-based software often works with its own customised apps or other apps, while some platforms incorporate self-tracking wearable devices as well. The Bellabeat Leaf digital self-tracker is one example that has been specifically designed for women in their reproductive years. The device has been designed to wear as jewellery: as a leaf-shaped pendant worn on a chain around a woman's neck, around her wrist as a bracelet or clipped to her clothing like a broach. It measures the wearer's sleep patterns, physical activity, heart rate, energy expended, stress level, breathing patterns as well as allowing her to log her ovulation and menstrual cycles. The data are synced to the Leaf app on the user's smartphone.

As part of interacting with these technologies, users upload a range of intimate details about their bodies, via both manual entry and, for some devices, automatic data generation facilitated by sensors. Fertility, sexuality and reproduction are often intertwined with other aspects of embodiment in such technologies and are thus extended into the realms of fitness and emotional well-being. A key selling point for many of these technologies, as with other health, sexuality and fitness information and self-tracking devices, is that use will provide better knowledge of the functions and behaviours of the reproductive body (Lupton, 2015). Thus, for example, the Glow platform and associated app provide daily predictors of the chance of conception and identifies the next fertile time based on users' data that they input. The Glow website advertises its services as enacting 'Womanhood: Demystified by Data'. It offers its Eve menstrual and sexual activity tracking app to allow users to 'Know What's Up Down There' and contends that its Glow app will allow users to 'Master Your Fertility'. Using Glow involves entering up to 40 different 'health signals' to configure a 'Daily Health Awareness Log'. These personal details include menstrual cycle, indicators of ovulation, intercourse, basal body temperature, cervical mucus, body mass index, cramps, use of contraception, exercise, spotting, period flow and period symptoms. Glow also provides a mirror app for users' partners so that they track the user's fertility. The software syncs with data entered from the physical activity trackers Google Fit and My Fitness Pal and assists women to refill their contraception prescriptions at selected pharmacies as well. Users are sent reminders to take medications and use their regular contraception if they are attempting to avoid conception.

When pregnancy is achieved (the Glow developers claim that by its first year, over 25,000 pregnancies have resulted from use of their software), a further Glow app—Nurture—is provided to assist women to 'Take care of you while you take care of your baby' by continuing to enter into the app details about their changing bodies (Sen, 2014). Users are encouraged to upload their details to 'receive more personal health insights' to 'guide you through a healthy pregnancy'. These information gathering and uploading practices, in conjunction with the algorithmic manipulations and data visualisations offered by the Glow suite of software offerings, are portrayed as allowing women to take control of their otherwise mysterious and unruly bodies. A 'Glow Community' of other users presents opportunities for women to interact with others using these technologies. The developers encourage pregnant women to include their partners in their self-surveillance efforts, using an app specially designed for partners so that they can send the women messages, for example, to nudge her to exercise or drink water.

Apps and associated platforms have also been designed in the interests of reducing health care costs for pregnant women. The Due Date Plus app, for example, was developed by the Wildflower Health company that produces a range of mobile health programmes for people on health care plans in the United States. As noted on the Wildflower website: 'Our smartphone programs help families plug into the healthcare system and focus on driving behaviors and decisions to reduce costs for our clients'. The Due Date Plus app provides a range of services for users, including targeted health information, information about what their health care plan covers and tools to monitor their weight gain or symptoms. Here, the neo-liberal imperatives of these type of programmes are made especially overt: the healthy reproductive citizen not only promotes her own health and that of her children but saves other citizens' money in doing so.

These technologies present reproductive citizenship ideals in mobile, accessible and often highly attractive and aestheticised forms. Platforms and apps such as those offered by Ovuline and Glow feature beautiful images of foetuses, pregnant women and happy, attractive young couples with laughing infants. Games for young girls involve players ensuring that pregnant woman characters are rendered glamorous via grooming, dressing up and makeovers so that they supposedly may develop the confidence of being stylishly pregnant (Lupton & Thomas, 2015). Menstrual- and ovulation-tracking apps use archetypal feminine images of colourful flowers or circle shapes (to symbolise fertility and reproductive cycles) or of babies or attractive young women (one enterprising app developer uses an image of a stylised smiling uterus to signify their ovulation-tracking app). Elements of gamification and ludification in many of these apps portray pregnancy self-tracking as fulfilling and exciting, the details worthy of sharing and celebrating with friends and family (Lupton & Thomas, 2015).

The appeal of technologies such as apps to women is evident. Several such apps have been downloaded by hundreds of thousands or millions of users. Among the top health and fitness apps on Google Play on 21 October 2015, for example, was Period Tracker at number 7, with between 10 and 50 million downloads. MyCalendar—Period Tracker—was at number 21, with 50–100 million downloads. The highest-ranked pregnancy apps featured at number 23 (What to Expect Pregnancy Tracker, 1–5 million downloads) and number 27 (Glow Nurture Pregnancy Tracker, 50–100,000 downloads). A market research report showed that pregnancy apps were used more often than fitness apps (Dolan, 2013). Academic research has also demonstrated that women are turning to the use of such apps in high numbers, finding them particularly useful for information, monitoring foetal and child development, connecting with other mothers and providing reassurance (Declercq et al., 2013; Kraschnewski et al., 2014; Lupton & Pedersen, 2016).

## THE DIGITISED REPRODUCTIVE CITIZEN

Several key discourses, meanings and practices are reproduced and configured in the kinds of digital technologies directed at female fertility and reproduction that I have described earlier. One central feature of these technologies is the tacit assumptions concerning the needs, desires and interests of women. They assume a subject who is ready and willing to generate information about her fertility and reproductive capacities and functions and who privileges the putative benefits offered by the technical affordances of digital technologies, such as the opportunity to input personal details, have these data algorithmically manipulated and presented in metricised or graphical formats. In pregnancy software and devices, there is a blurring of boundaries between concepts of the pregnant woman's needs and requirements and those of her unborn. Many of these technologies are explicitly oriented towards providing opportunities to manage and optimise the development and health of the foetus via the pregnant woman's body. Thus, for example, while numerous apps are directed at the pregnant woman keeping track of her diet, exercise, mood and so on, the ultimate beneficiary of her self-tracking efforts is represented as her foetus, for whom she is positioned as having care and responsibility.

These technologies further assume that the user conforms to the idealised subject position of the reproductive citizen. The reproductive citizen conforms to the broader idealised health-promoting citizen (Bell, McNaughton & Salmon, 2009; Salmon, 2011; Lupton, 2012). This citizen, a key figure in neo-liberal political climates, takes responsibility for her or his health status, well-being and productivity (Lupton, 1995). These practices now often take place using digital technologies as part of patient self-care and health promotion (Lupton, 2013b). When women's reproductive functions and capacities are the focus of neo-liberal notions of citizenship, it is not only women themselves who are implicated but their progeny (potential or actual) as well. Over the past few centuries, unborn entities have taken on these meanings attributed to infants as they have become increasingly valued as protohumans, individual personalities in their own right and beautiful, vulnerable creatures requiring the utmost care and protection (Lupton, 2013). These representations of the unborn have contributed to an adjacent discourse that represents the pregnant body as a vessel for the containment and nurturing of this precious entity. Pregnant women are positioned as being 'at risk' because a plethora of dangers and threats are imagined to surround their bodies, from which they must defend themselves, again principally in the interests of their foetuses. When they are considered to flout these expectations and place their unborn 'at risk', they are subject to intense levels of moral opprobrium and, in some cases, legal action (Mason, 2000; Bell, McNaughton & Salmon, 2009; Salmon, 2011).

The focus on the aestheticisation of menstruation and pregnancy reproduces ideas concerning the importance of retaining physical attractiveness during these bodily states, not allowing one's body to become uncontained or disorderly. Furthermore, in their offerings of metricisation and algorithmic analyses of personal data, these technologies offer rational monitoring and calculation, the provision of information, opportunities for playfulness and the celebration of female reproduction and pregnancy. They promise to discipline, aestheticise and contain the risks and anxieties concerning the messiness, unpredictability (and sometimes discomfort or pain) of the menstruating, ovulating, pregnant or labouring body. As the developer of Clue, a popular menstrual tracking app, put it in an interview for *The New York Times*: 'There is a basic need among women to understand their bodies and know more about it [. . .] When body awareness goes up, it creates a sense of being in charge and being in control' (Wortham, 2014).

Discourses of commodification are intertwined with healthy citizenship. In neo-liberal political environments, the ideal citizen is both productive and a consumer, contributing to economic growth. Pregnancy has long been subject to commodification, with the pregnant woman viewed as needing many new goods and services to help her maintain her health, well-being and physical appearance, use appropriate forms of information and purchase products for her new baby (Thomas & Lupton, 2015). Mobilising the engagement of women as digitised reproductive citizens has indirect economic and political effects. However, these effects extend well beyond attempts to reduce state expenditure on health care provision or to ensure the engendering of adequate numbers of new and potentially productive citizens (*qua* healthy infants). These data possess new forms of value, not only for pregnant women themselves and their friends and family but also for second and third parties. In the global digital knowledge economy, people's personal information has become commercialised, harvested from digital data archives and sold as commodities for marketing, advertising, research and managerial uses (Andrejevic, 2014; Marwick, 2014; Lupton, 2016). Just as women's uteruses and ova have become elements of the bioeconomy as part of the trade in reproductive medicine and surrogate motherhood, so, too, the data generated by women about their fertility and reproductive capacities and functions have taken on commercial value (Sunder Rajan, 2012). Like other digital data about human bodies, reproductive data may be considered to possess a type of biovalue (Lupton, 2016).

The intersections of the commodification of fertile and reproductive women's bodies and their personal data as part of the performance of reproductive citizenship raise concerns not only about their exploitation but also the privacy and security of their data. By encouraging pregnant women to upload apps or use other software (in itself requiring them to allow the developers access to some personal information) and then to personalise them with further intimate information about themselves and their foetuses, the activities of monitoring transformations in pregnancy, observing how one's foetus is growing and developing, recording its movements and heart rate and sharing these details with others are rendered into marketable commodities for second and third parties. The woman who is trying to conceive, already pregnant or has young children is part of an especially valuable demographic (Dembosky, 2013; Marwick, 2014; Vertesi, 2014). This woman is assumed to require a panoply of new goods and services for herself and her children. For these reasons, it has been estimated that online marketers pay far more for pregnant women's browsing data compared with other internet users (Dembosky, 2013). If a woman announces her pregnancy on her social media sites, downloads pregnancy-related apps, makes pregnancy-related purchases online or uses a customer loyalty programme in-store or carries out web searches relating to pregnancy, her status becomes quickly recognised by internet companies, retailers and the third parties that access the data that they collect (Vertesi, 2014).

Personal medical and health information is a prime target for a range of actors and agencies: not only legal enterprises such as the internet empires and data mining companies and the advertisers and health insurance companies to which they sell the data they collect but also to cybercriminals, who stand to profit from selling such information on the black market or by making fraudulent health insurance claims or gaining access to drugs and medical equipment (Humer & Finkle, 2014; Huckvale et al., 2015). Women who use digital reproductive technologies, therefore, may also be rendering themselves open to breaches of data privacy and security, risking the intimate details of their bodies becoming used illicitly or rendered public in unanticipated ways. Research suggests that they are not considering to any significant extent the ways in which their personal data (or those about their children) are used by other parties (Lupton & Pedersen, 2016).

## CONCLUSION

The concept of reproductive citizenship as it is practised and performed using digital media brings women's fertility and reproduction into the public domain in unprecedented ways. Women's bodies, especially when they are visibly pregnant, are already the subjects of intense surveillance: not only on their own part but also from family members, health care workers and people with whom they interact as part of their everyday lives. When women share details of their fertility and reproduction on public forums such as social media or inadvertently open their personal data to scrutiny by internet companies and data miners, their bodies are incorporated into further public modes of surveillance: potentially involving hundreds or thousands of audience members on social media, for example. Digital reproduction technologies allow women to measure elements of their bodies evermore closely, and to compare their data with other users of these devices. Their personal reproduction data become aggregated with others in big data sets to create new norms of female reproduction, which are then used to calibrate further the algorithms that are used to interpret women's information and make predictions. Such technologies, therefore, provide avenues by which personal details about often very intimate aspects of people's bodies can be joined with others' details, distributed and compared.

There are many pleasures potentially involved in using reproduction software and devices. Women who are menstruating, trying to conceive, pregnant or menopausal often experience their bodies as uncontained and unpredictable, and these experiences may be associated with feelings of embarrassment, shame, inadequacy and loss of control (Longhurst, 2005; Wilkinson, Roberts & Mort, 2015). In this sociocultural and political climate, it is not surprising that fertility and reproductive health technologies directed at helping women learn more about their bodies in the interests of 'demystifying womanhood' and 'mastering your fertility' are popular. These pleasures may include generating knowledge about one's body and achieving a sense of control over one's reproductive cycles, working towards the conception of a wanted baby, gathering details about one's pregnancy and sharing these with friends and family, monitoring progress, imagining how one's unborn is developing and changing. Engaging in pregnancy software use may serve to contain anxieties about the pregnancy and the unborn. Many of these media have playful and aestheticising elements that position monitoring of reproductive patterns and pregnancy as an experience to be enjoyed and celebrated. As such, they position the reproductive citizen as a woman who is positive about her fertility and pregnancy, who embraces pregnancy and the prospect of motherhood and is doing so carefully and responsibly to serve her child's best interests. This software tends not to acknowledge the possibilities of women who may be ambivalent about becoming pregnant, who choose not to take on detailed self-monitoring, who are unpartnered or in same-sex relationships or who do otherwise not subscribe to heteronormative stereotypes or ideals of reproductive citizenship. Across the digital reproductive technologies offered to women, female sexuality is represented as predominantly oriented towards such aspects as avoiding or achieving conception, preparing for pregnancy and avoiding risk (Lupton, 2015).

Research suggests that pregnant women and mothers with young children tend to believe in and adopt the principles of reproductive citizenship as part of the ideals of 'good motherhood' (Lupton, 2011; Wigginton & Lee, 2012). Given the burden of expectation and moral meanings that surround the conceptually leaking and potentially uncontained female body that requires stringent monitoring and regulation, it is very difficult for women to contest or resist the norms and imperatives that are embedded in these types of digital technologies. For women who are attempting to conceive and for pregnant women, in particular, to do so is to risk being framed as failing to conform to the idealised reproductive citizen. The weight of social opprobrium against such 'bad mothers' is heavy. While some women have turned to social media or online forums to challenge dominant norms of the contained and responsibilised pregnant or mother's body, they often find themselves subjected to public criticism (Boon & Pentney, 2015).

The exploitation of women's personal details as part of reproductive citizenship also requires acknowledgement. These devices recruit their users and their reproductive organs into the broader digital knowledge economy, in which digital users are configured as data assemblages, often for commercial profit. Women who are enrolled into the use of digital reproductive technologies, while conforming to expectations of reproductive citizenship are also contributing, and indeed donating, their valuable personal information to commercial entities in ways of which they may not be fully aware. As such, the private and personal reasons why women choose to engage as digitised reproductive citizens, and the labour that they invest in so doing, are open to exploitation by diverse actors and agencies. The novel digital practices of 'mastering your fertility', therefore, bring together the private with the public spheres in new ways.

## REFERENCES

Andrejevic, M. (2013). *Infoglut: How too much information is changing the way we think and know.* London: Routledge.

Bell, K., McNaughton, D., & Salmon, A. (2009). Medicine, morality and mothering: Public health discourses on foetal alcohol exposure, smoking around children and childhood overnutrition. *Critical Public Health, 19*(2), 155–170.

Boon, S., & Pentney, B. (2015). Virtual lactivism: Breastfeeding selfies and the performance of motherhood. *International Journal of Communication, 9*, 1759–1772.

Coole, D., & Frost, S. (2010). *New materialisms: Ontology, agency, and politics.* Durham, NC: Duke University Press.

Declercq, E. R., Sakala, C., Corry, M. P., Applebaum, S., & Herrlich, A. (2013). *Listening to mothers III: Pregnancy and birth.* New York, NY: Childbirth Connection.

Dembosky, A. (2013, Sep 29). Pregnancy apps raise fresh privacy concerns. *The Financial Times.* Retrieved from http://www.ft.com/cms/s/0/1c560432-2782-11e3-ae16-00144feab7de.html#axzz4F32BPdCZ.

Dolan, B. (2013, Feb 14). Report finds pregnancy apps more popular than fitness apps. *Mobile Health News.* Retrieved from http://mobihealthnews.com/20333/report-finds-pregnancy-apps-more-popular-than-fitness-apps/.

Grosz, E. A. (1994). *Volatile bodies: Toward a corporeal feminism.* Bloomington, IN: Indiana University Press.

Huckvale, K., Prieto, J. T., Tilney, M., Benghozi, P. J., & Car, J. (2015). Unaddressed privacy risks in accredited health and wellness apps: A cross-sectional systematic assessment. *BMC medicine, 13*(1), 1.

Humer, C., & Finkle, J. (2014, Sep 24). Your medical record is worth more to hackers than your credit card. *Reuters US.* Retrieved from http://www.reuters.com/article/2014/09/24/us-cybersecurity-hospitals-idUSKCN0HJ21I20140924.

Kraschnewski, J. L., Chuang, C. H., Poole, E. S., Peyton, T., Blubaugh, I., Pauli, J., Reddy, M. (2014). Paging "Dr. Google": Does technology fill the gap created by the prenatal care visit structure? Qualitative focus group study with pregnant women. *Journal of Medical Internet Research, 16*(6), e147.

Leaver, T. (2015). Born digital? Presence, privacy, and intimate surveillance. In J. Hartley & W. Qu (Eds.), *Re-orientation: Translingual, transcultural, transmedia* (pp. 49–60). Shanghai: Fudan Universtiy Press.

Longhurst, R. (2012). *Maternities: Gender, bodies and space.* London: Routledge.

Lupton, D. (1995). *The imperative of health: Public health and the regulated body.* London: Sage.

Lupton, D. (2012). 'Precious cargo': Foetal subjects, risk and reproductive citizenship. *Critical Public Health, 22*(3), 329–340.

Lupton, D. (2013). The digitally engaged patient: Self-monitoring and self-care in the digital health era. *Social Theory & Health, 11*(3), 256–270.

Lupton, D. (2014). Apps as artefacts: Towards a critical perspective on mobile health and medical apps. *Societies, 4*(4), 606–622.

Lupton, D. (2015). Quantified sex: A critical analysis of sexual and reproductive self-tracking using apps. *Culture, Health & Sexuality, 17*(4), 440–453.

Lupton, D. (2016). *The quantified self: A sociology of self-tracking cultures.* Cambridge: Polity Press.

Lupton, D., & Pedersen, S. (2016). An Australian survey of women's use of pregnancy and parenting apps. *Women and Birth.* Retrieved from http://www.ncbi.nlm. nih.gov/pubmed/26874938.

Lupton, D., & Thomas, G. M. (2015). Playing pregnancy: The ludification and gamification of expectant motherhood in smartphone apps. *M/C Journal, 18*(5).

Lupton, D. A. (2011). 'The best thing for the baby': Mothers' concepts and experiences related to promoting their infants' health and development. *Health, Risk & Society, 13*(7–8), 637–651.

Manovich, L. (2013). *Software takes command.* London: Bloomsbury Publishing.

Marwick, A. E. (2014, Jan 09). How your data are being deeply mined? Retrieved from http://www.nybooks.com/articles/archives/2014/jan/09/how-your-data-are-being-deeply-mined/.

Mason, C. (2000). Cracked babies and the partial birth of a nation: millennialism and foetal citizenship. *Cultural Studies, 14*(1), 35–60.

O'Riordan, K. (2011). Revisiting digital technologies: Envisioning biodigital bodies. *Communications, 36*(3), 291–312.

Salmon, A. (2011). Aboriginal mothering, FASD prevention and the contestations of neoliberal citizenship. *Critical Public Health, 21*(2), 165–178.

Sen, P. (2014, Aug 27). How Max Levchin's Glow App got 25,000 women pregnant. *Fortune.* Retrieved from http://fortune.com/2014/08/27/how-max-levchins-glow-app-got-25000-women-pregnant/.

Shildrick, M. (2015). *Leaky bodies and boundaries: Feminism, postmodernism and (bio) ethics.* London: Routledge.

Sunder Rajan, K. (2012). Introduction: The capitalization of life and the liveliness of capital. In K. Sunder Rajan, (Ed.) *Lively capital: Biotechnologies, ethics, and governance in global markets*, (pp. 1–41). Durham: Duke University Press.

Thomas, G. M., & Lupton, D. (2015). Threats and thrills: Pregnancy apps, risk and consumption. *Health, Risk & Society*, 1–15.

Tiidenberg, K. (2015). Odes to heteronormativity: Presentations of femininity in Russian-speaking pregnant women's Instagram accounts. *International Journal of Communication, 9*, 1746–1758.

Ussher, J. M. (2006). *Managing the monstrous feminine: Regulating the reproductive body.* London: Routledge.

Vertesi, J. (2014). My experiment opting out of big data made me look like a criminal. *Time*. Retrieved from http://time.com/83200/privacy-internet-big-data-opt-out/.

Wigginton, B., & Lee, C. (2013). A story of stigma: Australian women's accounts of smoking during pregnancy. *Critical Public Health, 23*(4), 466–481.

Wilkinson, J., Roberts, C., & Mort, M. (2015). Ovulation monitoring and reproductive heterosex: Living the conceptive imperative? *Culture, Health & Sexuality, 17*(4), 454–469.

Wortham, J. (2014, Jan 23). Our bodies, our apps: For the love of period-trackers. *New York Times*. Retrieved from http://bits.blogs.nytimes.com/2014/01/23/our-bodies-our-apps-for-the-love-of-period-trackers/.

*Part II*

# CONTEST

## Chapter 6

# Digital Citizen X

## *XNet and the Radicalisation of Citizenship*

### Eugenia Siapera

In the wake of the crisis that triggered austerity, the initial shock and numbness gave way to anger, strikes and protests across southern Europe. By the spring of 2011, the protests gave way to occupations of public spaces and squares in cities across southern Europe, from Syntagma in Athens to Puerta del Sol in Madrid. By the summer, most of the public squares had been violently evacuated by the police. However, rather than dissipating, the so-called movements of the squares merely changed tactics. In particular, in Spain, citizens joined forces in online environments and actively pursued some of the demands that were articulated in the squares, all revolving around demands for real democracy.

This chapter focuses on XNet, one of the citizen-led initiatives that fed into the Spanish movement of the squares and which continues its online activism for 'real democracy'. The main argument pursued here is that XNet helps propel the discussion to a different, more pragmatic level: by operating across oppositions such as online/offline, 'real' activism/clicktivism, participatory/ representative democracy, XNet and its offshoots manage to radicalise digital citizenship, actually contributing to a new conception of citizens' relationship to government that is continuous and collaborative.

In pursuing these arguments, the chapter begins with a brief discussion of approaches to citizenship in the context of representative democracies, followed by a discussion of conceptions of digital citizenship. It then moves to an empirical analysis of the techno-pragmatic citizenship assumed and implemented by XNet. This discussion is based on a series of informal exchanges with XNet activists and on the texts XNet has published. Finally, the chapter argues that XNet's radicalised version of citizenship is only made possible because of the assemblage of a set of socio-historical events and developments alongside certain technological factors. Technology and its appropriations cannot be read outside concrete historical events, but these events are themselves enabled and enacted through certain socio-political imaginaries.

## CITIZENSHIP IN POLITICAL THEORY

If we reduce the question of citizenship to one foundational question, then this must concern the rights, privileges and obligations that people have as members of a particular political community, namely the nation state. Citizenship therefore mediates between individuals and authority or power structures such as the state. In traditional liberal theory, citizenship revolves around a set of rights to be enjoyed by citizens, protecting them from state encroachment (Marshall, 1977). Conversely, the republican conception of citizenship revolves around shared notions of the public good, active citizenship and participation in the decision-making process (Walzer, 1989). In liberal theory, the state emerges as a necessary evil, while in republican theory it is understood as representing the public will. These positions that represent two distinct normative idealisations of citizenship and the state are thrown into disarray by empirical reality, which includes on the one hand historical and political developments, namely the rise of neo-liberalism that reordered drastically relations between the state, the public and the individual (Turner, 1992), and on the other hand technological developments, namely the rise of digital media that considerably expanded what citizens can actually do, leading to a reorganisation of citizenship from below (Barney, 2007). To this mix, we can add the voices of theorists who argue against a limited view of citizenship in terms of the political field only and suggest an expansion of the concept to include cultural citizenship as a means of realising the pluralism inherent in modern societies (Stevenson, 2001). But to fully understand the implications, possibilities and continued relevance of citizenship, we need to trace its origins in political theory.

In political theory, the debate on citizenship has been set by comparing and contrasting the two models of citizenship found in the republican and liberal traditions. Walzer (1989) traces the republican model in the works of Aristotle and the view that citizenship requires an active involvement in political life, where citizens rule and are subjected to the rule of others in turn. The communities, such as ancient Athens, where this notion applied were small and the citizenship was confined to Athenian men, excluding women, slaves and foreigners. This kind of active citizenship was neither desirable nor possible in the Roman Empire, thereby reducing the concept to a legalistic form of belonging, accompanied by a set of rights. This, more minimal understanding of citizenship has come to dominate liberal thought. However, it is not only rights that citizens are meant to enjoy in the liberal conception but also protection. Given that liberal thought emerged after and against the absolutism of the late middle ages, the idea that citizens have rights was enriched with the notion that they deserve protection from any centralised authority such as the state. For example, in Locke and Montesquieu, we find the notion that individuals enjoy rights and protection and that, moreover, this is guaranteed by a form of contractual agreement, such as a legal framework (Walzer, 1989). In early modern liberalism, citizenship therefore meant that individuals had certain rights and protection from the state, implying also that they enjoyed a degree of political freedom in the sense that they could pursue their interests without fear.

Rousseau, in *The Social Contract*, takes over this view and adds the notion of duties and obligations, lost since the days of Athens. According to Walzer (1989), Rousseau ties citizenship to a theory of consent, holding that the citizen is the free and autonomous individual who partakes in the construction of law and who therefore consents to obey this law. Freedom is located precisely in participating in public assemblies, in the public arena, where people meet, debate and eventually consent. While Rousseau locates freedom and the pursuit of happiness in the public domain, Walzer observes that the rise of the bourgeoisie moved happiness to the private domain of the market and the family. Nevertheless, during the French Revolutions and the years when Jacobinism dominated, the conception of citizenship was connected to this active notion of ongoing participation in politics. However, the forces of history led to the demise of Jacobinism and strong, active citizenship, as envisaged by Rousseau and the republican model, gave way to the minimal liberal conception of citizenship as rights and protection passively enjoyed by individuals.

But this minimal conception was not without its critics, who sought to update citizenship in line with historical developments. It is here that we can locate Marshall's (1977 [1949]) attempt to revise citizenship for the modern era. Marshall sought to reconcile the central contradiction in liberal theory, namely that while liberalism assumes a basic equality, in reality modern societies are structured on the basis of inequality. Marshall argued for the inclusion of social rights in an expanded notion of citizenship as a means of addressing this structural inequality. In his historical analysis of citizenship rights, Marshall argues that in the case of England, civil rights, as protection from the state, emerged in the eighteenth century, followed by political rights (e.g. the right to vote and be elected) in the nineteenth century. The twentieth century saw the emergence of social rights (e.g. the right to education, housing and health), thereby considerably expanding the notion of citizenship. Acknowledging the role of inequality and class divisions, Marshall argued that social cohesion can only be achieved if the poorest citizens are offered protection not only from the state but also by the state, against the risks associated with unbridled capitalism. Like most liberals, Marshall did not advocate elimination of inequality as this might go against individual and market freedom, but management of inequality through providing a minimal safety net (Jones and Gaventa, 2002).

Marshall's theory has been criticised because it does not take into account gendered citizens and the ways in which political and civil rights were constructed relied on gendered divisions between the public and private spheres (Fraser & Gordon, 1992). Multiculturalism has also challenged the liberal conception of citizenship, since the latter assumes that citizenship is blind to questions of cultural diversity (Kymlicka & Norman, 2000). Turner (2001 in Stevenson, 2001) argues in favour of an expansion of citizenship to include cultural rights. Nevertheless, the theory of citizenship whether minimal or expanded, has been thrown into disarray because its historical bases have been eroded: industrial capitalism, the nation state and the welfare state are undergoing massive changes. Turner, writing in 1992, was already tracing the end of the welfare state, the rise of 'disorganized capitalism' (Lash & Urry, 1989) and the pressures of globalisation and multiculturalism for the nation state.

## Post-Democracy and Citizenship

In the early twenty-first century, the welfare state is retreating even in the most advanced social democracies in Northern Europe under generalised austerity policies, in line with neo-liberal reforms. At the same time, the power of a localised state is seriously compromised both by globalised informational and finance-based capitalism (Castells, 1998) and by the increasing power of supranational institutions such as the European Union. These challenges have led some to argue that we have now entered a post-democratic political context in which political, civil and social rights are retreating. Colin Crouch (2004) argues that in post-democracy the democratic apparatus, such as parliament, courts and so on, is present, but its power is diminished, as more and more political decisions are taken elsewhere with no input from citizens. Multinational corporations can go for 'regime shopping', choosing where and under what circumstances they will invest. At the same time, under neo-liberalism, more and more governments subcontract their own activities to private firms, which can then have a say in public policy (Crouch, 2011). While one would expect that the financial crisis of 2008–2009 would lead to a decrease in the power of corporations, especially financial ones such as banks, in reality the opposite happened, with citizens compensating private corporations for their losses through the state.

With post-democratic conditions clear not only in states such as Cyprus, Ireland, Greece and Portugal, where bailout agreements supersede electoral preferences and parliamentary lawmaking, but also in states such as Italy and Spain, which were also hard hit by the crisis and legally bound by agreements relating to the Eurozone, the role and function of citizenship is drastically undermined. Even in its minimal liberal conception, citizenship was bound to a political community that enabled citizens to participate to some degree in political decision-making processes. But the post-democratic condition implies that this is no longer possible and that the democratic political process is itself increasingly meaningless in the light of globalised decision-making processes taking place in the absence of citizen participation and consent (Crouch, 2011).

## Digital Citizenship

Yet, at the same time as the states were ceding power to multinational corporations and neo-liberal policies undermined citizenship, the rise of new media forms led to hopes for a renewal of citizenship through the potential offered by new technologies. In part, this kind of literature assumes a normative perspective, understanding digital citizenship not only as a necessary but also as a desirable development. Mossberger, Tolbert and McNeal (2008) build on Marshall's work arguing that digital citizenship must address the economic inequalities that exclude some from participation in the digital world, while it must also expand the possibilities for political participation. For digital citizenship, in the sense of membership in digital society, it is crucial to have both access and skills or digital literacy (Mossberger et al., 2008). However, this once more would require a state that can address these prerequisites for digital citizenship.

Barney (2007) takes a more substantive view of digital citizenship, not merely as membership, but as the exercise of political judgement over both questions of morality (what is right) and ethics (what is good). But this exercise of political judgement requires a kind of citizenry that is accustomed to making such judgements, or in other words, a citizenry that actively participates in civic life. Couldry et al. (2014) studied the ways civic life and participation can be enhanced through digital media. Using digital storytelling as a method, and against the theoretical backdrop of Dahlgren's (2009) theory of civic culture as a circuit, Couldry and his associates examined the multiple ways people in different social contexts used digital media to narrate experiences and tell stories contributing to building their self-esteem, establishing social cooperation and relations of reciprocity, all of which are important prerequisites for citizenship practices. Moreover, following Couldry et al. (2014), digital media may help people to start reclaiming a public and social space that has been impoverished after years of neo-liberal policies. Useful though as this focus on civic culture may be, it limits itself to the preconditions for political participation and does not speak to pressing questions of political efficacy.

In other words, this literature on digital citizenship, although addressing important issues, dilemmas and tensions, does not seem capable of addressing the monumental challenges to citizenship posed by post-democracy. Numerous studies have shown how digital media have widened political participation (Carpentier, 2011), whereby the public sphere has been enhanced (Papacharissi, 2010), and they have enabled global transnational political actions (Bennett & Segerberg, 2013). However, the conditions of post-democracy as described by Crouch (2004; 2011) render all these increasingly powerless, leading to a widening gap between citizens and the political decision-making process. We have seen, for example, that although protests such as the Occupy movements had been very successful in generating public support and in mobilising digital media (Fuchs, 2014; Gaby & Caren, 2012), nothing really changed in terms of the policies being implemented. Additionally, the circulation of more and more contents in online environments contributes to what Jodi Dean has called communicative capitalism (2005; 2009), where contents circulate endlessly without any recipient, while people are captured in a seemingly endless circuit of content production and enjoyment (Dean, 2010). To these issues, we can add the increasingly problematic role played by social media platforms, whose power to order contents and visibility through algorithms and to condition users to the economy of likes and shares, prioritises popularity (measured in likes and shares) over everything else (Siapera, 2013; Gillespie, Boczkowski, and Foot, 2014). So, ultimately, what room is left for digital citizenship? Any response to this question must engage with empirical reality and with the ways people are actively creating new forms of political engagement, which seek to redress and reclaim the political field. The next section will look at XNet, a collective of activists, artists and everyday people, whose digital initiatives are on the one hand showing some of these creative appropriations, while on the other they help radicalise citizenship in a post-democratic context.


## XNET: TECHNO-PRAGMATISM AND DIGITAL CITIZENSHIP

XNet is a collective based in Barcelona and founded in 2008 with an agenda to defend citizens from the imposition of copyright and the monopolisation of culture and knowledge. From there, XNet expanded to issues such as online democracy, understood as involving participation mechanisms and citizen control of power and institutions; the advocacy of a neutral and free internet; freedom of information; political and financial corruption; and technopolitics defined 'as the practice of networking and taking action for empowerment, justice and social transformation' (XNet, 'About').[1] XNet is therefore grounded on the digital domain, defending on the one hand the internet and its potential and on the other using this in order to reclaim and radicalise citizen power, by creating new forms of political participation and in the process new understandings of what it is to be a citizen. In doing so, they seek to actively intervene in and shape the political agenda, making political parties notice citizens outside election periods, holding them accountable using the existing state apparatuses, such as the courts or the media, and insisting on the need for total transparency. In this manner, the work of this collective is instrumental in putting pressure on national governments from below, thereby seeking to counter post-democracy and reclaim the political power that citizens seem to have lost. Moreover, in creating transnational links and sharing their know-how with others across Europe, they are contributing to the global spread of these new forms of citizenship. The discussion below aims to show the founding principles and goals of XNet, and how integral technologies are to those, alongside political strategies that constitute an assemblage of technological and political practices.

## Principles, Structure and Goals

The starting point of XNet is the Internet. For it, the internet is an epoch (Levi, 2012),[2] and this epoch is characterised by the internet's potential for sharing and collaboration, thereby enabling a new kind of relationship between citizens and the polity. The first kind of necessary struggle therefore is against those who seek to enclose the internet and to use it for their own purposes. The foundational texts of XNet and its first iteration as EXGAE are all concerned with internet freedom, understood as the right to share. The name EXGAE is a direct reference to the Sociedad General de Autores y Editores (SGAE), which is responsible for collecting royalties. EXGAE organised against the imposition of copyright associated with SGAE and more broadly against the attempt to impose taxes and to privatise knowledge; SGAE reacted with the threat of legal measures and EXGAE eventually became XNet in 2010 (EXGAE, 2010).[3]

The focus on the internet is central to XNet activism, precisely because of the idea that internet is an epoch. If the internet is an epoch, then this is characterised by openness, sharedness and free exchange. Attempts to make the internet part of the culture industries must be resisted. The oXcars, a free culture event organised in the years 2008–2013, aimed at celebrating the culture of creativity and sharedness and opposing attempts to control this via commercialisation of (digital) culture, the criminalisation of sharing and P2P file transfers, active resistance to legislation that seeks to control the internet, the notorious ACTA-SOPA-PIPA acts and the net neutrality debate: the internet will not be another TV as XNet puts it (XNet, Net Neutrality).[4] This approach is two pronged: on the one hand, they fight against the monopolisation of the internet, and on the other they fight in support of sustainable creativity and cultural production. In practice, this is accomplished through the Free/Libre Culture forums—events that take place annually and are open to a wide variety of participants, including individuals, collectives and organised groups. The FCF website is tagged as 'Citizen Rights' Observatory in the Digital Age',[5] pointing to its role as a platform for citizens to intervene in attempts to control the internet. At the same time, XNet offers a host of tools and services for to people resisting or fighting against copyright and the criminalisation of the internet. These include the provision of free information about copyright, licences, the digital levy, etc.; downloadable self-defence tools, such as contracts; the provision of free legal advice; designing proposals for intervention in legislation, creating transnational networks, and viral campaigns raising awareness (e.g. the Save the internet campaign) (XNet, 'About').

However, the internet is at the centre because it can be used 'for sharing and connecting inputs, an opportunity to find new forms of action and to change the rules of the game' (Levi, 2012); the internet, as a tool and a battleground, is important only insofar as it contributes to the creation of what they refer to as 'real democracy'. This point links XNet to the well-known 15M movement in 2011 and the demand for democratic reforms associated with the umbrella movement of Democracia Real Ya! XNet was an active participant and organiser in the days of 15M and used it as a learning platform for the potentials and limits of this kind of activism (c.f. Postill, 2014). The struggle for net neutrality is therefore both a goal and a tool or method for citizens to learn how to develop and use digital media for their own empowerment. Social transformation, towards a direct democracy model, is the ultimate goal where 'we have the obligation as citizens to take advantage of its [the internet's] possibilities to make our society truly democratic, to eliminate the middle men in the process of accessing knowledge, and to empower ourselves against those who govern us' (XNet, Technopolitics, Activism and Cyberactivism).[6]

The internet and technopolitics have also been influential in structuring the collective. This structure in turn can serve as paradigm for a radicalised social structure more broadly speaking. In her article 'Working notes towards a r-evolution' Simona Levi, one of the founding members of XNet, refers to a new ethics based on 'maturity and autonomy thanks to the recognition of each individual's merits and skills, and the standardisation of forms of organisation that favour decentralised control, the empowerment of end users, and the shared distribution of resources' (Levi, 2012). This excerpt highlights XNet's central tenets and operational principles: meritocracy and sharedness. There is a clear recognition that different people have different skills and abilities, and it is through these that they can best contribute to changing social and political life; but their contribution is something that others can build upon and share.

A crucial parameter of XNet is that they do not revolve around ideologies. It is not the ideology of the left, for example, that motivates them, nor do they claim that they know how and what to implement. This is an incremental project, motivated by a quest for freedom, curiosity about things, and respect to difference and individuality. As we shall see below, the hacker ethos is a clear inspiration: this ethos which revolves around problems and collaborative problem solving is more central to XNet's politics than ideologies, and because of this, they put forward a notion of distributed leadership. Levi (2012) uses the analogy of the herd:

A herd is an association of a number of individual agents interacting with one another and with their environment. Their collective behaviour is decentralised and self-organised. The herd acts as a unit that moves in the same direction, but its function emerges from non-coordinated behaviour of individuals who follow their own impulses. In a herd, each individual spontaneously carries out different roles according to their ability during brief periods of time.

The internal structure of XNet is therefore one that revolves around the notion of meritocracy, and it is neither vertical nor horizontal: XNet understands itself as a network, with hubs emerging around specific merits, skills or abilities.

The above discussion aimed to illustrate the founding principles of XNet: the centrality of the internet and technopolitics, their view of democracy beyond ideological camps and meritocracy rather than top-down verticality or levelling horizontality. The highlighting of meritocracy is important because it speaks to dilemmas of equality versus difference in debates about citizenship. If we take meritocracy in the sense that XNet is using it to denote the specific skills, abilities and potential contributions of individuals, then we can see how valuable this is in understanding citizenship not in terms of the least common denominator but in terms of what each person has to contribute on the basis of their individuality or 'individual impulses'. Not as an obligation therefore, which is how communitarians or republicans would have it, but as a realisation of people's uniqueness and individuality.

## Strategies and Tactics: Doing Citizenship

An important aspect of XNet is its pragmatism: rather than losing time in criticising the existing situation—'we have to do our crying elsewhere', as Simona Levi puts it (Levi, 2012)—Xnet is interested in the 'cult of the done' or in other words in change in the here and now. Drawing again on ideas connected to hackers and hack-labs, the 'makers', XNet prioritises doing, but in a specific way: 'with specific goals, focused plans and quick, targeted victories' (Levi, 2012). If by strategy we understand a broader, long-term goal as to the 'what' XNet is trying to achieve, and by tactics the 'how', then their long-term strategy is a change of polity; and, in order to accomplish this, they use a variety of tactics in a variety of battlegrounds. The discussion on the internet earlier shows how important the battleground of the internet is, as it is a paradigmatic battle for the future. But it is not the only one: the main-stream political domain is another important battleground, both symbolically and pragmatically, and XNet's medium-term strategy is to use the existing political system against itself. In doing so, they have used two main tactics: BuzonXNet and the fight against corruption, and Partido X, the formation of a new political party.

Commensurable with its ideas for reuse, XNet works within the existing political model, seeking to revise it, using the tools of the system against it. This is not a repetition of the reform versus revolution dilemma, co-optation or exodus, but rather a belief that 'demands for reforms will destroy the current system, because the system is ready to face enemies, but it is not ready to have its own internal contradictions blown open'(Levi, 2012). This is why XNet is so focused on bringing to light and to their legal conclusion cases of corruption, holding the system accountable and imposing transparency from the bottom-up. The main way this is pursued is through Buzon XNet, a Wikileaks-inspired drop box, for citizens to submit cases of corruption for investigation. Any information submitted is then checked to see if it can be pursued legally, and/or to be sent to journalists. The pivotal case in which XNet has launched is the 15MpaRato, a citizen initiative[7] that led to the arrest and trial of the former IMF director and Finance Minister Rodrigo Rato, who, as president of the bank Bankia, was considered responsible for the scandal and eventual bankruptcy of the bank. The case is still ongoing, but the initiative of the citizen lawsuit was driven and launched by XNet in 2015 with the explicit aim 'to put an end to economic and political impunity while naming those who are responsible for the crisis' (XNET, '15Mparato Dossier').[8]

The 15MpaRato initiative is ongoing (in 2016) and supported by crowd-funding efforts which have currently managed to collect over €17,000. With the help of citizens, enough evidence to bring a legal case was collected in the space of two weeks. Based on the success of this case, this offshoot of XNet plans to bring more cases against other corrupt officials and those considered responsible for the banking crisis. It is with this in mind, and drawing on the model of Wikileaks, that XNet has set up the XNet Leaks through Buzon X. Another success of the XNet Leaks has been the case of 'Blesa's emails' and the 'Black credit cards' scandal, which uncovered €15.5 million in tax evasion by banks and corrupt officials, as well as the involvement of all major political parties and trade unions. This information came to light through XNet Leaks (XNet, '15Mparato Dossier'). Buzon X encourages citizens to speak out against corruption, but without exposing them to potential retribution and protecting their anonymity. Corruption and its inverse, transparency, are central to XNet's effort to expose the contradictions of the political system in Spain and elsewhere. A corollary of the 15MpaRato case and more broadly of the 15M movement has been the Citizens' Debt Audit Platform (PACD), a citizen initiative which seeks to audit public debt, in order to see which part is legitimate and which isn't. XNet collaborates with PACD in the initiative Citizen Group against Corruption launched in the 2015 Free Culture Forum in Barcelona.

Through naming names and holding specific people accountable, these citizen-based initiatives are actively reclaiming citizen power, lost in the post-democratic context. XNet views the debt crisis 'not as divine retribution but as an organized scam', as they put it—citizen initiatives such as XNet aim to end the impunity and the collusion involving governments and corporations, in so doing reclaiming the power of citizens over their governments (XNet, '15MpaRato Dossier'). Through the tactics of Buzon X and XNet Leaks, XNet involves other citizens in the process of reclaiming power, thereby spreading and sharing (digital) citizenship while at the same time enabling citizens to restructure their political subjectivities in a collaborative, bottom-up manner independent of political parties.

While the fight against corruption is crucial in exposing the system's contradictions, XNet's political strategy also involves another kind of struggle on the political battlefield: the formation and promotion of an alternative, radical political party, Partido X or, as it is formally known, Red Ciudadana Partido X: Democracia y Punto (Citizens' Network X Party: Just Democracy).[9] 'X' stands for any citizen, pointing to the distributed and citizen-based conception at the heart of this initiative. Moreover, the party is described as 'a minimum non-ideological cross-border pact among citizens on the basis of a common roadmap and working method' (Partido X, About)[10] and draws on some of the principles found at the core of XNet's organising. There is a disdain for ideology in favour of common sense and the idea that people know better—rather than the political elites—on the basis of their own skills and abilities. Partido X rests on four principles thought to bring forward 'just democracy' (democracia y punto): transparency in public office, wikigovernment and wikilegislation, continuous right to vote on any legislation, and binding referendums. Wikigovernment and Wikilegistlation refer to processes by which citizen involvement in government is direct and continuous: in Wikilegislation, citizens and experts in specific fields put forward a proposal, inform other citizens about it and ask for opinions and consultation citizens; in Wikigovernment, citizens participate in government through ongoing consultation in prioritising certain issues and in draft legislation (Partido X, Just Democracy).[11] While some might consider these ideas utopian, Partido X points to the implementation of such models in Brazil, where 160,000 citizens were involved in consultations of the Digital Cabinet of the state of Rio Grande Do Sul, and in Iceland's Better Reykjavik initiative, a platform where citizens 'debate and prioritise ideas to improve their city, creating open discourse between community members and city council and also giving the voters a direct influence on decision making' (Citizens' Foundation, Better Reykjavik).[12] Better Reykjavik is now integrated into Reykjavik's city council.

The party allows for any citizen to be nominated to stand as a candidate through the internet, and based on their knowledge, competencies and expertise. The decision-making process takes place through the Partido X method, a series of rules for the effective organising of the party. These are spelled out in some detail, but the two elements that run through them include, firstly, openness to all in principle, and, secondly, building upon the various competencies of people (Partido X, Method).[13] This ensures that the party remains a dynamic network, where people rotate on the basis of their varied skillsets, degree and ability of involvement and peer recognition. The operating principle comes directly from the internet's collaborative culture and its 90:9:1 rule: at any given time, 1% will be creating, 9% will be editing or modifying and 90% will be consuming or otherwise benefitting. Partido X relies on this rule, but understands that those that comprise these percentages will not always be the same people.

Concerning the question of openness to new members, XNet understands that there is a tension involved between accepting new people and ideas and having a core set of values that keep its identity and political goals stable. According to Levi, a slogan they have espoused is 'we want to be less', meaning that while they are interested in growing, this cannot be at the cost of their core values and principles. They therefore envisage a kind of democracy where small groups will network, confederate and collaborate on those goals they have in common and they know more about. If a group cannot reach consensus, there is always the possibility of 'forking' or going their separate ways until they meet again in issues where they can agree. In this respect, XNet differ from recent neo-populist hegemonic politics associated with Podemos and the Pirate Parties, as these place a high value on unity and scaling even, as XNet argue, at the expense of diluting or even discarding their core ideas. According to Levi, the idea of forking and going on separate ways allows XNet to talk against unity if the issue under question is one that is fundamental for the group and as such it allows them to operate in a coherent and consistent manner across time. On the other hand, forking, as we shall see below does not really address the question of dealing with or managing disagreement, while it may also be used in order to consolidate existing power dynamics in the group. However, broadly speaking, the non-fetishisation of unity is an important parameter in XNet which allows them to keep a strong and coherent identity.

In short, XNet, Citizen's Network X Party, and their associated initiatives articulate a new political model that is open to those who have a strong affinity for the group's principles, that relies on ongoing grass-roots participation, although understanding that this comes in different degrees, and that integrates the internet and new technologies not as a set of technical functionalities and affordances, but more fundamentally in terms of the culture they make possible.

## IMPLICATIONS

How might XNet's practices inform the debate on citizenship in the digital age? XNet's techno-pragmatic perspective radicalises existing abstracted notions of citizenship that are either minimal as in the case of liberal models or which assume too much involvement as in the communitarian or republican models. This techno-pragmatism posits the question of what kinds of citizenship and citizen actions are enabled by new technologies and what can citizens contribute on the basis of their different skills and interests. Rather than beginning with an idealised abstraction and then seeking to implement it, they begin with pragmatic issues and problems and seek to intervene and resolve them, through mobilising the potential of new technologies. The digital citizenship proposed by XNet is driven by a quest to restore citizen sovereignty and hence 'real' democracy. For XNet democracy is emptied of meaning by corrupt and incompetent elites on the one hand and by dogmatic ideologists on the other.

Unlike activist models of previous years, such as for example the anti-globalisation movement, which sought to exit the system altogether (Gerbaudo, 2016), XNet works within the existing order by seeking to revise it, using the tools of the system against it. This is not a repetition of the reform versus revolution dilemma, co-optation or exodus, but rather an attempt to have it all. Because these reforms are brought about by concerted citizen action through digital means, the subjectivity of citizens and the very character of liberal citizenship is actively changed in the process. So this is a kind of reform which actively radicalises citizens, in recognising and realising their own power to change things. The assumption is that once citizens realise their power and once the system has been forced to take into account the citizens, there is no going back.

While digital citizenship is often conceived in terms of ad hoc actions, primarily concerning cultural politics and/or politics belonging to the internet

XNet returns digital citizenship to the domain of politics proper (legislation and political decision-making). For Isin and Ruppert (2015) digital citizenship is understood in terms of its performative dimension, comprised of digital speech acts, recognising both the ad hoc character of a lot of action in online environments as well as the different outcomes of different digital acts. Meikle (2016, p. 123) develops a normative or aspirational account of citizenship in and through social media, which refers to a version of citizenship distributed across networks, in terms of responsibility and spatiality. Both accounts are useful in contextualising and understanding XNet's digital citizenship, but none explicitly links the online digital environment with the material, political domain, which is precisely what XNet is doing. While Isin and Ruppert as well as Meikle are concerned with interpreting digital acts and understanding their ontology, XNet's actions are pragmatically oriented to the present seeking to address specific problems through specific actions. But in so doing, their political work has an impact on the very ontology of digital citizenship, which for them concerns pragmatic and systematic actions and hence the development of conscious and strategic digital organising.

This is crucial especially in the light of the post-democratic context that appears to dominate the political domain. Unsystematic ad hoc digital acts with political relevance, even if they are subversive or even if they draw on the hacker ethic, risk ending up as more contents feeding into communicative capitalism (Dean, 2005) or taken up and co-opted by the system. It is only through concerted digital action that both the digital element—in the sense of having bottom-up control of the internet—and the citizenship element—in the sense of having rights, responsibilities and a say in political decision-making processes, are addressed, and this is precisely what XNet's citizen activism is looking to do. Moreover, this digital strategic and tactical political action enabled by the tools and methods of XNet is significant for another reason: because of the complete integration of the technological and digital with the political and socio-historical. XNet's action is part of an evolving socio-historical moment with great political significance. We have argued here that this is comprised on the one hand by the movement towards a post-democratic model of governance where citizen power is diminished and on the other hand the technological evolution and expansion of the digital domain, which in turn feeds back into the culture and politics of the era. It is at this crossroads that XNet has emerged, and its efforts to keep the internet free and to empower citizens through direct political action are crucial for the future of democracy. Finally, instead of prioritising the technological and online over offline political action, XNet transcends these pseudo-dilemmas, fully integrating both the technological and political, the digital and the material in order to address the specific socio-political challenges of neoliberalism and post-democracy.

While XNet's actions are crucial for the future, they are also liable to some criticisms. These include at least three, the question of ideology, the issue of scalability and the dilemmas of disagreement. In terms of ideology, the contempt shown by XNet to this can be partly explained by the tendency of political parties in Spain (and elsewhere) to identify with broad ideologies of the right and left. This kind of thinking, which they associate with the old order, the political parties, hierarchical models of governance and so, is seen as obsolete and problematic. The problem here is that the founding ideas and beliefs of XNet and their associates, which are implicit in both their methods and operating principles, are offered as a result of practical, pragmatic solutions for efficient organising. In so doing, the ideological work that has gone into developing these is black-boxed, meaning that they are made opaque and that they cannot be subject to critique and change. However, unless the question of ideology is fully addressed, XNet might find itself usurped, driven to different directions or rendered meaningless. While XNet have a core set of ideas comprising a logic specific to the group, and a clear set of methods, which form a crystallised version of this logic, this insistence on methods and procedures may hide the very substance of what democracy and democratic citizenship is—Cornelius Castoriadis (1997) argues against views of democracy as a procedure, positing that instead we have to see it as a regime. While procedures are an important part of a democratic regime, for democracy to properly exist it must also address the substantive question of the common good, and how to attain it. In this respect, digital citizenship must also be something beyond the application of the methods and the realisation of the internet's culture of sharedness and openness. In these terms both the substance, and the methods, which are partially derived by the substance must be addressed, and made subject to critiques and peer-based revisions.

This question becomes more pressing if we take into account the issue of scalability. What happens if the XNet and Partido X models begin to scale and attract more and more people? The problem is that as more and more people participate the method might become unwieldy and the criteria of expertise and involvement might appear arbitrary and undemocratic unless they become bound to the substance of what is understood as the common good. This is especially because the method may veer towards elevating technocracy, the rule of the experts, as the ultimate arbiter, thereby forgetting the basic democratic principles of the rule of the many. On the other hand, it may also veer towards populist hegemony, relying on up and down-votes. Additionally, it is likely that there are disagreements between experts in which case decisions must be taken in a different manner. This points to the last issue, the issue of disagreement. How is disagreement managed? Levi has addressed this implicitly through the notion of 'forking', or going towards separate directions, at least temporarily. While this may work as long as this remains an activist project but it may not work as model of governance. More fundamentally, as Ranciere (1999) argued, disagreement is the fundamental condition of politics because it denotes that something is wrong, that someone is excluded, that someone is affected disproportionately and this has to be made right again—in this manner, substance and ethics returns once more to haunt techno-pragmatism.

Notwithstanding these issues, the efforts by XNet to reimagine digital citizenship are important and urgent. While often the assumption is that there will be some kind of spontaneous polity change where citizens will be endowed with the right to participate, implementing republican models of citizenship, which would then lead to better, more inclusive forms of democracy, we see in XNet's action the inverse: they claim this participation for themselves in the here and now and through this seek to bring about a r-evolution as they put it, that involves both a return of democracy with the citizens in power once again and an evolution of democracy towards a more direct participatory model. Will they succeed? The odds are stacked against them, against all of us as citizens in the context of neo-liberal globalised capitalism and the post-democratic regime. But at the very least, they try.

## NOTES

1. XNet, About, retrieved from: https://xnet-x.net/es/about/.
2. Levi, Simona, 2012 Working Notes for a R-evolution 2, retrieved from: http://conservas.tk/working-notes-for-a-revolution/.
3. EXGAE, 2010, Cambio de Nombre (Change of Name), retrieved from: https://xnet-x.net/es/exgae-cambio-de-nombre/.
4. XNet, Net Neutrality, retrieved from: https://xnet-x.net/en/areas/net-neutrality/
5. Free/Libre Culture Forum, retrieved from: http://2015.fcforum.net/en/participants/.
6. XNet, Technopolitics, Activism and Cyberactivism, retrieved from: https://xnet-x.net/en/areas/technopolitics-hacktivism-cyberactivism/.
7. XNet, 15MpaRato: Citizens against corruption, retrieved from: https://xnet-x.net/docs/15MpaRato-dossier-english.pdf.
8. XNet, 15MpaRato: Citizens against corruption, retrieved from: https://xnet-x.net/docs/15MpaRato-dossier-english.pdf.
9. Partido X. What Is, retrieved from: http://partidox.org/what-is/.
10. Partido X, About, retrieved from: http://partidox.org/what-is/.
11. Partido X. Just Democracy, retrieved from: http://partidox.org/just-democracy/ Partido X, Method, available at: http://partidox.org/method/.
12. Citizens' Foundation, Better Reykjavik, retrieved from: http://www.citizens.is/portfolio/better-reykjavik-connects-citizens-and-administration-all-year-round/; Better Reykjavik, https://betrireykjavik.is/.
13. Partido X, Method, retrieved from: http://partidox.org/method/. Chapter 6

# REFERENCES

Barney, D. (2007). Radical citizenship in the republic of technology: A sketch. In L. Dahlberg & E. Siapera (Eds.), *Radical democracy and the internet* (pp. 37–54). Basingstoke, UK: Palgrave Macmillan.

Bennett, W. L., & Segerberg, A. (2013). *The logic of connective action: Digital media and the personalization of contentious politics.* Cambridge: Cambridge University Press.

Carpentier, N. (2011). *Media and participation: A site of ideological-democratic struggle.* Bristol: Intellect Books.

Castells, M. (1998). *The rise of the network society: The information age: Economy, society, and culture.* Malden, MA: John Wiley & Sons.

Castoriadis, C. (1997). Democracy as procedure and democracy as regime. *Constellations, 4*(1), 1–18.

César, R., & Sola, J. (2015). Podemos and the Paradigm Shift. *Jacobin.* Retrieved from https://www.jacobinmag.com/2015/04/podemos-spain-pablo-iglesias-european-left/.

Couldry, N., Stephansen, H., Fotopoulou, A., MacDonald, R., Clark, W., & Dickens, L. (2014). Digital citizenship? Narrative exchange and the changing terms of civic culture. *Citizenship Studies, 18*(6–7), 615–629.

Crouch, C. (2004). *Post-democracy.* Cambridge: Polity

Crouch, C. (2011). *The strange non-death of neo-liberalism.* Cambridge: Polity.

Dahlgren, P. (2009). *Media and political engagement.* Cambridge: Cambridge University Press

Dean, J. (2005). Communicative capitalism: Circulation and the foreclosure of politics. *Cultural Politics, 1*(1), 51–74.

Dean, J. (2009). *Democracy and other neoliberal fantasies: Communicative capitalism and left politics.* Durham, NC: Duke University Press.

Dean, J. (2010). *Blog theory: Feedback and capture in the circuits of drive.* London: Polity.

Fraser, N., & Gordon, L. (1992). Contract versus charity. *Socialist Review, 22*(3), 45–67.

Fuchs, C. (2014). *OccupyMedia!: The Occupy Movement and Social Media in Crisis Capitalism.* Hants, UK: John Hunt Publishing.

Gaby, S., & Caren, N. (2012). Occupy online: How cute old men and Malcolm X recruited 400,000 US users to OWS on Facebook. *Social Movement Studies, 11*(3–4), 367–374.

Gerbaudo, P. (2016). *Mask and the Flag: The Rise of Anarchopopulism in Global Protest.* Oxford: Oxford University Press.

Gillespie, T., Boczkowski, P. J., & Foot, K. A. (Eds.). (2014). *Media technologies: Essays on communication, materiality, and society.* Cambridge, MA: MIT Press.

Isin, E., & Ruppert, E. (2015). *Being digital citizens.* London: Rowman & Littlefield International.

Jones, E., & Gaventa, J. (2002). Concepts of citizenship: A review. *IDS Development Bibliography 19.* Retrieved from https://www.ids.ac.uk/files/dmfile/Db19.pdf.

Kymlicka, W., & Norman, W. (2000). *Citizenship in diverse societies.* Oxford: Oxford University Press.

Lash, S., & Urry, J. (1987). *Disorganized capitalism.* Cambridge: Polity Press.

Marshall, T. H. (1977). *Class, citizenship and social development: Essays by TH Marshall. With an introduction by Seymour Martin Lipset.* Chicago: University of Chicago Press.

Meikle, G. (2016). *Social Media: Communication, Sharing and Visibility.* New York: Routledge.

Mossberger, K., Tolbert, C. J., & McNeal, R. S. (2007). *Digital citizenship: The Internet, society, and participation:* MIT Press.

Papacharissi, Z. (2010). *A private sphere: Democracy in a digital age.* Cambridge: Polity.

Postill, J. (2014). Freedom technologists and the new protest movements A theory of protest formulas. *Convergence: The International Journal of Research into New Media Technologies, 20*(4), 402–418.

Ranciere, J. (1999). Disagreement: Politics and Philosophy. London: University of Minnesota Press.

Siapera, E. (2013). Platform infomediation and journalism. *Culture Machine, 13,* 1–29.

Stevenson, N. (Ed.) (2001). *Culture and citizenship.* Thousand Oaks, CA: Sage.

Turner, B. S. (2001). Outline of a general theory of cultural citizenship. In N. Stevenson (Ed.), *Culture and citizenship* (pp. 11–32). Thousand Oaks, CA: Sage.

Turner, B. S. (1992) *Regulating bodies: Essays in medical sociology.* London: Routledge.

Walzer, M. (1989). Citizenship. In T. Ball, J. Farr, & R. L. Hanson (Eds.), *Political innovation and conceptual change* (pp. 211–220). Cambridge: Cambridge University Press.

*Chapter 7*

# Indigenous Activism and Social Media

## *A Global Response to #SOSBLAKAUSTRALIA*

Bronwyn Carlson and Ryan Frazer

#SOSBLAKAUSTRALIA was born far from any big city. The Bieundurry family, comprising residents of the remote Aboriginal community Wangkatjungka (population of 200, located 130 km southeast of Fitzroy Crossing in the Kimberley region of Western Australia), were deeply concerned about the future of their community and dozens of others across the state (Stein, 2015). On 12 November 2014, Western Australia Premier Colin Barnett announced the closure of 150 of the state's 274 remote Aboriginal communities, displacing up to 12,000 people. Funding arrangements between state and federal governments were in transition, he explained (Kagi, 2015). The supply of essential services, including water and electricity, would now be the responsibility of the state rather than Commonwealth. The state government, headed by Barnett, had decided that it was not economically viable to continue servicing most of the smaller, more remote communities. Without these services, the communities would be forced to relocate to larger regional centres, such as Broome or Perth. No information was given as to which communities would be selected or what criteria would be used. The Bieundurry family, like thousands of other Aboriginal people across the state, did not know what they could do to influence the decision-making (Kagi, 2015). 'All they know is that the government is trying to push them off their land, once again', the *Guardian Australia* reported (Wahlquist, 2015).

It was clear the issue was not simply about economic efficiencies. Rather, it was implicated in a long, complex colonial history of Indigenous dispossession of land, citizenship rights and justice. Taking to the internet, made available in Wangkatjungka a few years prior, the Bieundurry family connected with kin across the state and country (Wahlquist, 2015). Together on a private Facebook group chat, they strategised options and settled on a decisive plan of action—what would soon materialise as a social media–driven activist movement under the hashtag–moniker #SOSBLAKAUSTRALIA.

The purpose of this chapter is to explore the nexus of political activism and Indigenous peoples' use of social media in Australia. It is structured by three sections. We first situate #SOSBLAKAUSTRALIA within the context of a long tradition of Aboriginal resistance and political expression, particularly with regard to movements that struggled for formal and substantive citizenship rights for Aboriginal people in Australia. Second, we discuss the recent and enthusiastic uptake of social media technologies by Indigenous people across Australia, and implications for identity, culture and politics. We present here some preliminary results from a survey of Indigenous peoples' engagement with online activism—the first such data made available in the Australian context. And last, we describe in detail the origins and development of the #SOSBLAKAUSTRALIA campaign, mapping its connections across local, national and global scales. We offer analysis of some of the movement's strategies that aimed to resist and subvert the political status quo. We conclude by arguing that involvement in #SOSBLAKAUSTRALIA is essentially a question of citizenship: of which Australians are considered citizens and which are not.

## ACTIVISM: CITIZENSHIP AND SOVEREIGNTY

The notion of citizenship is complicated for Indigenous people of Australia who were denied it for so long. The political gains of the latter half of last century were not due to benevolent governments, but rather were the result of decades of Indigenous activism. Early demands for citizenship began in the 1920s after Indigenous soldiers who fought in the First World War returned to find they were not considered citizens by the state (Maddison, 2009, p. 52). Established shortly after the war, the 'Australian Aboriginal Progressive Association' (AAPA) was the first Aboriginal political organisation in Australia. The AAPA was founded by Aboriginal activist Fred Maynard who was inspired by international events and in particular the activism of Marcus Garvey, the president of the 'Universal Negro Improvement Association' in the United States. From the late 1800s, Aboriginal people on reserves had farmed the land, raised livestock and built homes. Following the war, they were forcibly removed from the reserves so the land could be given to non-Indigenous soldiers (Maddison, 2009, p. 52). Fred Maynard's grandson, John Maynard, comments, 'The black fellas were thrown off' (cited in Maddison 2009, p. 52). Maynard refers to many Indigenous activists from the 1920s to the 1940s as 'eminent Aboriginal freedom fighters', noting their efforts to gain full citizenship rights for Indigenous people (2007, p.3).

By 1948, the *Nationality and Citizenship Act* was passed, granting citizenship to those born in Australia. However, due to a range of discriminatory laws and administrative practices formed during the Protection Policy era, the situation was different for Indigenous people (Cuneen, 2005). Instead, Australian citizenship was granted only to Indigenous people who held 'exemption certificates'. These were authorised government identification documents issued to Indigenous people deemed of 'good character and industrious habits . . . [and who had demonstrated] the manner and habits of civilised life' (Flood, 2006, p. 227). In theory, those who held an exemption certificate were entitled to receive the benefits afforded to non-Indigenous citizens. However, any relative benefits and freedoms were conditional and the 'good character' criterion associated with exemption certificates could be revoked by colonial officials without substantiation. The contingency of 'citizenship' therefore rendered Indigenous beneficiaries vulnerable to the vagaries, perceptions and whims of white officials, white community opinion and shifting interpretations of policy (Carlson, 2016).

The 1950s and 1960s saw a shift in the government's approach to Aboriginal issues with an emphasis on encouraging assimilation through citizenship for all Indigenous people. As noted by anthropologist A. P. Elkin, 'these "true" Aborigines are not going to become "white" in the foreseeable future, though they can and will become worthy Australian citizens' (1964, p. 379). Elkin's considerable influence as an anthropologist must not be disregarded; governments of this era depended on the work of anthropologists, who often acted in an advisory capacity. Elkin's comments that the process of assimilation was now seen to be fundamental to the achievement of full citizenship had a significant influence on policymakers throughout the 1950s and 1960s.

The 1960s was a time of increased Indigenous-led political activism (see Broome, 2010). Inspired by the civil rights movement in the United States, Aboriginal activist Charles Perkins organised the 'Freedom Rides' through New South Wales (NSW) to expose the racism towards Indigenous Australians. In the Northern Territory, Vincent Lingiari led the Gurindji walk-off at Wave-Hill protesting against low wages and poor conditions, a political protest that led to the movement for Indigenous land rights. Indigenous political campaigning also played a significant role in achieving the overwhelming 'Yes' vote in the 1967 referendum to remove two references in the Australian Constitution that discriminated against Indigenous people. The success of the 1967 referendum saw the Australian Constitution amended to allow the Commonwealth government to make laws in relation to Indigenous people and to include Indigenous people in the census.

Not all Indigenous people accept Australian citizenship, however. There is a strong Indigenous sovereignty movement, which is in part a rejection of Australian citizenship for the recognition of Aboriginal sovereignty. On

Australia Day in 1972, in a protest that demanded land rights for Indigenous people, Indigenous activists erected a beach umbrella on the lawns of Old Parliament House and hung a sign bearing the words 'Aboriginal Embassy' (Robinson, 2014, p. 5). Efforts by the government to forcibly remove what is popularly known as the 'Tent Embassy' have been futile; the site remains a reminder of the ongoing struggle for land rights and sovereignty. The 1972 Tent Embassy has inspired the erection of many other Tent Embassies asserting Aboriginal sovereignty. For instance, the political organisation Sovereign Union was officially formed in 1999.[1] In 2012, organisers and representatives from across Australia met in Wollongong at the Kuradji Tent Embassy intent on forming the National Unity Government of the Sovereign Union of First Nation Peoples in Australia.

The Aboriginal Provisional Government (APG) was formed in the 1990s and is founded in the principle that Aboriginal people are and always have been a sovereign people. The APG was spearheaded by political activist Michael Mansell, who originally introduced the Aboriginal passport in the 1980s. Mansell argues:

> Citizenship is not offered without strings attached—it comes at a heavy price. The price to be paid . . . is the abandonment of Indigenous sovereignty, and with it the loss of self-determination. (Mansell, 2003, p. 8)

As this brief and highly fragmented account of Indigenous activism demonstrates, the question of citizenship for Indigenous people in Australia is fraught with much tension and ambivalence. There are two main lines: the past political activism of Indigenous people, where the recognition of citizenship was enshrined in mainstream definitions of 'citizenship', and the present activism of Indigenous people that seeks the recognition of either a more substantive citizenship or full Indigenous sovereignty.


## INDIGENOUS PEOPLES' USE OF SOCIAL MEDIA

Australian Indigenous peoples have always been early adopters of communication technologies. Comparing cultural systems of communication to social media, Justin Mohamed notes, 'For over 40,000 years Aboriginal people have used a culturally based form of social media called Songlines to connect, share, engage and record news and information' (Sweet, 2015). Although accurate statistics are difficult to obtain, recent research suggests that Indigenous people use social media at rates 20% higher than non-Indigenous Australians, and that over 60% of Aboriginal people in specifically 'remote' communities are active Facebook users (Callinan, 2014). These findings contradict common racist stereotypes of Indigenous people as somehow anti-technology. As Carlson argues, the use of social media is now an 'everyday, typical activity' for Indigenous people in Australia (2013, p. 147). This is significant. Indigenous people comprise just 3% of the total national population, and families, kin and communities are spread across the entire antipodean continent. Social media offer opportunities to connect across vast territories and disparate populations.

A string of recent research has found that the use of social media has had significant cultural implications for Indigenous Australians by affording possibilities for both practising culture and producing new forms of cultural expression (see Kral, 2011). In an early paper on the topic, Corbett, Singleton and Muir explored the ways in which new media could be used in a remote Western Australian Aboriginal community to 'revitalise their culture and enhance community development both socially and economically' (2009, p. 73). Likewise Singleton et al., who explored the use of communication technologies, including social media, in Walkatjurra Cultural Centre in Leonora, Western Australia, found this technology 'contributes to keeping knowledge alive within the community' (2009, p. 73).

In another study, Edmonds et al. found young Aboriginal people were using mobile devices and social media technologies for 'maintaining connections and for pathways to assist them when facing big decisions' (2012). Facebook in particular has become a significant conduit for cultural expression. It is used to promote the formation and maintenance of relationships across distance, to establish and maintain Indigenous identities and subjectivities and as a means of participation in community politics (Edmonds et al., 2012, p. 8). Carlson and Frazer (2015), for example, examined the intersections between Aboriginal people's use of Facebook and Sorry Business (the diverse practices that centre on responding to death and loss). Sorry Business, while varying considerably across cultural groups, is often implicated with strict protocol and responsibility. These responsibilities, which may be punitively enforced, can be difficult to fulfil for populations spread throughout the length and breadth of Australia. However, Carlson and Frazer found that Facebook 'empowers some [participants] to fulfil cultural responsibilities across distance' (2015, p. 222). Ultimately, they argue, Aboriginal people's engagement with social media is 'creating new and dynamic forms of cultural expression and connection' (p. 222). This is a significant study as it seeks to examine the manifold ways Indigenous people are using online platforms to reinforce the continuity of cultural protocols.

## SOCIAL MEDIA AND POLITICS

There has been sustained academic interest in the increasing politicisation of social media (Kahn & Kellner, 2004). While not specifically designed for facilitating political activism, a 2009 survey by DigiActive found that social media is now the most common entrance to online activism (Brodock & Zaeck, 2009). From the Arab Spring to the global Occupy Wall Street movements of the '99%', social media has cemented itself as a key feature of democratic politics. Advocates of online activism point to the resounding successes of these movements: the unexpected toppling of despotic rulers, the shutting down of centres of global commerce the mass rallying of support— all mediated through the expedient affordances of social media. However, internet sceptics such as Evgeny Morozov argue the role of social media in political change is overstated. Rather, naïve optimists are caught in the fever of internet 'slacktivism', and what Morozov defines as 'feel-good but useless Internet activism' (2009, p. 13).

There is a dearth of research on Indigenous people's use of social media for political purposes. Notable exceptions include Petray's research on online Aboriginal protests, in which she argues social media can both enable and restrict individual and collective agency (Petray, 2011). In a later paper, Petray argues that 'self-writing'—where Indigenous Australians freely express their identities on social media—is an already widespread form of everyday political activism that can work to deconstruct essentialist assumptions about Indigenous people (Petray, 2013). More recently, Dreher, McCallum and Waller drew on concepts of participation, mediatisation theory and 'political listening' to explore the potential and limitations of social media in influencing policy debates affecting Indigenous Australians (Dreher, McCallum & Waller, 2016). They analysed the mainstream and social media responses to two social media–driven Indigenous political movements: the Recognise campaign (a movement pursuing the recognition of Indigenous Australians in the Australian Constitution) and the protest movement of interest to the current chapter, #SOSBLAKAUSTRALIA. They argued that while there is 'no doubt that Indigenous Australians are harnessing emerging technologies to voice opinions and share contributions on policy developments', they also expressed 'uncertainty of being heard in the key spheres of influence—mainstream media and policy-makers' (p. 34).

The limited work on Indigenous Australian online activism thus suggests ambivalent outcomes. On the one hand, social media clearly affords opportunities to muster geographically disparate populations under a common political cause. On the other, Petray (2011) and Dreher, McCallum and Waller (2016) have demonstrated the limitations of social media in effecting political change for Indigenous people.

## SURVEY ON INDIGENOUS ONLINE ACTIVISM

Statistics on the rates and range of Australian Indigenous peoples' engagement with activism online are currently non-existent. Here, we present preliminary results from a survey of Indigenous people's use of social media in Australia conducted by this article's lead author, Bronwyn Carlson, through a project funded by the Australian Research Council (ARC). Between April 2014 and April 2015, the survey drew on a variety of opportunistic, purposive and snowball sampling techniques. Direct links to the survey were provided through the ARC project's dedicated Facebook and Twitter accounts, whose followers number in the hundreds. However, related Facebook pages and Twitter accounts, such as the influential Twitter account for Indigenous politics @IndigenousX, distributed the survey to larger online networks through 'sharing' and 'retweeting'.

It is important to note that the results below cannot be considered representative. There are three main reasons for this. First, the information provided was unverified and anonymous. Second, there was a skewed geographical distribution of responses, with the majority of respondents being located in the major urban centres of Sydney and Wollongong, NSW. And, third, there was modest sample size ($n = 70$). However, the primary purpose of the survey was to scope engagement in online activities by Indigenous Australians. Thus, in presenting these preliminary results, we hope only to provide some background context for exploring the #SOSBLAKAUSTRALIA movement.

The survey asked Indigenous social media users: 'Have you ever supported a political cause on social network sites?' The vast majority indicated they were politically active online, with an overwhelming 79% of respondents answering 'yes' and only 15% answering 'no' (and 5% 'not sure'). Those supporting political causes expressed a wide range of interests and standpoints, which often conflicted. For example, respondents reported supporting the Recognise campaign, the anti-Recognise campaign, the Greens party, climate change initiatives, the Redfern Aboriginal Tent Embassy, Black Nationalism, the Aboriginal Sovereignty Movement, LGBTQI rights and anti-Tony Abbott (former Australian Prime Minister) sites. One participant answered that he supported 'Anything run by blacks for blacks' (MV37). Online activities included liking pages, sharing information, links and events, signing online petitions, posting comments and 'reposting' statuses, and donating funds. The results show that Aboriginal political involvement is evidently not just limited to activities on social media, but blends with offline activism. One male participant from Sydney captures the range of pursuits: 'I have raised funds, held membership/follower drives, promoted causes & petitions, provided offline support to improve online causes/campaigns etc—all voluntary' (MN72).

However, reservations were expressed among some respondents in participating in political activity online, as exemplified by the concern of a male respondent from Melbourne: 'I don't want to "politicise" my social media, as I also post stupid, fun things, [I] don't need possible backlash that I sometimes see' (MV24). Another woman from Brisbane feels constrained by her profession and its public profile: 'Now that I'm a public servant it really limits

my ability to support' (FA19). A man from Wollongong indicated the resistance many Aboriginal people meet when expressing their opinions online:
'We also meet a lot of prejudice when we assert our ideologies amongst varying audiences with a range of political stances' (QN62).

As these respondents suggest, despite the burgeoning use of social media
by Aboriginal people, participation in political activities online is not unproblematic and is at times met with reservations about 'politicising' online
spaces. These misgivings include restrictions by employers and racism from
political opponents. But at another level, they might also be understood as
a response to the negative historical consequences of political resistance by
Aboriginal people in Australia. While this data is unlikely to be representative
of all Indigenous Australians, it does suggest there are sustained, widespread
and highly diverse political engagements among Indigenous social media
users.

Building on the small body of existing work on Indigenous online activism, in what follows we map the unfolding of a single political movement:
#SOSBLAKAUSTRALIA. We hope to demonstrate the power of Indig-
enous online activism in forming political connections, giving voice to
Indigenous citizens and speaking back to official government discourse.
While the Freedom Rides of the 1960s made connections through physically
transporting their message from town to town across Australia, today social
media affords the instantaneous transmission of communication across
local, national and international borders. As this chapter aims to show,
Indigenous movements—such as #SOSBLAKAUSTRALIA—are taking
advantage of these expedient technologies, developing creative strategies
for resisting, subverting and challenging the political status quo. In this
way, we offer a timely counterpoint to Morozov's pessimistic view: a social
media–driven political movement born in a remote Indigenous community
in Western Australia, which would ultimately lead to tens of thousands of
people connecting online and marching on the streets of cities the world
over. In doing so, we respond to calls for more critical inquiry into the topic
(see Harlow, 2009).

## 'LIFESTYLE CHOICE': THE TRIGGER
## NEEDED TO POLARISE A NATION

Western Australian Premier Colin Barnett's initial announcement of the closure of up to 150 remote Aboriginal communities—discussed in this chapter's
introduction—instantly polarised public sentiment. However, it was not until
four months later that opposition to the policy would solidify into collective
political action.

On 10 March 2015, then Prime Minister Tony Abbott, talking to Australia's public broadcaster, ABC Radio, confirmed the federal government's support for Premier Barnett's policy: 'What we can't do is endlessly subsidise lifestyle choices if those lifestyle choices are not conducive to the kind of full participation in Australian society that everyone should have'.[2] His explicit insinuation was that Aboriginal people were only living in remote communities as a 'lifestyle choice'. This view was widely condemned as an offensive misunderstanding of Aboriginal cultures, ontologies and histories. It was especially inflammatory coming from a prime minister who held the self-elected title of minister for Indigenous affairs, ostensibly charged with representing the interests of Indigenous people at a federal level. There was no acknowledgement of the importance of connection to the country for Indigenous people and no reflection on the proposed closure's parallels with the long history of forced Indigenous dispossession from land.

Abbott's comments inflamed the fear and anger of Indigenous and many non-Indigenous people nationwide. The notion of Indigenous people living in the country as a 'lifestyle choice' set in motion the white nationalist myth of egalitarianism and a level-playing field where Indigenous people enjoyed the same 'choices' as non-Indigenous people. That this comment was an obliteration of colonial history goes without saying. Emanating from the highest political voice in government, it had a considerable impact and spoke to a widely disgruntled populace of Indigenous people and their non-Indigenous supporters—although no doubt also reaching a projected audience of supporters of Abbott's rhetoric. However, Abbott's words, as #SOSBLAKAUSTRALIA's Facebook page explained, while encapsulating the 'ongoing disdain toward Aboriginal people and the flippant nature of disregard toward Aboriginal culture', also became 'the trigger needed to polarize a nation'. In this sense, the remark can be considered what Harlow calls the necessary 'critical event' of political movements, animating the ire of citizens to the point of collective action (Harlow, 2011, p. 231).

## THE BIRTH OF A MOVEMENT

Two days later, late on Thursday evening on 12 March 2015, a lively Facebook conversation thread was transpiring across Western Australia's Kimberley region. Members of the Bieundurry family in Wangkatjungka and a small group of other Kimberley women across the state were strategising a response to the impending threat of community closure (Harlow, 2011, p. 231). At 2 am the following morning, Sam Cook, a Nyikina woman, activated the Facebook page titled 'Stop the Forced Closures of Aboriginal Communities'. Cook had created a website for #SOSBLAKAUSTRALIA in the weeks following

Premier Barnett's initial announcement. The website '[called] for Aboriginal communities to register their needs and individuals to offer skills that could aid the community' (p. 231). However, the Facebook page was intended for a different, more explicitly radical purpose. Layangali Bieundurry explained: 'We knew that all our family were on Facebook, so what we did, we just set the page up and started sending out messages throughout Facebook and that is how most of our family knew' (Blackstar Radio, Facebook).[3] They hoped by sunrise the page might garner 1,000 'likes'. But the word spread faster than they had either anticipated or hoped. 'And then other communities started to jump on Facebook and started realising what the Government [was] going to do to us in the remote communities', Bieundurry continued. In just seven hours, the page had attracted over 2,000 likes.

From these beginnings in a remote community on the edge of Australia's Great Sandy Desert, the virtual campaign's growth was exponential. Within three weeks, the page had attracted 50,000 likes. A sister Twitter account, @sosblakaust, was also launched. The connections afforded through social media meant the message could reach not only people who were geographically distant but also people from vastly disparate social and cultural contexts. High-profile celebrities and other important figures publicly offered their support to the cause, sharing and creating their own messages and images on their Facebook and Twitter accounts. Endorsements included actors Hugh Jackman and Russell Crowe, musicians Talib Kweli and Michael Franti, and US Civil Rights campaigners Angela Davis and Dr Cornel West, extending the virtual reach of #SOSBLAKAUSTRALIA to further unknown millions across the world (Blackstar Radio, Facebook). This supports Petray's assertion that 'The interactivity enabled by Web 2.0 serves to expand the "virtual we" of Indigenous solidarity, encompassing not just Indigenous people but their supporters, and many sympathetic individuals from around the world' (Petray, 2011, p. 933).

## THE GLOBAL CALL TO ACTION

A call to action was put out within days of launching the #SOSBLAKAUS-TRALIA Facebook page. The protest would transfer from the virtual world to the streets of Australia's major capital cities. On April 12, an estimated 4,000 people in Melbourne and 800 in Sydney took part in marches and 'sit-ins' through the cities' CBDs. Harlow, who explored the use of Facebook in a protest movement against the Guatemalan government (a country where around 50% of the population is Indigenous), found that Facebook was used 'to mobilize and advance an online justice movement that activated an offline movement' (Harlow, 2009, p. 226). This, Harlow argues, is the essence of what she calls 'Activism 2.0'. In this vein, Petray argued that for online activism to be effective, 'it needs to be integrated as one component of the over-arching social movement, rather than the only component' (Petray, 2011, p. 936). Thus, in contrast to Morozov's (2009) pessimistic and ultimately ineffective 'slacktivism', #SOSBLAKAUSTRALIA—a movement born entirely online—made itself present in the 'real world'. Protesters successfully interrupted significant spaces of global commerce in Australian capital cities by filling them with politicised bodies and emphatic demands for change.

Although the Melbourne protest was regarded as unequivocally peaceful, because the crowd disrupted activity on two main streets for several hours during peak hour, the response by the mainstream media was decisively unfavourable. Social scientists have deconstructed the discursive techniques deployed by mainstream media to delegitimise and undermine grass-roots political movements (see McFarlane & Hay, 2003). In Australia, there has been a long historical trend of inimical media responses to Indigenous civil rights protests (Bennett 1999, p. 183). In this vein, the following day, Victoria's major daily newspaper, the *Herald Sun*, ran the front-page headline 'Selfish Rabble Shut City'. The article foregrounded the 'selfish' disruption of the 'innocent' commuters' homeward journey (Watson, 2015). The newspaper sought comment from Melbourne Lord Mayor Robert Doyle, who criticised and dismissed the protesters as 'self-indulgent' (Watson, 2015). Voices of the Indigenous and other protesters themselves were relegated to the final few lines of the article, by which time any chance of sympathetic sentiment in the reader had been precluded by the newspaper's demonisation of the protesters.

## SUBVERSION AS POLITICAL ACTIVISM

But the demonising discourse was not totalising. In response, the movement subverted the pejorative descriptor 'selfish rabble' by appropriating it in their posts on Twitter and Facebook. Just before midday 11 April, #SOS-BLAKAUSTRALIA tweeted: 'We think #selfishrabble should trend today— an honouring of sorts for @theheraldsun. They got their wish, as hundreds of sympathetic tweeters began sharing tweets and photos with the subversive new hashtag. One of the first incantations of the newfound meme was, perhaps predictably, an image of Rupert Murdoch, owner of Melbourne's *Herald Sun* and global media empire News Corp, accompanied by the hashtag #selfishrabble (Watson, 2015). Other politicians were soon to follow, including then Prime Minister Tony Abbott and Melbourne Lord Mayor Doyle. Tweeters began playing around with the hashtag, making puns about #Shellfish-Rabble and #ElfishRabble, before drawing clever parallels with other protest movements. Iconic historical images of activists occupying city streets were juxtaposed with #selfishrabble. These included Australia's first gay and lesbian Mardis Gras in 1978, Martin Luther King Jr.'s 'I have a dream' address and the haunting photo of the sole Tiananmen Square protester confronting a line of tanks (Watson, 2015). The hashtag remains an 'official hashtag' of the movement.

Thus, back online, #SOSBLAKAUSTRALIA and its followers demonstrated their joy and creativity in protest through play and humour. Much like Waitoa, Scheyvens and Warren found in reference to Maori engagement online, the #SOSBLAKAUSTRALIA Facebook and Twitter accounts provided alternative platforms for both Indigenous and non-Indigenous people to share and explore 'political discussions and political perspectives alternative to those in mainstream media' (2015, p. 46). Social media offered, in the form of subversive memes, opportunities to respond to a mainstream media that aimed to contain the movement. It is also clear that the online and offline aspects of the movement did not form some clearly delineated dichotomy. Rather they constituted a synergic unit with myriad actors all working towards a common goal in creative ways (see also Garcia et al., 2009). An idea catches on, takes off and pushes the movement in new directions—but the trajectory towards justice remains. In this case, it was a simple hashtag.

## THE SECOND GLOBAL CALL TO ACTION

The organisers of #SOSBLAKAUSTRALIA decided the virtual movement needed to once again materialise on the streets. On Friday 1 May, protesters now in the tens of thousands marched in solidarity across both Australia and the world (Davidson, 2015). A reported 97 rallies were held: from remote Aboriginal communities in outback Australia to all the major Australian capitals, from New Zealand to New York, from Hong Kong to Honolulu. Many of these were organised spontaneously by existing groups sympathetic to the cause.

The largest protest again took place in the Victorian capital of Melbourne (Davidson, 2015). Up to 10,000 protesters marched from Town Hall to Flinders Station in the city's CBD. Throughout the Friday afternoon peak hours, protesters disrupted commuters' journey home by staging a 'sit-in' in front of the station. Indigenous leaders gave passionate speeches, dancers performed, and branches from gum trees were burned as part of a smoke ceremony. As dusk approached, the crowd transformed into a makeshift camp in Kings Domain, where some would stay for two nights to hold discussion and information sessions. The Sydney protest also shut down peak-hour traffic in the city's CBD. Exact numbers of protesters are difficult to ascertain, but estimates suggest up to 30,000 across the 98 protests. What is known is that by the afternoon, the protest's hashtag, #SOSBLAKAUSTRALIA, was trending globally on Twitter (Davidson, 2015). The movement, which was sparked by a small group on the edge of Australia's Great Sandy Desert, made its demand heard in city streets the world over: *Stop the forced closures of Aboriginal communities.*

Once again, mainstream media chose to either ignore the protests—some of the numerically largest and most geographically expansive in Australian history—or depoliticise the events, instead emphasising the inconvenience they caused 'regular' Australians. Much like the *Herald Sun*'s 'selfish rabble' criticism, Premier Barnett attempted to delegitimise and ultimately contain the movement by suggesting that because few (or, in Barnett's mind, none) of the people participating in protests were actually from the communities concerned, it was not their business to have a say in the matter (Davidson, 2015). According to Barnett, the 30,000 protesters' opinions were invalid, their anger groundless. This convenient shift from the idea that Aboriginal peoples' political interests reflect an homogenous, unified set of values, to the notion that only 'remote' Aboriginal people could have a say in this particular case, was not lost on those protesting, or indeed, on the vast number of Aboriginal activists and the non-Aboriginal supporters of this cause.

Again, social media afforded possibilities to 'speak back' in ways traditional, mainstream media had foreclosed. Twitter user @callapilla, for instance, working as a Perth correspondent for the *Guardian* Australia, sent out a tweet at 6 pm: 'From Broome march. Barnett asked if protestors [sic] were from Aboriginal communities—these guys are. #SOSBLAKAUSTRALIA'. The tweet was accompanied by a photo of four Aboriginal men, white paint striped across their face, staring down the camera. Another Twitter user @MJLovegrove wrote: 'Does it matter? Remote community #SOSBLAKAUSTRALIA closures are an issue for everyone'. Barnett's strategy to contain the anger through delegitimising protesters' involvement if they were not from the affected areas was, itself, undermined and lampooned. Through giving space and amplifying the voices of those ignored by mainstream media, social media afforded opportunities to subvert the government's official discourses of containment, which were being widely bolstered by mainstream media. This is not to suggest that the power of social media is unlimited or unrestricted, or to deny the surveillance measures available to social media administrators for the purpose of containing and delimiting expression. But rather it demonstrates the diverse opportunities social media opens for political activism, where individuals and loose collectives may speak back to dominant narratives, subvert them in creative ways and convey their messages to potentially global audiences.

## CONCLUDING REMARKS

This chapter aimed to explore the intersection of political activism and Indigenous people's use of social media through mapping a single contemporary movement. We argued that #SOSBLAKAUSTRALIA's single demand and organised effort to 'stop the forced closures of Aboriginal communities' can be read as an extension of a long tradition of Indigenous activism. From the Freedom Rides of the 1960s to the Aboriginal Tent Embassy that is now approaching half a century old, Indigenous activists have long developed creative ways to make heard their demands as citizens. As the survey data presented above demonstrated, it is apparent that these strategies are increasingly implicated in internet technologies, where heterogeneous Indigenous individuals and groups can engage in political debate, organisation and action across national and global borders.

Like Dreher, McCallum and Waller (2016), we are cautious in claiming that Indigenous online activism has the ability to effect changes at a governmental policy level—in the case of #SOSBLAKAUSTRALIA, the ultimate outcome is still uncertain. But it is clear social media effected a mass galvanisation, politicisation and animation of geographically diverse bodies; it offered opportunities to creatively subvert the official discourse of government, which so often works to contain the voices of Indigenous people; and, perhaps most importantly, it afforded possibilities for Indigenous Australians to powerfully assert their presence through exercising their right to protest against government policy. Support for and alliance with #SOSBLAKAUSTRALIA took many forms: joining Facebook and Twitter pages; liking, sharing and producing supportive digital content; creatively appropriating the political discourse of the government, subverting it, being ironic and playful, and in the process revealing the questionable basis for closing the communities; organising or attending the mass rallies, shouting out demands and shutting down streets. In every case, these activists were expressing themselves as citizens.

## NOTES

1. For more information on the Sovereign Union, see http://nationalunitygovernment.org/.
2. 'Prime Minister Tony Abbott's interview with the ABC Goldfields-Esperance'. ABC Goldfields Radio, accessed December 15, 2015, http://www.abc.net.au/local/videos/2015/03/10/4194973.html.
3. Blackstar Radio, Facebook Post, May 1, 2015, accessed June 17, 2015. Retrieved from: https://www.facebook.com/permalink.php?story_fbid=89693530369 6039&id=502449413144632.

# REFERENCES

Bennett, S. (1999). *White Politics and Black Australians*. Leonards: Allen & Unwin.

Brodock, K., Joyce, M., & Zaeck, T. (2009). *Digital activism survey report 2009*. Retrieved from http://akgul.bilkent.edu.tr/DigitalActivisim-SurveyReport2009.pdf.

Broome, R. (2010). *Aboriginal Australians*. Sydney: Allen & Unwin.

Callinan, T., (2014, Aug 26). Remote Indigenous Australians rely on Facebook to stay in touch. *SBS*. Retrieved from http://www.sbs.com.au/news/article/2014/08/26/remote-indigenous-australians-rely-facebook-stay-touch.

Carlson, B. (2013). The 'new frontier': Emergent Indigenous identities and social media. In M. Harris, M. Nakata, & B. Carlson (Eds.), (pp. 147–168). Sydney: University of Technology Sydney E-Press.

Carlson, B. (2016). *The Politics of Identity: Who Counts as Aboriginal Today*. Canberra: Aboriginal Studies Press.

Carlson, B., & Frazer, R. (2015). 'It's like going to a cemetery and lighting a candle': Aboriginal Australians, Sorry Business and social media. *AlterNative: An International Journal of Indigenous Peoples, 11*, 211–224.

Corbett, J. O. N., Singleton, G. U. Y., & Muir, K. (2009). Web 2.0 for Aboriginal cultural survival: A new Australian outback movement. *Participatory Learning and Action, 59*, 71–78.

Cunneen, C. (2005). Colonialism and Historical Injustice: Reparations for Indigenous Peoples. Social Semiotics, *15*(1), 59–80.

Davidson, H., (2015, May 01). Melbourne city centre blocked by protests over closure of Indigenous communities—as it happened. *The Guardian*. Retrieved from http://www.theguardian.com/australia-news/live/2015/may/01/protests-at-proposed-closure-of-remote-indigenous-communities-live.

Dreher, T., McCallum, K., & Waller, L. (2016). Indigenous voices and mediatized policy-making in the digital age. *Information, Communication & Society, 19*(1), 23–39.

Edmonds, F., Rachinger, C., Waycott, J., Morrissey, P., Kelada, O., & Nordlinger, R. (2012). Keeping Intouchable: A Community Report on the use of Mobile Phones and Social Networking by Young Aboriginal People in Victoria. *Institute of a Broadband Enabled Society*, 1–32.

Elkin, A. P. (1964). *The Australian Aborigine: How to Understand Them*. Sydney: Angus and Robertson.

Flood, J. (2006). *The original Australians: Story of the Aboriginal people*: Allen & Unwin.

Garcia, A. C., Standlee, A. I., Bechkoff, J., & Cui, Y. (2009). Ethnographic Approaches to the Internet and Computer-Mediated Communication. *Journal of Contemporary Ethnography, 38*(1), 52–84.

Harlow, S. (2011). Social media and social movements: Facebook and an online Guatemalan justice movement that moved offline. *New Media & Society, 14*(2), 225–243.

Kagi, J. (2015, Nov 12). Plan to close more than 100 remote communities would have severe consequences, says WA Premier. *ABC News*. Retrieved from http://www.abc.net.au/news/2014-11-12/indigenous-communities-closures-'will-have-severe consequences'/5886840.

Kahn, R., & Kellner, D. (2004). *New media and internet activism: From the 'battle of Seattle' to blogging. New Media & Society, 6*(1), 87–95.

Kral, I. (2011). Youth media as cultural practice: Remote Indigenous youth speaking out loud. *Australian Aboriginal Studies, 1,* 4–16

Maddison, S. (2009). *Black politics: Inside the complexity of Aboriginal political culture*: Allen & Unwin.

Mansell, M. (2003). Citizenship, assimilation and a treaty. *Treaty: Let's Get it Right!* 5–17.

Maynard, J. (2007). *Fight for liberty and freedom: The origins of Australian Aboriginal activism*. Canberra: Aboriginal Studies Press.

McFarlane, T., & Hay, I. (2003). The Battle for Seattle: Protest and Popular Geopolitics in the Australian Newspaper. *Political Geography, 22*(2), 211–232.

Morozov, E. (2009). Iran: Downside to the "Twitter Revolution". *Dissent, 56*(4), 10–14.

Petray, T. L. (2011). Protest 2.0: Online interactions and Aboriginal activists. *Media, Culture & Society, 33*(6), 923–940.

Petray, T. L. (2015). Self-writing a movement and contesting indigeneity: Being an Aboriginal activist on social media. *Global Media Journal: Australian Edition, 9*(2), 1–20.

Robinson, S. (2014). The Aboriginal Tent Embassy: An account of the protests of 1972. In G. Foley, A. Schaap, & E. Howell (Eds.), *The Aboriginal Tent Embassy: Sovereignty, black power, land rights and the State* (pp. 49–63). Milton Park: Routledge.

Singleton, G., Rola-Rubzen, M. F., Muir, K., Muir, D., & McGregor, M. (2009). Youth empowerment and information and communication technologies: A case study of a remote Australian Aboriginal community. *GeoJournal, 74*(5), 403–413.

Stein, G., (2015, Apr 30). Family harness power of social media to drive protests against forced closures of Aboriginal communities. *ABC News*. Retrieved from http://www.abc.net.au/news/2015-04-30/protest-against-forced-closure-aboriginal-communities/6431558.

Sweet, M., (2015, Jun 14). From Songlines to Twitter: Communicating and connecting for Aboriginal health. *Crikey*. Retrieved from http://blogs.crikey.com.au/croakey/2012/06/14/from-songlines-to-twitter-communicating-and-connecting-for-aboriginal-health.

Wahlquist, C., (2015, Mar 11). Of three remote communities here, why are the two Aboriginal ones under threat? *The Guardian*. Retrieved from http://www.theguardian.com/australia-news/2015/mar/11/of-three-remote-communities-here-why-are-only-the-two-aboriginal-ones-under-threat.

Waitoa, J., Scheyvens, R., & Warren, T. R. (2015). E-Whanaungatanga: The role of social media in Māori political empowerment. *AlterNative: An International Journal of Indigenous Peoples, 11*(1), 45–58.

Watson, M., (2015). The Herald Sun has dismissed 4,000 Indigenous rights protesters as a "Selfish Rabble." *Junkee*. Retrieved from http://junkee.com/the-herald-sun-has-dismissed-4000-indigenous-rights-protestors-as-a-selfish-rabble/54833.

*Chapter 8*

# Platforms Are Eating Society

*Conflict and Governance in Digital Spaces*

Andrew Quodling[1]

When Marc Andreesen (2011) told us that 'Software is eating the world', he was referring to the growth in affordability and availability of computing hardware and internet access, which would allow software services to operate at scale and influence major societal change. Social networking platforms are an obvious beneficiary of this evolving status quo, as platforms like Facebook and Twitter have grown to attract user bases and economies that dwarf some nations (Deloitte, 2014). These platforms are host to public and personal aspects of their users' lives, and act as governmental actors, providing rules, regulatory structure and policing.

The roles of organisations like Facebook and Twitter as owners, operators and adjudicators of these digital spaces are complex. Diverse groups of stakeholders, including users, investors and external governmental actors often have different expectations of how these spaces should be governed. James Grimmelmann (2009) has characterised the governance of the massively multiplayer online game *Second Life* as 'Virtual Feudalism', where the rights and responsibilities of both users and operators balance the complicated social ecosystem and economy of the platform. With this frame, we can examine expressions of user rights in governed digital spaces, particularly those that contest the power exerted by platform operators, to critically appraise what it means to be a citizen of a digital space.

To this end, we can also use conflicts in digital spaces as opportunities to interrogate the operating and social structures of social networking platforms. For this, we must consider the disproportionate power wielded by platform operators and owners in social platforms. Whilst some stakeholders (users) are given affordances with prescribed uses, others (platform operators) have the ability to create and shape affordances and to implement policies as *de facto* laws of the platform. This disproportionate power is reflected in the governing strategies of platform operators and the tactical responses of users (de Certeau, 1998).

In this chapter, I sketch three conflicts that reveal how users and platforms navigate the dynamic interplay of 'personal expression' and 'safety' in digital platforms, in a manner that reveals unequal relations of power operating through user-user interaction and platform-user interactions. The 'Austengate' and 'Gamergate' conflicts present cases where groups of belligerent users campaigned to bully, harass and intimidate other users on Twitter. This provides an opportunity to interrogate the rights and responsibilities of users on Twitter, and the expectations that users have of the platform's governance. Similarly, Twitter's targeted advertising system 'Promoted Tweets' has been used in concert with these campaigns, to broadcast offensive and harassing speech. With this, we can observe the subversion of Twitter's governance—wielded in the design of platform architecture and policies— and more closely examine the influence of technological affordances on the social dynamics of the platform. The tactics of user activism in these conflicts reveal user perceptions of failed governance on behalf of operators, and provide an opportunity to examine the tactics users wield to protect their rights on the platform.

## 'AUSTENGATE'

In 2013, the departing Bank of England governor, Sir Mervyn King, announced that from 2016 onwards, the Bank of England would introduce polymer notes into circulation. Coinciding with this change was the announcement that Sir Winston Churchill's portrait would replace Elizabeth Fry on the reverse side of the £5 note. This drew the ire of some observers, who noted that, with Fry's replacement, there would no longer be any women represented on Bank of England currency. Previously, this representation had celebrated the achievements and contributions of historic Britons since the introduction of Series D notes in the 1970s.[2]

After complaining to the Bank of England about the resulting lack of female representation and finding their response 'inadequate' (Hinge, 2013), Criado-Perez, feminist activist and journalist, launched a legal challenge under the *Equality Act, 2010 §149(1)*. She argued that the bank had failed to give 'due regard' to the need to 'eliminate discrimination' and 'advance equality of opportunity' for women (Criado-Perez, 2013a). Criado-Perez also started a petition and public campaign to suggest Jane Austen as a replacement (Criado-Perez, 2013b). The campaign was successful, generating over 36,000 signatures and supporting letters from members of parliament. The Bank of England announced its intent to feature Austen on the reverse of the £10 banknote on 24 July 2013. Criado-Perez hailed this as a victory for women, but the celebrations were quickly overshadowed by a gender-based counter-campaign against Criado-Perez herself.

A litany of grotesque and intimidating threats ensued on Twitter, primarily delivered through public tweets. Many employed the use of sexist slurs and violent, threatening language:

> 'this Perez one just needs a good smashing up the arse and she'll be fine'
>
> 'Everyone jump on the rape train > @CCriadoPerez is conductor'
>
> 'Wouldn't mind tying this bitch to my stove. Hey sweetheart, give me a shout when you're ready to be put in your place' (Criado-Perez, 2013c)

Criado-Perez wrote at the height of the campaign that she would receive one or more intimidating tweets every minute (Criado-Perez, 2013c).

The campaign against Criado-Perez drew significant media attention with journalists, columnists and politicians who reported or spoke out against the campaign also becoming the target of threats and harassment. Writers India Knight and Laurie Penny wrote that credible bomb threats were made against them (Knight in Quinn, 2013). Similarly, Labor MP Stella Creasy, who was involved in Criado-Perez's banknote campaign, received dozens of threats from Twitter users:

> *@CarolineIsDead:* 'I'm going to pistol whip you over and over until you lose consciousness, then burn ur [sic] flesh.'
>
> *@rapey1:* 'I will rape you tomorrow at 9pm, Shall we meet near your house?' (Roiphe, 2013)
>
> *@protectys:* 'You better watch your back, I'm going to rape your arse at 8pm and put the video all over.' (Jozuka, 2014)

Over 147 Twitter accounts were associated with this campaign of harassment and intimidation against Creasy, Criado-Perez and other prominent women in the United Kingdom (Creasy, 2014). Whilst it's not possible for external observers to determine how many users were behind these accounts, as it is a common practice for users to create multiple accounts on Twitter. Police investigations resulted in three arrests. Peter Nunn, Isabella Sorley and John Nimmo were arrested and charged under §127 of the *Communications Act 2003* for sending messages that were 'grossly offensive or of an indecent, obscene, or menacing character' (Creasy, 2014). According to accounts from Sorley and Nimmo, the bilious counter-campaign was more about the sense of celebrity and community they earned from participation in an online mob: 'I saw it was trending, so I looked into what it was about and, stupid me,

I decided to join in. And I was getting, like, retweets, I was getting favourites and all that' (Nimmo, 2014). Nimmo wrote in his blog, 'The irony of it all is that I wasn't even passionate about the subject or the people I was bullying. I was simply bored, saw what was trending and leaped on to the bandwagon' (Nimmo, 2014).

A year later, this style of misogynistic and anti-feminist campaign would appear again in the shape of *'Gamergate'*, an amorphous crusade against women, people of colour, LGBTIQ+ people, and others who were seen as unwelcome interlopers in video gaming culture by a vocal segment of that community (Mantilla, 2015).

## GAMERGATE

The *Gamergate* conflict began early in August 2014 after Eron Gjoni, the ex-boyfriend of independent game developer Zoë Quinn, published 'the zoe post'. The post was a 'rambling online essay' (Jason, 2015) in which Gjoni accused Quinn of having an affair with a journalist associated with Gawker Media's popular gaming website, *Kotaku*. Although posts associated with Gjoni's blog were deleted from the *Penny Arcade* and *Something Awful* forums (Jason, 2015), they were still shared on several websites, including 4chan's */r9k/* 'Robot 9001' board and the gaming and culture website *The Escapist*'s forums.[3]

This prompted a loosely organised campaign of ongoing harassment (Thomsen, 2014), which continued unabated for the remainder of the month, focusing largely on Quinn and the allegations made by Gjoni—with some gaming commentators alleging that Quinn's relationship with *Kotaku* journalist Nathan Grayson was a *quid pro quo* for favourable press coverage and reviews. The assertion was found to be false (Totilo, 2014); however, the allegations continued, and the scope of harassment extended not just to Quinn but also to supporters like Phil Fish and others who identified as, or were labelled, a 'feminist' or a 'social justice warrior' (*SJW*),[4] like cultural critic Anita Sarkeesian (Johnston, 2014). The campaigns' gender-based harassment of Quinn and other women in the gaming industry earned it an early admonition as misogynistic and hateful, though its proponents often insisted that their campaign was 'actually about ethics in gaming journalism', a refrain that would eventually become the punchline of jokes about the movement.[5]

By the end of August, the controversy earned a name: '#Gamergate', ascribed in a tweet from television actor and conservative activist Adam Baldwin. A host of video gaming websites, including the developer-focused website *Gamasutra*, had begun to criticise the campaign against Quinn, with a number of writers railing against exclusionary behaviours in gaming culture, and the notion of 'gamer' as an elitist subcultural identity (Alexander, 2014).

The 'gamer' identity has been particularly fraught with controversy, as the proponents of Gamergate often discuss their identity as 'gamers' in a manner that appropriates minority politics and language to construct 'gamer' as a 'simulated ethnicity' (Kunyosying & Soles, 2012). Through Gamergate, we can observe the melodramatic construction of 'gamers' as members of a marginalised identity, which functions to secure validity or authenticity for their concerns. Similarly, the 'gamer' identity is constructed as a supra-identity that subsumes other identities. As Cross argues, women and minorities are welcome to identify with this constructed identity in a limited capacity, contingent on 'checking all other identities in at the door' (2015, p. 88).

*Gamasutra* writer Leigh Alexander, and others who oppose the 'gamer' identity, argue that producers should attempt to meet the needs of a broader, growing demographic of people who play games, rather than just 'hard-core' audience members for whom 'gamer' is a central part of their identity. These sentiments mirror the conclusion of Ian Bogost's book '*How To Do Things With Videogames*':

> As videogames broaden in appeal, being a 'gamer' will actually become less common, if being a gamer means consuming games as one's primary media diet or identifying with videogames as a primary part of one's identity. . . . Soon gamers will be the anomaly. . . . Instead we'll just find people, ordinary people of all sorts. And sometimes those people will play videogames. And it won't be a big deal, at all. (Bogost, 2011, p. 154)

By contrast, it is not difficult to see the Gamergate campaign as a conservative, reactionary revolt against the perception that newcomers and progressive interlopers have come to drastically change their way of life (Cross, 2014).[6]

Gamergate proponents were quickly excommunicated from 4chan, after the website's owner Christopher '*moot*' Poole decided that its proponents violated 4chan's 'rules' regarding the publication of private, personal information (Kushner, 2015). The movement consolidated its discussion and organisation to Reddit's */r/KotakuInAction/* forum and 8chan, a 4chan-style image board (Machkovech, 2015) that is notable mostly for its association with Gamergate and its removal from Google search results for reportedly hosting 'suspected child abuse content' (Machkovech, 2015).

In light of these issues, Gamergate was quickly characterised as a new, technologically advanced style of 'culture war' (Chituc, 2015)—a protracted, ideological conflict between advocates for change, and proponents of the status quo. Indeed, influential figures in conservative, reactionary and 'alt-right' political movements have associated themselves with the campaign, and are regularly afforded celebrity status on the */r/KotakuInAction* forum (Schubert, 2014).

There's much more that can be written about Gamergate—from the cross-platform loose organisation of their campaigns to the semiotics of 'Vivian James', the movement's coded rape joke-cum-mascot (Melendez, 2014).[7] For now, the core allegations of 'unethical journalism' alleged by 'GamerGate' proponents have largely been exposed as a mess of misinformation (Lomas, 2014), wilful misunderstanding (Petit, 2015) and *chart brut*-style conspiracy theories[8]—used to obscure troublingly sexist perspectives and behaviours. Although 'Gamergate' is waning in public significance,[9] a dedicated base of harassers and culture warriors remain tightly associated with the movement and its media.


## TWITTER'S POLICIES

As an organisation, Twitter has long been a fierce advocate of free speech for its users—with former Chief Executive Officer Dick Costolo asserting that Twitter strives to be the 'free speech wing of the free speech party' (Barnett, 2011). This is represented both in the rules of Twitter, which are broadly permissive of user expression—even to the point of allowing nudity and pornography on the platform—and in their actions contesting United States Department of Justice subpoenas for user data relating to *Wikileaks* (Barnett, 2011). Similarly, their reticence to censor anti-Semitic tweets in response to requests from German and French governments resulted in the development of a location-based censorship mechanism, which created affordances for tweets to be hidden in the countries in which the governments had sanctioned them.

Whilst permissiveness and freedom of expression are important values held by Twitter's platform operators, as communicated in the company's blog and public statements, issues of user safety have become a higher priority as recent internal and public communications show. Dick Costolo's leaked communiqué provides a clear example of this attitude:

> We suck at dealing with abuse and trolls on the platform and we've sucked at it for years. It's no secret and the rest of the world talks about it every day. We lose core user after core user by not addressing simple trolling issues [. . .] I'm frankly ashamed of how poorly we've dealt with this issue during my tenure as CEO. (Tiku & Newton, 2015)

Twitter General Counsel Vijaya Gadde (2015) argues that the recent focus on user safety is core to the platforms' focus on free expression, noting that if they allow belligerent users to threaten, harass and intimidate other users into silence, then this value is compromised. With this, Twitter has begun to embrace the nuance that Owen Fiss explored in *The Irony of Free Speech* (1996)—that censorship can modestly enhance freedom, to the extent that governmental actors can use censorship to ensure that the 'underfunded, underrepresented, or disadvantaged voice' can be heard (Bernstein, 2014, p. 2).

## TWITTER'S DESIGN AND PLATFORM AFFORDANCES

Twitter's policies speak clearly and definitively about the importance of user safety, but are undermined by organisational issues and design issues. At an organisational level, Twitter does not prioritise user safety to the same extent as other commercial, technological or ideological concerns. An example of these priorities can be seen in Twitter's short-lived attempt, in 2013, to change the 'blocking' function (Sippey, 2013). At the time, 'blocking' another user on Twitter would remove their ability to view your user profile or tweets whilst logged in, and would prevent them from using your username to @reply and @mention you. Twitter briefly changed the function of 'blocking' to be more akin to a 'mute' function, which would allow blocked users to follow and interact with the users who blocked them—but would simply not send notifications to the users who blocked them. Whilst both 'block' and 'mute' functions are useful to users in different ways, the outright replacement of the more powerful 'block' with a less effective 'mute' was of great concern to users, many of whom were strongly critical of the change. Twitter changed the function back within 12 hours of its launch (Sippey, 2013). It was later revealed that Del Harvey, Twitter's vice president of trust and safety, had internally counselled against the change, warning that it was a 'terrible idea' that 'would make cyberbullying easier' (Hill, 2015).

As a technological structure, Twitter's platform has affordances that can support users that are abusive to other users. This can be seen in the ease with which serial harassers can set up multiple accounts.[10] By having multiple accounts, users inclined to harassment can simply log into new accounts and continue their campaigns after being banned or punished for breaking Twitter's rules, or use multiple accounts at the same time to create the illusion of a more populated campaign (Seife, 2014). This is the same tactic of abuse that was deployed in the Austen and Gamergate campaigns.

Even Twitter's '*Promoted Tweets*' advertising system is susceptible to abusive behaviour. The system adds tweets to users' Twitter timelines based on the demographic options, email addresses or Twitter usernames provided by the advertiser, as well as providing flexible affordances not available to ordinary tweets. This allows for either broad or small-scale targeting for the purposes of harassment and abuse-focused tweet campaigns.

One such campaign offers a clear example of how Twitter's 'Promoted Tweets' system can be used for harassment:

> *@Caitlin_Roperr:* Trannies, getting surgery won't change your gender. It will only turn you into a deformed freak. End your miserable existence. Kill yourself.

> *@Caitlin_Roperr:* Trannies, you will never be the opposite gender.

> *@Caitlin_Roperr:* Trannies, your families will never love you. You are living a lie & you know it. End your miserable existence. Commit suicide now. (Gibbs, 2015)

> *@Caitlin_Roperr:* Trannies, everyone is laughing at you. You will never be able to change your chromosomes. End your miserable existence & kill yourself now. (Payton, 2015)

The preceding four tweets were targeted at users of Facebook who were identified as transgender[11] all originated from '@Caitlin_Roperr', an account set up to impersonate Caitlin Roper, an Australian feminist campaigner. On 4chan's */pol/* board, an anonymous user claimed credit for the campaign (Hathaway, 2015). This anonymous 4chan user reportedly used similar tactics in a campaign to impersonate an Australian lawyer, using his name to blog post to the *Times of Israel*'s website calling for the genocide of the Palestinian people (Bornstein, 2015). At the time of writing, the 4chan user was arrested on suspicion of encouraging an attack in Kansas City, Missouri, on the fourteenth anniversary of September 11 (Zavadski, 2015), and has been charged with 'distribution of information relating to explosives, destructive devices, and weapons of mass destruction' (Moyer, 2015).

The progenitor of these efforts to use Twitter's Promoted Tweets for targeted harassment is Andrew Auernheimer (also known as 'weev') (2015), who used his @rabite Twitter account and the Promoted Tweets tool to target tweets about 'white discrimination' and 'white pride' to women and progressives:

> *@rabite:* Whites need to stand up for one another and defend ourselves from violence and discrimination. Our race is dying.

> *@rabite:* White pride, world wide. Do you know the 14 words?[12] /

As both Auernheimer (2015) and Baio (2015) note, the affordances available to advertiser's tweets are significantly more flexible than those available to non-paying users, and include the ability to make a 'nullcasted' tweet—that is, a tweet that appears neither in the creator's timeline nor in the results for Twitter search.[13]

To be clear, Promoted Tweets is neither a tool created for abuse nor a tool solely used for abuse, and much of its usage is likely for traditional advertising purposes. The design and implementation of this system, however, has provided avenues for abuse without appropriate safeguards.

## USER'S POWERS: TACTICAL RESPONSES

Users who have borne the brunt of the hostilities in campaigns like those mentioned against Criado-Perez and Gamergate deploy a range of tactics in navigating Twitter and negotiating the affordances of the platform. We can classify three key tactics as follows:

- *Advocacy*—The use of rhetoric and argument to advocate for changes in policy and/or enforcement on a platform
- *Circumvention*—The use of third-party software and/or the platform's application programming interface (API) to alter the harassed user's experience of the platform
- *Intervention*—The use of social intervention or social engineering to appeal directly to a harassing user's friends or family

These tactics are seen in many other types of platform-user conflict, but are particularly common to conflicts relating to harassment and user safety

## ADVOCACY

In the aftermath of the campaign of tweets and threats following Criado-Perez's banknote campaign, users turned their attention to the platform, with over 140,000 people signing a petition demanding better reporting tools (Graham, 2013). Whilst Twitter was not criticised for hosting or facilitating the campaign, users saw both a failure of moderation and a failure of affordances, and lobbied accordingly for Twitter to make changes to address these flaws. Similarly, the lengthy Gamergate campaign saw users and observers campaign not only for better protections against harassment and harassing campaigns on Twitter and other social platforms (Eleveth, 2014) but also for the response and intervention of traditional law enforcement agencies (Clark, 2015). A key part of these campaigns is attracting the attention of 'mainstream' media sources to gain public legitimacy. This is often accomplished by users writing publicly about their experiences and being interviewed in mainstream news publications. The attention of policymakers and major news outlets often necessitates responses from the operators of social platforms. The *meae culpae* from Twitter's United Kingdom General Manager Tony Wang and then Chief Executive Officer Dick Costolo are key examples of these responses—both coming after significant public consternation about Twitter's failures to protect users.


## CIRCUMVENTION

Twitter's relatively extensible platform infrastructure allows users the opportunity to navigate the platform in atypical ways. A notable example of this is the rise of third-party blocking applications that use Twitter's API to outsource or collaborate on blocking accounts that are known, or deemed likely, to harass users. Some examples of these third-party systems include '*The Block Bot*', '*Block Together*' and '*Good Game Auto Blocker*'. Though each of these systems has different implementations and different designs, their goal is fundamentally quite similar.

'*The Block Bot*' is an application that includes an updating set of block lists. It is developed and organised by members of the 'Atheist+' community, a movement that attempts to accommodate diversity of gender, race, sexuality and class in Atheist discourse. It is operated by a team of moderators who classify Twitter accounts under three tiers based on levels of harm and aggression. The highest 'Level 1' tier criteria include a bevy of behaviours that are already against Twitter's rules, including 'threats, harassment . . . impersonating someone, . . . encouraging self-harm, . . . promoting hate speech'. The lowest tier 'Level 3', expands the list to include accounts that the moderators deem likely to be 'tedious or obnoxious', especially from accounts that 'appear to frequently engage in micro-aggressions [, or] show a sense of entitlement to have a conversation'. Users who activate '*The Block Bot*' with their Twitter accounts can choose their preferred level of severity to pre-emptively block according to their desires.

In comparison, '*Block Together*' provides a more flexible system for users 'to reduce the burden of blocking when many accounts are attacking you, or when a few accounts are attacking many people in your community' (Hoffman-Andrews, 2015). '*Block Together*' provides the option for users to privately manage their own block lists, or share them amongst others. It also provides a number of blocking affordances designed to counteract behaviours commonly associated with harassing accounts. In particular, '*Block Together*' provides options for users to block 'young' Twitter accounts that are less than a week old, as well as Twitter accounts with less than fifteen followers. Both of these options provide some remedy to the harassing tactic of 'sockpuppetting'[14]—creating new, disposable Twitter accounts to avoid the punishments associated with breaking Twitter's rules.

The *'Good Game Auto Blocker'* (often shortened to GGAutoBlocker) uses the underlying *'Block Together'* system, along with an associative algorithm that adds Twitter users to a shared block list on the basis of who they're following. If a user follows more than one of a handful of Twitter accounts associated with the Gamergate movement, including Breitbart columnist Milo Yiannopolous and blogger Ethan Ralph, they are added to the list. This dragnet method is efficient at weeding out potentially harassing users, but also flawed, as 'following' a Twitter user does not particularly indicate support for them or their views. To counteract this, *'Good Game Auto Blocker'* has an appeals process by which Twitter users can publicly appeal their ban and request to be added to a white list of accounts that the algorithm will not block.

At a less-comprehensive level, third-party Twitter clients like Tweetbot and Twitterrific allow flexible 'mute' and 'muffle'[15] options to create personalised filters that hide or make less visible tweets from certain users, including hashtags or tweets that conform to user-specified regular expressions (Gonzales, 2014). Although Twitter now offers rudimentary block list sharing and both 'mute' and 'block' functions, these third-party offerings predate Twitter's provision of these services and functions and continue to offer more flexible options to users who find Twitter's affordances lacking.

## INTERVENTION

For some users, an effective tactic is to directly or indirectly engage their harassers through social means. A particularly well-known instance of this is of writer Alanah Pearce's response to a harasser who turned out to be a young boy. Pearce used Facebook to investigate the harassing user (who had seemingly used his real name) and used Facebook's messaging function to contact the boy's mother, providing a screenshot of the threat and asking her if she'd like to discuss his threat with him. The mother replied, 'Omg little shit', 'IM SO SORRY', 'YES ILL TALK TO HIM' (Essert, 2014), and reportedly asked her son's school to talk about online harassment and bullying. This sort of social intervention can be a powerfully discouraging factor. Zoë Quinn, one of Gamergate's key targets, notes that in her discussions with self-identified 'former trolls', many stopped their belligerent behaviour because 'more often than not . . . someone they were close to, respected, or looked up to said that wasn't cool—that the social network supporting this kind of feeding frenzy was no longer reinforced' (Quinn, 2015).

## CONCLUSION: CONTESTED GOVERNANCE

Platforms such as Twitter have policies that are ignored by belligerent users and technological affordances that can be abused to cause harm to others. In the conflicts examined in this chapter, we can see divergent groups of users attempting to tactically use the structure and affordances of Twitter in their user-user conflicts. In these conflicts, belligerent users make use of Twitter's lax moderation practices and permissive account creation tools to facilitate the dissemination of their messages to other users. Targets of harassment on the other hand lobby the platform operators to more effectively enforce their rules. In response to the perceived failure of Twitter's operators to effectively and efficiently govern their platform, targets of harassment have also used Twitter's technological affordances to supplement their use of the Twitter platform with more comprehensive tools for controlling their experience and interactions with other users.

By using the affordances of the platform to subvert their intended uses and instead mitigate and combat abuse, users can also bring attention to the ways in which platform operators fail to effectively regulate the use of their space. Similarly, they provide opportunities for more complex discussion and analysis of the digital spaces users inhabit, and the rights, responsibilities and regulatory norms of these spaces.

Both the failures of platforms to effectively govern their space and the tactical advances of users to subvert the platform or address these failings are indicative of the challenges present in creating digital realms where users can truly participate as citizens. Whilst social networking platforms have thrived as notionally self-regulating entities, continued failures that risk the safety of users will likely bring the spectre of regulatory reform, either by external governmental actors (e.g. traditional broadcast and communications regulators) or by increased participation in governance by users seeking representation as citizens and stakeholders in these platforms. Twitter, and other social platforms like it, will continue to grapple with their own roles as governors, their social and political responsibilities to their users, and the resistance and activism of politically engaged users.

## NOTES

1. In this chapter, I quote and reproduce text that could *charitably* be described as hateful and abusive. These include violent threats, incitements to suicide and white supremacist rhetoric. I reproduce this text in this work not to be gratuitous or offensive, but to give context to the discussion of the policies and technological structures that support their publication. A term like 'hate speech' can be more easily dismissed

in the abstract, but in order to understand the dynamics of its effects on people and on discourse, we must be ready to engage these texts and challenge the systems that support their propagation.

2. Queen Elizabeth remains on the obverse side of the note. However, this is a function of her role as head of state, rather than recognition of her accomplishments or contributions to British society.

3. *The Escapist*, Retrieved August 17, 2014. http://www.escapistmagazine.com/forums/read/18.858347-Zoe-Quinn-and-the-surrounding-controversy#21276142.

4. 'Social Justice Warrior' is often used as a pejorative epithet to dismiss the arguments of feminist, anti-racist and social justice–focused campaigners as radical or ludicrous. The term is also adopted by many of those it is intended to disparage, who argue that being described as a fighter for social justice is not insulting.

5. For examples of these, see the 'Actually It's About Ethics' entry in the 'Know Your Meme' website: http://knowyourmeme.com/memes/actually-its-about-ethics.

6. This 'revolt' grew most notably amongst gaming community hubs, including 4chan's /v/ video games board and a handful of Reddit's 'subreddit' forums.

7. The colour scheme of Vivian James, and much of Gamergate's branding, are a reference to an animated GIF file called 'Piccolo Dick' that had regularly circulated on 4chan from 2008 onwards. In 'Piccolo Dick', the green-skinned, purple-clothed Piccolo character from popular anime Dragon Ball Z rapes another character, Vegeta. After 4chan moderators started to ban users who used the image, users rebelled and began posting abstract green and purple images in reference.

8. 'Chart Brut' refers to the aesthetic of crudely annotated images associated with online conspiracy theories and mob activity.

9. Google Trends searches for 'gamergate' reveal the term's steady decline in search traffic from late 2014 onwards. Retrieved from: https://www.google.com/trends/explore#q=gamergate.

10. Twitter typically only requires a username and an e-mail address to register an account. A mobile phone number may also be required if Twitter's systems determine it likely that a user is creating multiple accounts. Given the relative ease of creating new email addresses, or obtaining short-use 'burner' mobile phone numbers, it is relatively trivial for a dedicated user to create multiple Twitter accounts.

11. The anonymous 4chan user who claimed credit for this campaign did not reveal whether he supplied a list of users accounts that he suspected to belong to transgender users, or if Twitter's advertising system directed it to users with interests in transgender issues—as the Twitter platform does not offer users the ability to indicate their gender in their user profile and settings pages.

12. The 14 words is a well-known reference to an 88-word passage from chapter 8 of Adolf Hitler's *Mein Kampf*. It is often used to refer to the phrase 'We must secure the existence of our people and a future for White Children', which was popularised by white supremacist David Lane.

13. Although, some third-party applications with access to the full gamut of Twitter data—including promoted tweets—can find 'nullcasted' tweets.

14. Sockpuppet refers to an online identity used with the intention of misleading others. Sockpuppet identities are often used to praise, defend or criticise another

member of an online platform under the guise of offering an independent or correlating third-party viewpoint.

15. The distinction between 'mute' and 'muffle' relates to the design of the functions. Whilst 'mute' features do not display tweets that conform to the rules of the applied mute filters, 'muffled' tweets still appear in a user's timeline, but are given a visual design treatment that shows that a tweet has been hidden in the timeline, and the filter responsible for the removal.

# REFERENCES

Alexander, L. (2014, Aug 28). "Gamers" don't have to be your audience. "Gamers" are over. *Gamasutra*. Retrieved from http://www.gamasutra.com/view/news/224400/Gamers_dont_have_to_be_your_audience_Gamers_are_over.php.

Andreesen, M. (2011, Aug 20). Why software is eating the world. *The Wall Street Journal*. Retrieved from http://www.wsj.com/articles/SB10001424053111903480 904576512250915629460.

Auernheimer, A. (2015, May 09). So I'm banned from Twitter's ad console. *Storify*. Retrieved from https://storify.com/weev/twitter-ads-copycat-roundup.

Baio, A. (2015, Feb 04). Stupid tricks with promoted tweets. *Medium*. Retrieved from https://medium.com/message/stupid-tricks-with-promoted-tweets-57325552109d#.p2k7i5yfj.

Barnett, E. (2011). Twitter chief: We will protect our users from Government. *The Telegraph*. Retrieved from http://www.telegraph.co.uk/technology/twitter/8833526/Twitter-chief-We-will-protect-our-users-from-Government.html.

Bernstein, A. (2014). Abuse and harassment diminish free speech. *Pace Law Review, 35*.

Bogost, I. (2011). *How to Do Things with Videogames*. Minneapolis: University of Minnesota Press.

Bornstein, J. (2015, May 06). White supremacists stole my identity to spew hatred on the Times of Israel. *The Guardian*. Retrieved from http://www.theguardian.com/world/2015/may/05/identity-stolen-white-supremacists-times-of-israel.

Chituc, V. (2015, Sep 11). GamerGate: A culture war for people who don't play video games. *New Republic*. Retrieved from https://newrepublic.com/article/122785/gamergate-culture-war-people-who-dont-play-videogames.

Creasy, S. (2014, Sep 29). Twitter troll hell: "I can't get the last year of my life back". *The Telegraph*. Retrieved from http://www.telegraph.co.uk/women/womens-life/11127782/Stella-Creasy-Twitter-troll-hell-I-cant-get-the-last-year-of-my-life-back.html.

Criado-Perez, C. (2013a). After the Jane Austen announcement I suffered rape threats for 48 hours, but I'm still confident the trolls won't win. *New Statesman*. Retrieved from http://www.newstatesman.com/media/2013/07/after-jane-austen-announcement-i-suffered-rape-threats-48-hours-im-still-confident-tro.

Criado-Perez, C. (2013b). We need women on British banknotes. *Change.org*. Retrieved from https://www.change.org/p/we-need-women-on-british-banknotes.

Criado-Perez, C. (2013c). Women on bank notes: Is the Bank of England finally listening? *The Guardian.* Retrieved from http://www.theguardian.com/lifeandstyle/the-womens-blog-with-jane-martinson/2013/jul/04/women-bank-notes-bank-england.

de Certeau, M. (1998). *The Practice of Everyday Life.* (S. Rendall, Trans.) Berkeley, California: University of California Press.

Deloitte. (2014). The global economic impact of Facebook. *Deloitte.* Retrieved from http://www2.deloitte.com/uk/en/pages/technology-media-and-telecommunications/articles/the-global-economic-impact-of-facebook.html.

Essert, M. (2014). This Woman's Response to Online Rape Threats Deserves a Standing Ovation. Indentities. Mic, November 28, 2014. URL: https://mic.com/articles/105272/one-woman-has-the-perfect-response-to-online-rape-threats#.zmR3ZfTC2.

Eleveth, R. (2014, Dec 02). A new harassment policy for Twitter. *The Atlantic.* Retrieved from http://www.theatlantic.com/technology/archive/2014/12/new-harassment-policy-for-twitter/383344/.

Gibbs, S. (2015, May 21). Troll uses Twitter adverts to urge transgender people to kill themselves. *The Guardian.* Retrieved from https://www.theguardian.com/technology/2015/may/20/troll-uses-twitter-adverts-to-urge-trans-people-to-kill-themselves.

Gonzales, C. (2014, Aug 07). Quick Tip: Use Tweetbot to mute unwanted tweets - The Sweet Setup. *The Sweet Setup.*

Graham, K. (2013). Add a Report Abuse Button to Tweets. *Change.org.* Retrieved from https://www.change.org/p/twitter-add-a-report-abuse-button-to-tweets.

Grimmelmann, J. (2009). Virtual world feudalism. *The Yale Law Journal*, 118, 126.

Hathaway, J. (2015, May 20). 4chan troll claims he framed feminist for transphobic promoted tweet. *Gawker.* Retrieved from http://gawker.com/4chan-troll-claims-he-framed-feminist-for-transphobic-p-1705889031.

Hill, K. (2015). The Ashley Madison hack, and the value of averting your eyes. *Fussion.* Retrieved from http://fusion.net/story/185749/the-ashley-madison-hack-and-the-value-of-averting-your-eyes/.

Hinge, D. (2013, Jun 11). Bank of England faces legal challenge over all-male banknote roster. *Central Banking.com.* Retrieved from http://www.centralbanking.com/central-banking/news/2274214/bank-of-england-faces-legal-challenge-over-allmale-banknote-roster.

Jason, Z. (2015, Apr 28). Game of fear: The story behind GamerGate. *Boston Magazine.* Retrieved from http://www.bostonmagazine.com/news/article/2015/04/28/gamergate/.

Jozuka, E. (2014, Sep 29). Twitter troll jailed for abusive tweets against UK MP. *Wired.* Retrieved from http://www.wired.co.uk/news/archive/2014-09/29/twitter-troll-nunn-jailed-mp-creasy.

Kunyosying, K., & Soles, C. (2012). Postmodern geekdom as simulated ethnicity by Kom Kunyosying and Carter Soles. *Jump Cut - A Review of Contemporary Media.*

Lomas, N. (2014, Oct 18). #Gamergate shows tech needs far better algorithms. *TechCrunch.* Retrieved from http://techcrunch.com/2014/10/18/gamergate-tactics/.

Machkovech, S. (2015, Aug 18). 8chan-hosted content disappears from Google searches. *Ars Technica.* Retrieved from http://arstechnica.com/tech-policy/2015/08/8chan-hosted-content-disappears-from-google-searches/.

Mantilla, K. (2015). *Gendertrolling: How misogyny went viral.* Santa Barbara, CA: Praeger.

Melendez, S. (2014, Nov 03). The secret meaning behind GamerGate's branding. *Fast Company.* Retrieved from http://www.fastcodesign.com/3037941/the-secret-meaning-behind-gamergates-branding.

Moyer, J. W. (2015, Sep 11). Florida man plotted Sept. 11 attack on Kansas City, Mo., FBI says. *The Washington Post.* Retrieved from https://www.washingtonpost.com/news/morning-mix/wp/2015/09/11/florida-man-plotted-sept-11-attack-in-kansas-city-fbi-says/.

Nimmo, J. (2014, Nov 29). My experience as a convicted twitter bully. *Trolls Life.*

Payton, N. (2015, May 20). Twitter users shown transphobic promoted tweets from account impersonating feminist writer. *PinkNews.* Retrieved from http://www.pinknews.co.uk/2015/05/20/twitter-users-shown-transphobic-promoted-tweet/.

Petit, C. (2015, Jan 02). GamerGate gets one right. *A Game of Me.* Retrieved from http://agameofme.tumblr.com/post/106975098317/gamergate-gets-one-right.

Quinn, B. (2013, Aug 06). Twitter bomb threats made against more women in public eye. *The Guardian.* Retrieved from https://www.theguardian.com/technology/2013/aug/05/twitter-bomb-threats-women.

Quinn, Z. (2015, Nov 02). Zoe Quinn, crash override—XOXO festival (2015). *YouTube.* Retrieved from https://www.youtube.com/watch?v=vAcdKTXtx1k.

Schubert, D. (2014, Sep 20). How GamerGate's right wing nutjob heroes are betraying a hidden ideological purge. *Zen of Design.* Retrieved from http://www.zenofdesign.com/what-their-right-wing-nutjob-heroes-say-about-gamergates-hidden-ideology/.

Seife, C. (2014, Jul 29). The weird reasons why people make up false identities on the internet. *Wired.* Retrieved from http://www.wired.com/2014/07/virtual-unreality-the-online-sockpuppets-that-trick-us-all/.

Sippey, M. (2013, Dec 13). Reverting the changes to block functionality. *Twitter Blog.* Re-trieved from https://blog.twitter.com/2013/reverting-the-changes-to-block-functionality.

Thomsen, M. (2014, Oct 16). Gamergate and the unbearable maleness of computers. *Forbes.* Retrieved from http://www.forbes.com/sites/michaelthomsen/2014/10/16/gamergate-and-the-unbearable-maleness-of-computers/#7dabb6ba7487.

Totilo, S. (2014, Aug 20). In recent days I've been asked several times about a possible breach of ethics. *Kotaku.* Retrieved from http://kotaku.com/in-recent-days-ive-been-asked-several-times-about-a-pos-1624707346.

Zavadski, K. (2015, Sep 11). "Terrorist" troll pretended to be ISIS, white supremacist, and Jewish lawyer. *The Daily Beast.* Retrieved from http://www.thedailybeast.com/articles/2015/09/11/terrorist-troll-pretended-to-be-isis-white-supremacist-and-jewish-lawyer.html.

*Chapter 9*

# Intimate Citizenship 3.0

## Sonja Vivienne

In this chapter, I explore the good, the bad and the complicated of what I call Intimate Citizenship 3.0. These are constitutive digitally mediated practices that intersect across intimacy, privacy, publicness and difference. I use '3.0' in alignment with Tim Berners-Lee's evocation of the semantic web as 'fractal' (Berners-Lee and Kagal, 2008) and challenged by vastness, vagueness, uncertainty, inconsistency and deceit (Lukasiewicz and Straccia, 2008). These variables similarly invoke the uncertainty and inconsistency of navigating digitally amplified self-representation and civic participation. Ubiquitous engagement with technology, particularly social media, has made everyday maintenance of a congruent private/public identity increasingly complex. Digital technologies amplify what Bakhtin called polyphonic discourse, or multivocal speech that is 'overlapping' and 'always unfinished' (1970). There are currently endless communicative variables across textual genres (SMS, photos, blogs, status updates), spaces (home, work, public transport, f2f, numerous online platforms), publics (familiar, unknown) and time (revisiting past, present, anticipating future). boyd (2008) has dubbed this 'social convergence' or 'context collapse' whereby 'persistent, replicable and searchable' (boyd, 2008) dimensions, and digital 'exhibitions of self', overlay and intersect with embodied daily realities.

Digital Citizenship explicitly canvasses shifting understandings of inclusion/exclusion, private/public and negotiations of the intimate and personal in a way that previous understandings of traditional citizenship do not. The average teenager must negotiate their digital self-representations with many people—teachers, parents, friends, prospective employers, possible romantic interests—who are stakeholders in their daily life. I use 'negotiate' here because power resides in these processes, with adults and/or hegemonic structures and discourses positioned to lock down, censure and censor any representations that are deemed unsuitable for, or threatening to, homogeneity. One example of this is the moral panics that are routinely built around the dangers of 'over sharing' intimacies in online spaces, and the expectations placed upon guardians and parents to monitor and intervene in these practices. This has ramifications for marginalised and/or stigmatised identities (crossing intersections of race, class, faith, sexuality and gender) that can be simultaneously mundane and profound.

When Ken Plummer originally coined 'Intimate Citizenship' in 2003—to encapsulate the right to choose what we do with 'our bodies, our feelings, our identities, our relationships, our genders, our eroticisms and our representations'—he could not have anticipated the complications invoked by ubiquitous use of technologies that bring disparate social spheres together. In acknowledgement of these complications, Intimate Citizenship 3.0 is a conceptual framework that defies out-of-date digital dualisms like 'real life' and 'online'. It is a toolbox of pragmatic and contextual strategies that circumnavigate the strictures of stigmatised digital self-representation. Working with a cohort of people whom I call 'everyday activists'—those who advocate for social change through routine embodied encounters with norms, rather than formal participation in social movements—I have observed and analysed exceptionally sophisticated navigation of the complex terrains of intimacy, identity and networked life (Vivienne, 2016). These inform the refinements I make to Plummer's theoretical lens of 'Intimate Citizenship.'

While I draw on previous work with queer and gender-diverse communities, it seems possible that their strategies—used to counter the high risks of networked self-disclosure—might also be utilised by a broad majority of young people, who are similarly vulnerable as they navigate emergent and fluid identities, and personal change. I argue that these strategies enhance social connectedness and expression of diverse activist voices. These in turn, contribute to the regeneration of norms for self-representation, privacy and publicness that constitute what I call erosive cultural change. I use 'erosive cultural change' rather than 'social change', which is a term that is more easily quantifiable and may be measured by law reform or policy updates. Like waves on a cliff face, erosive change has impact over extended periods and is effected by many incremental elements and shifts in climate. These nevertheless add up to empirical differences in the cliff, and in values and beliefs, and eventually institutions and social infrastructure.

In this chapter, I offer a theoretical backdrop for this analysis and some emergent definitions of digitally mediated cultural engagement. Then, I describe four exemplars of people engaged in the practice of Intimate Citizenship 3.0. I describe people who are themselves embodied sites of culture war, framed in terms of intimate personal rights. Lisa Barrett is an Australian birth activist and digitally savvy feminist who is caught between legal and medical interventions and the right to choose the circumstances of birth. Philip Nitschke is an Australian medical doctor who is caught between divergent international laws on assisted suicide and the right to choose the circumstances of death. Jasper and Louise are transgender, and they are caught between rigid social expectations of gender, timeline versions of personal history (as mediated by Facebook), and the right to inhabit a legal identity of their choosing. The line between networked privacy and public everyday activism, for all of them, is unclear and difficult to navigate. Finally, I consider whether the conceptual frame of Intimate Citizenship 3.0 is constitutive of erosive cultural change, in which people confront and dismantle outmoded models of 'coherent' self-representation (Giddens, 1991; Hyvärinen et al., 2010) in favour of curated personal congruence.

## THEORETICAL AND SOCIAL CONTEXT

One of the benefits of working out what groups one is 'a part of', or 'apart from', is the very practical and affirming experience of social connectedness. Nearly 20 years ago, Lauren Berlant wrote about the formation of groups of affinity (principally in North America), calling them 'Intimate Publics' (1997). In an exploration across genres and subjects (i.e. *not* exclusively 'chest-baring autobiographical confession') that range from cult TV, children and sexuality, home video and live sex acts, Berlant illuminates the ways that people coalesce around a shared world view. This shapes the content they consume, their experiences of belonging and their self-representations.

In 2003, Ken Plummer developed a frame for what he called 'Intimate Citizenship', focusing on what he perceived as an increase in public awareness and discussion of 'the decisions people have to make over *the control (or not) over* one's bodies, feelings, relationships; *access (or not) to* representations, relationships, public spaces etc.; and *socially grounded choices (or not) about* identities, gender experiences, erotic experiences' (Plummer, 2003, p. 14). He canvasses the identity construction practices surrounding emergent social issues—new forms of 'family life', choices around sexuality and gender, IVF, cosmetic surgery, post-human cyborgs and unacceptable approaches to intimacy (e.g. sexual harassment, child abuse and sex-murders). From Berlant and Plummer, I derive a conceptual research frame that focuses on public (and inevitably digital) encounters over the norms of embodied and bodily intimacy.

Long prior to ubiquitous internet use Nancy Fraser (1990) and Iris Marion Young (1997) argued that an inclusive public sphere should accommodate diverse speaking styles and narrative modalities along with capacity to listen across difference. More recently, a growing field of internet scholars have explored the relationship between public spheres and citizenship, arguing that, in order to participate publicly, we draw on private lived experiences and constraints, many of them mediated by digital technologies (Livingstone, 2005; Papacharissi, 2010). Modern daily life is perpetual connectedness, a phenomenon that has arisen from a 'triple revolution'. According to Rainie, Rainie and Wellman (2012) these are social networking, the internets' capacity to facilitate voice, and the always-on connectivity of mobile devices. Building on this, Jurgenson (2011) argues against digital dualisms, pointing out that most people are not singularly, discretely online *or* face-to-face—but both, simultaneously. Interactions that take place in one space influence the other and vice versa, effectively (digitally) augmenting a (embodied) reality. The intersections are opaque and sometimes it is difficult to fathom finite meaning. Where previously we might have risked being overheard by five people co-located in space and time, now inept utterances or #fails may be simultaneously witnessed by hundreds of acquaintances in different places and even at different times. Where previously news might spread via gossip (and early technologies like the printing press, telephone and later television), now virtually anyone has access to and can redistribute news to virtually unlimited new contexts. Networked individualism and digitally mediated identity construction therefore calls forth skills and strategies to juggle multiple overlapping publics, while expanding opportunities for learning, sharing, problem-solving and decision-making (Benkler, 2006; boyd, 2011; Rainie et al., 2012)

Considerations of personal 'orientation' in social space, and understandings of 'performance' and 'exhibition of self' are also pertinent. While Sara Ahmed (2006) draws attention to phenomenological perceptions that orient otherness in socially constructed spaces. danah boyd (2014) suggests that, due to increasingly complex digital mediation of communication and identity, 'it's complicated'. Bernie Hogan (2010) compares performances that take place in synchronous 'situations', and artifacts, that reside in asynchronous 'exhibitions'. Hogan builds on Goffman's stage metaphor to argue that social media platforms like Facebook operate to curate identity as an *exhibition* rather than a *performance* of self. Questions of agency and ownership (or production and distribution) of self-representation are central to surveillance, activism and everyday engagement in networked public life.

In Australia in 2016, a predominantly conservative political leadership combined with concentrated ownership of mainstream media to inflame debate about issues of citizenship and belonging. Both new arrivals, and those who walked the land prior to colonial invasion, were excluded by accusations of being 'un-Australian', while 'free speech' was reframed to include what was formerly known as 'hate speech'.[1] Public servants were encouraged to report colleagues that posted anti-government commentary on social network sites, while those who did so were likely to receive legal notice via Twitter.[2] Public protests like the 'March in March'[3] also bear forth some of the discontent that marked 'Occupy Wall Street'. Overtly moralistic discourses concerned with 'protecting' innocent children from explicit discussions of gender, sexuality[4] and gay marriage still divide the population, and the legislative assembly.[5]

In this context, how are discourses about what groups one is 'a part of' or 'apart from' evolving among networked publics and how are ideas of citizenship, speaking across difference and intimacy being mediated by technology? With these discourses increasingly intertwined, how does the framework of Intimate Citizenship 3.0 connect with current regulatory and/or legal processes? While Australia has no formal Bill of Rights, the right to freedom of political expression is arguably implicit in the constitution. Meanwhile state-based Bills of Rights distinguish between political expression and cultural politics. In practice, freedom of speech most clearly applies in the context of electioneering, while online expression is regulated for the most part by the Australian Communications and Media Authority (ACMA).

An extensive list of media and communications ranging across film, television broadcast, games and any content distributed via the internet can be refused classification for an equally lengthy list of infringements ranging from representations of child abuse to instruction in crime. On the other hand, material that does not require classification, but is distributed in media form (e.g. blogging or broadcast in the 'public interest'), is moderated by 'public standards' that are determined through investigating formal complaints. Criminal law is different again and applies to issues of harassment, stalking and violent threats that may also be mediated by technology. Unfolding from these complex and overlapping frameworks, any public discussion of issues that verge upon criminality (including supporting suicide, illegal importation of regulated hormones or drugs like Nembutal and, in some circumstances, home birth) can also be regulated following complaint from a member of the public. ACMA can impose takedown orders and refer potentially criminal discourse to authorities.

## EMERGENT DEFINITIONS

In the following text, I clarify my usage of key that are, including 'congruent self-representation' and the 'everyday activism' at the heart of 'Intimate Citizenship 3.0'. My notion of 'congruence' is derived from usage in transgender and queer communities. Gender dysphoria remains the dominant clinical diagnosis for a 'mis-match' between gender assigned at birth and understanding of self. Alignment between gender presentation and self-concept (with or without sex reassignment surgery, or SRS) may therefore be referred to as achieving 'congruence'. Giddens regards 'the reflexive project of the self' as an effort to maintain coherent self-representation in the face of the 'standardising influences' of commodification that are 'core components of modernity's institutions' (Giddens, 1991, p. 5). He nevertheless regards self-identity as, primarily, an 'internally referential system':

> It has no morality other than authenticity, a modern version of the old maxim 'to thine own self be true'. Today, however, given the lapse of tradition, the question 'Who shall I be?' is inextricably bound up with 'How shall I live?' (Giddens, 1992, p. 198)

Giddens points out that conformity with an external social judgement of 'coherence' is somewhat arbitrary and emphasises, 'A combination of imbalanced power and engrained psychological dispositions keeps dualistic sex divisions quite firmly in place; but in principle matters could be organised quite differently' (Giddens, 1992, p. 199). This argument rests on the power of social traditions, and, while Giddens' focus here is on sexuality and intimacy, it applies equally to gender and other intimate concerns like birth and death. These concerns are so primal and embodied that transgressions push against long-held conventions. The people who articulate ways of transgressing boundaries (and indeed regulations) must achieve personal congruence in the face of pressure to perform 'coherence' in compliance with social norms. This is not a question purely of identity so much as a process of steadfast resistance that brings new possibilities into being. Rather than 'who shall I be?' their everyday activism probes 'how shall I live?'. Personal congruence, achieved through curated and digitally mediated self-representation, also underpins the emergent practices of Intimate Citizenship 3.0.

Personal storytelling has a long legacy in political activism (Poletta, 2006; Solinger et al., 2008). Building on this tradition, I use 'everyday activism' to signify the sharing of personal stories in public spaces (Vivienne, 2013) often driven by mundane lived experiences in which simply 'being oneself' does not permit any other alternative. Like Giddens, Foucault (1979) draws attention to the ways that social surveillance, and being monitored everywhere, all the time, by everyone, enables iterative moralities to appear 'natural' and unchanging. The everyday activists I describe in the following are interested in social change, but not necessarily as a part of an organised social movement. Rather, they engage in slow erosion of cultural norms through everyday transgressions both online and offline.

The frame of Intimate Citizenship 3.0 combines everyday activism, as defiant personal congruence that transgresses social norms, with technological affordances. These in turn reinforce individual capacity to speak across differences in values, capabilities, social capital, locative time and space; their processes are simultaneously embodied/virtual, networked and distributed. Intimate Citizenship 3.0 requires digital agency and fluid but congruent self-representation, and assumes negotiation of privacy and publicness, and self-exposure in the face of surveillance and risk of retribution.

## CASE STUDIES IN TRANSGRESSIVE TRANSITION

In this section, I describe four examples of people engaging in Intimate Citizenship 3.0. To a large degree, their identities or the issues they wish to speak about, publically, are contentious and socially maligned. As well as engaging in everyday activism, they have a common interest in what I describe as 'transgressive' transition. They speak about processes or journeys across socially accepted norms. While the use of 'transgression' infers infringement, I reclaim it here (in allegiance with the reclamation of 'queer') because it accurately captures their perceptions of exclusion and of embodying otherness. From this oppositional stance, their everyday activism challenges boundaries, subverts marginalisation and erodes cultural conventions. Their representations are risky, and consequently self-exposure is carefully curated and undertaken in full awareness of surveillance, both formal and social.

In a wider social context, transgressive transitions occur across minutiae of boundaries and include the following:

• Sense of belonging to a place (becoming homeless, stateless)
• Way of being (gender, sexuality, disability)
• Rite of passage (birth, death, becoming family, becoming coupled)

Some transitions are more socially acceptable than others—for example, while becoming a teenager can be quite disturbing, it is generally accepted that teenagers are engaged in exploration of identity. We know that they will probably become adults who are different, in many ways, to the children they have been. Having said that, puberty is easier to deal with if identity transformation is within the parameters of social norms and does not involve transgressions in gender or sexuality. Similarly, the intimate transitions into and out of life—birth and death—are scripted by social norms that, at least in many contemporary western contexts, are highly medicalised. Refusing hospital care involves transgressive choices that are frequently penalised, both socially and legally.

## Birth in Private . . . and Public

Currently, in Australia, choosing home birth in so-called high-risk scenarios is held to jeopardise the well-being of the child. High-risk categories are culturally arbitrary and range quite broadly from previous caesarean, twins, breech babies and even first-time mothers over 38. In some of these circumstances, it is difficult to find a medical provider who will support vaginal delivery, even in a hospital context, and the rare obstetricians and midwives who do risk their own medical indemnity insurance and registration if something goes wrong and they are deemed liable. Lisa Barrett was an independent midwife and a staunch advocate for women's right to choose, even those who are traditionally determined 'high risk'. Barrett opposes medical dogma and systemic hospital authority and expresses her views in an articulate and passionate blog.[6] Her blog also serves as a hub for prospective mothers, midwives and interested people (mostly like-minded women), and many have used it to share stories about their birth experiences (including anecdotes of being subjected to medical interventions against their will).

Between 2007 and 2011, Barrett attended several home births in which babies died When something went wrong. Accidental deaths at home are routinely investigated by police, whether the family lays blame or not. In Barrett's case none of the families involved wished to pursue charges, however subsequent Coroner's inquests raised questions about her fitness to practice. The Nurses and Midwifery Board brought charges of professional misconduct against Barrett. When further changes were made to maternity and midwifery policy in 2009, Barrett chose to hand in her registration rather than compromise her personal values and convictions. She continued to advocate informally for a range of birth choices. Social surveillance increased, fanned by media interest that bordered on hysterical.[7]

Barrett continued to defend herself and what she and many women believe to be safe home birth practices, supported by substantial medical research. Barrett's 'most-commented' blog post, refuting accusations and inaccurate news reports, received 295 comments, both supportive and inflammatory. The following extract, encoded with ironic affect, evokes her frustration at routine public misrepresentation:

> The amount of hate mail I've received over the last few days has been remarkably low. I suppose all the uninformed must be spreading vitriolic opinions in the comment section of the national rags. I forgive you if you're basing your opinion on sloppy, lazy, sensationalistic journalism. You have an excuse. They don't.[8]

Barrett is now subject to a prohibition order that bans her from any public discussion of birth-related issues that may be construed as 'consulting' or 'offering an opinion' in Australia. Shortly, I will explore some of Barrett's emergent practices for maintaining a public voice.

## Death in Private . . . and Public

While choosing to end your own life is technically not illegal, supporting someone who wishes to end their life can attract ramifications, ranging from unwanted media attention (and informal social surveillance) to criminal charges for assisting suicide and/or manslaughter. Philip Nitschke is a well-known euthanasia advocate and medical doctor who believes that all elderly or terminally ill people should have choices available to them regarding the time, place and circumstances of death. He runs a non-profit organisation called 'Exit International' and is active both politically and in mainstream media and social media. On numerous occasions, he has been investigated for 'fitness to practice' and has faced accusations that claim his work in informing people of their death options is in breach of his Hippocratic oath. In 2014, he appealed a Medical Board of Australia (MBA) suspension of his licence. In late 2015, the MBA lifted their suspension but imposed extensive conditions on his practice. Nitschke called this 'a heavy-handed and clumsy attempt to restrict the free flow of information on end-of-life choice' and chose to resign his registration, burning his medical practicing certificate in a symbolic gesture of defiance.[9]

In his autobiography 'Damned if I do', Nitschke points out that it was initially his stature as a high-profile doctor that enabled him to fight on behalf of people who are marginalised by terminal and/or mental illness and/or poverty and/or old age. However, it is in his role as an advocate that Nitschke has encountered opposition on numerous occasions, particularly when travelling across national borders to deliver educational euthanasia workshops, when his citizenship status or licence to practice medicine has been questioned: 'Since when is public speaking "practising medicine"!' (Nitschke and Corris, 2013, p. 127). While acknowledging the inherent complexity of digital platforms, Nitschke describes feeling heartened by public support expressed online:

> It is nice to know that others are of like mind, that my message is on target, and that I am not alone. But the blogging and twitterspheres have also brought out the mad and downright dangerous, particularly among the fundamentalist Christians. (Nitschke and Corris, 2013, p. 159)

Nitschke's uses of online spaces (and select mainstream media) are sophisticated and responsive to social and political context, and I discuss them further shortly.

## Gender in Private . . . and Public

Jasper and Louise (pseudonyms chosen by interviewees) are exemplars of grass-roots everyday activism. They use social media and digitally mediated self-expression for personal advocacy, and on behalf of the transgender community. Jasper has made numerous Digital Stories[10] (Vivienne, 2012; 2013) that explicitly challenge socially perceived norms about gender and well-being. He engages in practices of Intimate Citizenship 3.0 when he negotiates with family members about how their collective history is revealed in public documents. When his dad chose to be excused from a family photo that Jasper wished to use in his digital story, Jasper responded with acceptance:

> When I was younger I would probably have just seen that as a rejection of me and my identity but yeah, now I know that it's more to do with his own perspectives and sense of power or powerlessness. He wasn't quite ready to stand up and be proud and, you know, there's a fair percentage of his own paranoia about technology. (Jasper, interview, 2010)

Both Jasper and Louise test the boundaries of social and political engagement with their networked publics on a routine everyday basis. This was something they learnt as children, long before they were digitally active. As Larry Gross quips:

> Queer folk are past masters at this game [of selective self-representation], as nearly every one of us went through the training program during childhood. Even if we weren't singled out for special (unwelcome) attention as sissies, tomboys or other gender non-conformists, most of us survived society's sexual boot camp – high school – either by masquerading and passing, or living on the margins. (Gross, 2007, p. vii)

Even with this hard-won expertise, digitally mediated privacy, selective publicness and the curation of congruent identity are most often acquired through trial and error, despite many claims made on behalf of so-called 'digital natives'.

## TRANSFORMATIVE NETWORKED STRATEGIES

Jasper and Louise, Lisa Barrett and Philip Nitschke all engage a toolbox of strategies for negotiating privacy and publicness among their networked publics. For prominent public figures like Barrett and Nitschke, free speech and advocacy is liable to be monitored not only by the mainstream media but also by moral vigilantes and political opponents. Censure in a social context, once reported to authorities, can translate into censorship by ACMA. Ramifications can effect employment, economic status and emotional well-being, right through to freedom of movement as citizens. On a more personal scale, the right to self-determination for gender-diverse people is currently limited not only by social norms that patrol appearance, mannerisms and usage of public bathrooms but also by medical and legal processes that restrict access to cross-sex hormones and surgical interventions. The strategies that underpin Intimate Citizenship 3.0 afford access to carefully curated public participation and advocacy alongside selective withdrawal from scrutiny. These strategies can be broadly categorised in six intersecting themes. Intimate Citizenship 3.0 affords:

- A platform for speaking across difference
- An opportunity to connect (being 'a part of' or 'apart from')
- Advocating (for) and proselytizing (to)
- Traversing geographical, social, legal boundaries
- Education (us) and provocation (them)
- Curation of privacy through selective self-representation

In the following sections, I will explore these strategies in practical use by everyday activists in my case studies.

## Blogging and Tweeting, a Counterpublic Voice

Since its inception, Lisa Barrett's blog has been a visible and populated platform for highly polarised discussion of birth choices. On some occasions, it directly contributed to conflict between medical practitioners, hospitals and the Nursing and Midwifery Board. Arguably, Barrett's embodied presentation of self—dreadlocks and brightly coloured natural fibre clothing—and irreverent manner also made a contribution. Forced to engage with the Coroner's Court in what was initially a legal argument over what constitutes life, she learnt that some opinions were best spoken quietly to a few, or not expressed at all. Barrett recalls opting for her right to remain silent rather than defend herself, because in her opinion, speaking meant violating the privacy of a woman and a family who were already traumatised by the loss of a child. This choice to *not speak* about something deeply personal, with widespread impact upon intimate publics, was the action that brought her closest to a criminal conviction, for contempt of court.

In contrast to social and legal judgements on Barrett's home birth practice, a body of research indicates that the number of complications in home birth environments equate with those undertaken in hospital environments (Jackson et al., 2012; Miller et al., 2012) and that, in some cases, outcomes for women and babies can be better in the familiar environment of the home. Despite this evidence, Lisa Barrett transgresses social norms when she chooses to publicise the choices available to women, especially the 'high risk' women who are offered limited options.

Barrett has not updated her blog since mid-2012 because she has been ordered to post a splash page containing a 'medical warning' and feels uncomfortable doing so. The blog nevertheless remains an archive for women and families seeking alternative points of view on birth choices. Barrett has closed the Facebook account she had (with 6000 or so friends) and opened another under a pseudonym that exists solely to engage with six or seven family members. Despite the prohibition order, she chooses to engage on Twitter under a pseudonym, which allows her to be actively involved in other resistance movements. She maintains a public voice through speaking about generalised experiences of oppression at activist forums, including events like 'Control of our bodies! Control of our Lives!' hosted by 'Radical Women' to coincide with International Women's Day in Melbourne.[11] Further, nationally enforced limitations on her free speech do not prevent Barrett from speaking about birth choices in international forums, engagements she may not have secured were it not for her outspoken online profile.

While Barrett never undertook blogging (and later tweeting) as a political act, it has become a means of circumnavigating suppression. Engaging with the world in this way affords her opportunity to connect and to be 'a part of' belief systems that are fundamental to her identity. She is astute in recognising that capacity to easily traverse boundaries and norms is correlated to power and privilege, and not so easy for home birth midwives. She is currently studying law.

## Strategic Storytelling and Networked Subversion

Philip Nitschke is an accomplished strategist in his relationship with mainstream media, which enables him to engage broadly with publics that do not share his point of view. Like Barrett, his authority and legitimacy as a healthcare provider is routinely challenged; however, he has not yet been banned from social media. He nevertheless walks a fine line and limits his self-representation on mainstream media to offering editorial opinion in occasional high-profile cases, while encouraging other people from the euthanasia activist community to share their personal stories in public. Like 36-year-old, terminally ill, Jay, speaking on 'Four Corners',[12] Nitschke argues that 'a very human face' serves the purpose of speaking across differences, engaging even antagonists in the personal importance of death choices (Nitschke & Corris, 2013, p. 146).

Philip Nitschke was motivated to take a public stance on censorship issues when the 'Peaceful Pill Handbook' was banned along with a pro-euthanasia

TV advertisement and billboard. Further, in 2009, WikiLeaks published the government blacklist of web pages likely to be banned and/or excised should the government be successful in implementing a mandatory internet filter.

> At a grassroots level, Exit responded to the threat of the clean feed by introducing our elderly members to concepts such as 'virtual private networks' and 'internet tunnels', which are technological means of getting around an internet filter. We placed our regular workshop information program on hold and focused on ways to subvert government censorship. With expertise from the twenty-something geeks of the Pirate Party, we held hacking meetings on the east coast of Australia. (Nitschke & Corris, 2013, p. 174)

While Nitschke uses online spaces and mainstream media to catalyse discussion, he also uses online and face-to-face networks for educative purposes. When the 'Peaceful Pill Handbook' was banned, Exit International took the opportunity to offer an e-publication. Perhaps ironically, the e-book exploits the responsive and interactive aspects of the medium with updates six times per year covering the latest information on international law reform, purchase of materials and equipment, etc. Hyperlinks point to alternate sources of online information. Membership of online forums is strictly monitored and thereby offers safe space in which people can discuss their concerns regarding euthanasia, free of accusations of complicity. They are encouraged to fully engage in negotiations with extended family and friends, considering both current and future circumstances.

This, in some cases, being an engaged citizen in a networked public involves advocacy; in others being 'a part from' involves a degree of proselytizing. Philip Nitschke leverages his former status as a medical doctor to command respect in deliberations in the public sphere. He is meticulous in maintaining this status—it offers congruence between his personal and public self-representations, and he understands that this position is both tenuous and powerful. It enables him to amplify the voices of the many terminally ill and/or elderly individuals he has everyday contact with.

Nitschke has also discovered another platform for storytelling and subversion of the firmly drawn lines between life and death. In 2015, he collaborated with terminally ill comedian Mel Moon, in a show for the Edinburgh Comedy Festival,[13] and performed 'Dicing with Death' at the Melbourne International Comedy Festival this year.[14]

## The Line between Education and Provocation

Louise and Jasper engage in gentle lobbying through routine provocations of their intimate networked publics, composed of carefully selected friends, family and colleagues. Posting links that share generic international news stories of transgressive transition and gender diversity, whether triumphant or harrowing, have the effect of reminding their audiences that external appearances are not always as they seem and that gender presentation is highly responsive to social constructs.

When Jasper and Louise travelled overseas together for Louise's gender reassignment surgery, they were keen to keep loved ones informed of their adventure. Rather than engaging with the tiresome labour of organising selective Facebook friendship groups around who may or may not wish to know, Louise opted to invite a select handful to a Facebook 'event'. Simply put, those 'attending' could read all updates; to everyone else, their respective timelines appeared as usual.

On LinkedIn, Louise and Jasper have many acquaintances in common. However, the same network of acquaintances can be interpreted as an asset or deficit, depending on what job and sector one is seeking employment. For Jasper, who works in community health, queer connections might be well regarded; for Louise, in white-collar administrative positions, ranging across a variety of sectors, the same networks might be regarded as troublesome. She tells of an unpleasant period of job seeking that occurred during gender transition. Louise had applied for positions according to her current legal stature, with a male moniker, but by the time of interview was living full time as a woman. She described calling employers to let them know she would be attending the interview as Louise, and went to the additional effort of preparing a pack of resources to assist with gender awareness in the workplace. Clearly, this additional labour was not called for in the job description, and yet it was a requisite undertaking for Louise and an excellent example of Intimate Citizenship 3.0—always, already, speaking across differences.

The four individuals I refer to here experience embodiment, citizenship and harm in different ways, while sharing potential risk to their intimate well-being by virtue of self-expression and stigmatised public exposure. Both Barrett and Nitschke have experienced invasions of privacy by media and lawmakers; however, on a routine basis, they manage their privacy by selectively withdrawing from public debate. Meanwhile, Jasper and Louise both utilise a range of strategies to draw a line between front- and back-stage selves (Goffman, 1959). Jasper has 'time off' from Facebook whenever he finds himself getting drawn into ongoing conflict. He admits that 'I have no filters' (interview, 2014) when it comes to speaking back to perceived injustice and sees periods of abstinence from social media as pro-active management of mental well-being. Louise, on the other hand, deliberately posts unusually upbeat material when she's feeling down, a form of coded sharing that only her very close friends are able to interpret. She is quite conscious of how she presents herself both online and face-to-face and is careful to keep track of who knows what personal information. She recalls, after social transition, the experience of 'Googling myself'. When she first came out as transgender, she was heavily reliant on a special-interest community forum for support and insight. Much later she realised that, despite the forum's illusion of privacy, these early, very revealing posts were clearly tagged with her chosen female name and were visible to a broad general public with little access to or understanding of the original context. She sifted through every digital trace she could find, either deleting the original posts or changing spellings or monikers on specific accounts so that the links to her current identity were obscured. This conscious selection and arrangement of artefacts, as if in a personal art gallery, resonates with Hogan's notion of online 'exhibition' of self (2010). While complete privacy and pseudonymity are as illusory as most forms of human control, Louise has nevertheless made a concerted effort to own what versions of herself she shares.

Jasper and Louise don't have a clearly formulated approach to engaging in Intimate Citizenship 3.0. Rather, in an ongoing dance between education and provocation, advocacy and proselytism, they bring new understandings of Intimate Citizenship into being. In traversing binary gender and selectively curating privacy, they enact an iterative process that is eroding the values of pre-modernity and bringing other possibilities into existence.

## INTERVENTIONS—INTIMATE CITIZENSHIP 3.0 IN PRACTICE

What are the possibilities for facilitated interventions that harness both the viral energy and the chaotic, fragmented inclusivity of digital platforms? Can they promise greater agency over self-representation, ownership of personal congruence *and* sustainable change? In the early moments of Occupy Wall Street, blogs, tweets, hash tags and sharing via memes facilitated public personal storytelling as everyday activism (Milner, 2013). Followers were encouraged to share brief personal handwritten anecdotes of their experience of living as one of the bottom #99percent of wage earners, photographed at chest height so as to frame out their faces. These circulated as online memes but also found material form photocopied and taped to power poles.

When amplification by conventional megaphones was banned, activists took up the 'human microphone' allowing speech to be amplified across huge 'general assemblies' through a series of call and repeat. The fractal and self-replicating nature of the human microphone finds parallel, in some ways, with the 'story circle' at the heart of most digital storytelling workshops. Everybody takes a turn to answer questions like 'tell a story about your name . . . a favourite object, person, memory'. Trust is established in an environment of mutual vulnerability, encouraging listening across difference. Participants are asked to reflect upon their typical engagement in social spaces and challenge themselves to 'step out of the comfort zone'. If one is used to holding forth, quiet down and sit with silence; if one is normally quiet, try speaking up. Depending on the storytelling cohort and the issues that draw them together (i.e. what makes them an intimate public), some of the listening and speaking skills acquired are replicated as participants negotiate the content of their story with the friends and family who are part of it. These practices, sustained over an extended time frame and reaching multiple publics, might also represent the slow creep of erosive cultural change.

Mapping these networked strategies has the function, like much narrative practice (Myerhoff, 1982; White & Epston, 1990), of bringing awareness and insight into communal and personal meanings that have previously been obtuse, including definitions of privacy. As a conceptual frame, Intimate Citizenship 3.0 makes apparent the emergent digital expertise and resilience of 'transgressive' communities and people. At an education, policy and advocacy level, this toolbox of networked strategies could be implemented for better listening, sharing and acceptance of 'the other'. Mapped even more broadly, this toolbox is of use to anybody navigating contemporary life beyond digital dualisms. Meanwhile, the personal benefits of practicing Intimate Citizenship 3.0 may include a consolidation of networked connections that support agency and ownership of curated congruence.

The practices of Intimate Citizenship 3.0 as manifest in these case studies—Lisa Barrett's acceptance of the ramifications of birthhome activism and her journey into more general and carefully curated activism; Philip Nitschke's crafted congruence on behalf of himself and those he represents; Jasper and Louise's everyday curation of trans-identity across multiple platforms—are demonstrations of networked engagement that deconstruct digital dualism.

Undertaking Intimate Citizenship 3.0, as a facilitated (by people or platforms or both) and creative everyday practice, constitutes an intervention—a strategic and targeted experiment in catalysing erosive change. In some cases, it may result in explicit and measurable law reform; in other instances, it represents the slow shifting of understandings of privacy and publicness and of 'coherence' (consistency judged by others) and 'congruence' (as determined by self and acknowledging fluidity and ongoing change). It exemplifies speaking back to power and is a response to the transitions, perceived to be transgressive, which disrupt social norms. These well-articulated strategies are likely to map broadly onto banal transitions (e.g. young person to adult) that are currently tangled in digitally mediated concerns about privacy and publicness. Thus, the selective curation undertaken by those at the most extreme at-risk borders of intimate transgression is equally useful to the confused teen and the overwhelmed caregiver, alongside social service providers and policymakers. When understanding of the selective self-representation strategies of Intimate Citizenship 3.0 becomes widespread and routine, we may witness greater acceptance of the multitude of intimate differences among us.

## NOTES

1. Chan, G. (2014, March 24). George Brandis: 'People have the right to be bigots' [World News]. Retrieved April 10, 2014, from http://www.theguardian.com/world/2014/mar/24/george-brandis-people-have-the-right-to-be-bigots.
2. Sparrow, J. (2014, July 4). Dob in your tweeting mate at work? So much for free speech [Political Editorial]. Retrieved April 10, 2014, from http://www.theguardian.com/commentisfree/2014/apr/07/dob-in-your-tweeting-mate-at-work-so-much-for-free-speech.
3. March in March | People Power—a vote of no confidence in the current government. (n.d.). Retrieved April 9, 2014, from http://marchinmarch.com.au/.
4. McNally, L. (2015, March 24). Gender Neutrality or Enforcement? 'Safe Schools' isn't as Progressive as it Seems [commentary]. Retrieved 17 February 2016, from http://www.abc.net.au/religion/articles/2015/03/24/4204018.htm.
5. Hutchens, G., & Hasham, N. (2016, March 6). Prime Minister Malcolm Turnbull refuses to endorse same-sex marriage pledge [News]. Retrieved 28 April 2016, from http://www.smh.com.au/federal-politics/political-news/same-sex-marriage-plebiscite-promised-this-year-if-coalition-wins-election-20160305-gnbma9.html; Australian Marriage | Think of the Child. (n.d.). Retrieved April 28, 2016, from http://australianmarriage.org/.
6. Homebirth: Midwife Mutiny in South Australia: www.homebirth.net.au/.
7. Mamamia News, 2013. Warning: this woman should not be allowed to attend births [WWW Document]. Mamamia. URL http://www.mamamia.com.au/news/news-homebirth-advocate-lisa-Barrettt-faces-professional-misconduct/ (accessed 4.8.14).
8. Barrett, L., 2011. Free for all [WWW Document]. Homebirth Midwife Mutiny S. Aust. URL http://www.homebirth.net.au/2011/10/free-for-all.html (accessed 4.8.14).
9. Breen, J., 2015. Euthanasia advocate Philip Nitschke sets medical certificate alight, rejects Medical Board's conditions [WWW Document]. ABC News. URL http://www.abc.net.au/news/2015-11-27/philip-nitschke-sets-medical-certificate-alight/6981522 (accessed 4.13.16).
10. including 'Back to Happiness' viewable at URL www.rainbowfamilytree.co.
11. Radical Women revolutionary socialist feminism [WWW Document], n.d. URL http://www.radicalwomen.org/melbourne.shtml (accessed 4.9.14).
12. Jackson, L., Fallon, M., 2013. My Own Choice [WWW Document]. Four Corners. URL http://www.abc.net.au/4corners/stories/2013/09/16/3847237.htm (accessed 11.10.14).
13. Russell, P. (2015, August 4). MercatorNet: Comedy is deadly serious for Philip Nitschke [Collaborative blog and commentary]. Retrieved 3 May 2016, from http://www.mercatornet.com/careful/view/comedy-is-deadly-serious-for-philip-nitschke/16619.

14. Woodhead, C. (2016, April 4). Melbourne International Comedy Festival review: No one dying of laughter in Philip Nitschke's Dicing With Death [News]. Retrieved 3 May 2016, from http://www.smh.com.au/entertainment/comedy/melbourne-comedy-festival/melbourne-international-comedy-festival-review-no-one-dying-of-laughter-in-philip-nitschkes-dicing-with-death-20160404-gny6oz.html.

# REFERENCES

Bakhtin, M. M. (1970–1986). *Speech genres and other late essays.* (M. Holquist & C. Emerson, Eds.). Austin: University of Texas Press.

Benkler, Y. (2006). *The wealth of networks: How Social production transforms markets and freedom.* New Haven: Yale University Press.

Berners-Lee, T., & Kagal, L. (2008). The fractal nature of the semantic web. *AI Magazine, 29*(3). Retrieved from http://dig.csail.mit.edu/2007/Papers/AIMagazine/fractal-paper.pdf.

boyd, d. (2008). *Taken out of context: American teen sociality in networked publics.* (PHD in Information Management and Systems), University of California, Berkeley.

boyd, d. (2011). Social network sites as networked publics: Affordances, dynamics, and implications. In Z. Papacharissi (Ed.), *Networked self: Identity, community, and culture on social network sites* (pp. 39–58). New York: Routledge.

boyd, d. (2014). *It's complicated: The social lives of networked teens.* New York: Yale University Press.

Foucault, M. (1979). *Discipline and punish: The birth of the prison.* London: Vintage Books.

Fraser, N. (1990). Rethinking the public sphere: A contribution to the critique of actually existing democracy. *Social Text,* (25/26), 56–80.

Giddens, A. (1991). Modernity and self-identity: Self and society in the late modern age. Cambridge, UK: Polity.

Giddens, A. (1992). *The transformation of intimacy: Sexuality, love and eroticism in modern societies.* Stanford, CA.: Stanford University Press.

Goffman, E. (1959). *The presentation of self in everyday life.* New York: Anchor Books.

Hogan, B. (2010). The presentation of self in the age of social media: Distinguishing performances and exhibitions online. *Bulletin of Science, Technology & Society, 30*(6), 377–386.

Hyvärinen, M., Hyden, L.-C., Saarenheimo, M., & Tamboukou, M. (Eds.). (2010). *Beyond narrative coherence.* Amsterdam: John Benjamins Publishing Company.

Jackson, M., Dahlen, H., & Schmied, V. (2012). Birthing outside the system: Perceptions of risk amongst Australian women who have freebirths and high risk homebirths. *Place of Birth, 28*(5), 561–567.

Jurgenson, N. (2011, Feb 24). Digital dualism versus augmented reality. *New Inquiry.* Retrieved from http://thesocietypages.org/cyborgology/2011/02/24/digital-dualism-versus-augmented-reality/.

Livingstone, S. M. (2005). *Audiences and publics: When cultural engagement matters for the public sphere.* Bristol, United Kingdom: Intellect.

Lukasiewicz, T., & Straccia, U. (2008). Managing uncertainty and vagueness in description logics for the Semantic Web. *Web Semantics: Science, Services and Agents on the World Wide Web*, (6), 291–308.

Miller, Y. D., Prosser, Samantha J., & Thompson, R. (2012). Going public: Do risk and choice explain differences in caesarean birth rates between public and private places of birth in Australia? *Place of Birth, 28*(5), 627–635.

Milner, R. M. (2013). Pop polyvocality: Internet memes, public participation, and the Occupy Wall Street movement. *International Journal of Communication, 7,* 2357–2390.

Myerhoff, B. (1982). Life History among the elderly: Performance, visibility and re-membering. In J. Ruby (Ed.), *A Crack in the mirror: Reflexive perspectives in anthropology* (pp. 99–117). Philadelphia: University of Pennsylvania Press.

Nitschke, P., & Corris, P. (2013). *Damned if I do.* Melbourne: Melbourne University Publishing. Retrieved from http://books.google.com.au/books?id=yZlwAAAAQBAJ.

Papacharissi, Z. A. (2010). *A private sphere: Democracy in a digital age.* Cambridge: Polity.

Plummer, K. (2003). *Intimate citizenship: Private decisions and public dialogues.* Washington, D.C: University of Washington Press.

Poletta, F. (2006). *It was like a fever: Storytelling in protest and politics.* Chicago, Illinois: University of Chicago Press.

Rainie, H., Rainie, L., & Wellman, B. (2012). *Networked: The new social operating system.* Cambridge, MA: MIT Press.

Solinger, R., Fox, M., & Irani, K. (2008). *Telling stories to change the world: Global voices on the power of narrative to build community and make social justice claims.* New York: Routledge.

Vivienne, S. (2016). *Digital identity and everyday activism: Sharing private stories with networked publics.* London, New York: Palgrave Macmillan.

Vivienne, S., & Burgess, J. (2012). The digital storyteller's stage: Queer everyday activists negotiating privacy and publicness. *Journal of Broadcasting & Electronic Media, 56*(3), 362–377.

White, M., & Epston, D. (1990). Narrative means to therapeutic ends. New York: Norton.

Young, I. M. (1997). Intersecting voices: Dilemmas of gender, political philosophy, and policy. Princeton: Princeton University Press.

*Part III*

# CULTURE

*Chapter 10*

# 'Somewhere in America'

## *The #MIPSTERZ Digital Community and Muslim Youth Voices Online*

Amelia Johns[1] and Abbas Rattani[2]

The modes of participation, representation and voice that have been enabled by the internet and digital technologies have brought into question long-held beliefs about who the citizen is and what constitutes political life (Isin & Ruppert, 2015). This has prompted serious questions about whether groups marginalised from formal decision-making, including young people, are using digital media to enact or renegotiate traditional features of democratic participation: from modes of speaking and representation to forms of activism that contest social, economic and political inequalities (Papacharissi, 2009; Couldry, 2010; van Zoonen, Vis & Mihelj, 2010).

In particular, attention has turned towards digital cultures which foster and amplify youth voices 'othered' within national frames. Studies of diaspora and minority media highlight these possibilities, with diaspora communities using digital media to shape alternative, diverse and transnational expressions of culture, identity and belonging (Siapera, 2010; Georgiou, 2013, p. 84); these also open up new possibilities for performing citizenship in online spaces. And yet, while digital media tools and platforms are celebrated for empowering marginalised groups, 'on the other hand national boundaries have become increasingly reinforced through systems of surveillance', including digital surveillance and control (Georgiou, 2014, p. 85), particularly since 11 September 2001, and most acutely for Muslim communities (Johns, 2014). This has undermined and constrained Muslim youth agencies and political practices. However it has also led to the formation of digital cultures which 'contest this marginal location' (Leurs & Ponzanesi, 2010).

Nonetheless, as Siapera (2010, pp. 107–08) notes, the techno-utopian visions that sometimes accompany analysis of digital communities often overlook how power operates *within* the social media forums of diaspora communities, with common problems of who gets to define and represent the community often leading to conflict and reinforcement of social inequalities and hierarchies, posing questions regarding their capacity to promote inclusive and pluralistic spaces of participation.

We engage with these debates via a digital ethnography of the Mipsterz ('Muslim Hipsters') online community. The Mipsterz phenomenon came to prominence in the United States in 2013 following the YouTube upload of a video depicting headscarf-observing Muslim women riding skateboards, taking selfies, and performing everyday selves to the backing of Jay Z's 'Somewhere in America', which went viral upon its release.[3] For the young Muslims who joined Mipsterz after viewing the video, it circulated an image of their everyday negotiations of faith and culture often missing from racialised post-9-11 representations and from formal religious spaces. Given the internalisation of struggles over representation since 9-11, a large number of negative responses to the video came from within US Muslim diaspora communities, with sensitivities around class-, race-, religion- and gender-provoking questions over whether the video was broadly representative of young American Muslims.

However, rather than this revealing a flaw in characterising digital communities like Mipsterz as 'counter-publics' (Warner, 2005) which contest dominant representations by presenting alternative voices, this chapter will highlight the value of analysing digital interactions involving dynamics of *agonism and conflict* (Papacharissi, 2009; van Zoonen et al., 2011), and *intimate forms of exchange* (Plummer, 2003) as crucial expressions of pluralistic democracy (Mouffe, 2000, 2013; Paparachissi, 2009; Couldry, 2010) and digital citizenship (Dahlgren, 2004, 2005; Couldry, 2014). Importantly, it is claimed that these interactions open up and modify (without replacing or completely resolving) the rational modes of deliberation demanded of the liberal citizen-subject, in a political field which all too often excludes voices which contest these dominant and normative modes of citizen participation.

## RADICAL PLURALISM AND MINORITY VOICE

Online cultures have been analysed as spaces which enable the inclusion of 'voices' marginalised from hegemonic, national public spheres. Fraser (2007), Warner (2005), Siapera (2010) and Georgiou (2013) have considered how the globalisation and fragmentation of the media landscape into a multiplicity of direct spheres of communication has facilitated the inclusion of minority groups in new sites of activism and struggle. Leurs and Ponzanesi (2010) similarly argue that everyday digital cultures are revitalising democracy by including diasporic and subaltern actors, who are able to use their marginal location and digital media tools to 'express their multivocality and negotiate cultural differences'.

Papacharissi (2009) and van Zoonen et al. (2010) identify the emotion-filled and passionate forms of disagreement which often characterise participation in digital communities as performances of 'agonistic pluralism' (Mouffe, 2000, 2013). Here, they make reference to the radical democratic theory espoused by Chantal Mouffe, where she claims the aim of democracy is not to eradicate passions and hostilities from the public sphere—but instead the media and other institutions of democracy should allow 'collective passions . . . to express themselves' (Mouffe, 2000, p. 103). Mouffe considers Habermas' (1992 [1989]) concept of the public sphere, where free and equal citizens enter into rational modes of deliberation to form a common consensus, to be an impossible fantasy. Papacharissi elaborates:

> Mouffe's (2000) critique is based on the impossibility of true plurality within a modern or postmodern deliberative democracy. Thus she proposed agonistic pluralism as a 'vibrant clash of democratic political positions', guided by undecidability, and more receptive to the plurality of voices that develop within contemporary pluralist societies than the deliberative model (Papacharissi, 2009, p. 232)

Papacharissi claims that this 'foreshadows' the types of interaction that occur in social media forums, which provide a platform for the inclusion of conflict-ridden and emotional exchanges between positions that are passionately held and often irreducible to consensus. While Papacharissi acknowledges that the inclusion of agonistic claims and discourse can lead to undecidability and inaction over matters of public concern, by being 'receptive to a plurality of voices' (Mouffe, 2000, p. 104) agonistic forms of deliberation are also understood to have a greater capacity to transform existing power relations and address exclusions (Papacharissi, 2009, p. 241).

Couldry considers how the affordances of networked digital spaces and the ephemeral nature of flows and connections in and across these spaces allow new forms of 'distributed' voice to emerge that challenge dominant narratives and modes of representation (Couldry, 2010). Following Butler, the aspect of voice which matters most for Couldry, particularly in pluralist democracies, is the right of citizens to 'give an account of themselves' (citing Butler, 2005) and the 'world within which they act' (Couldry, 2010, p. 7). For Couldry, narrating the self is a political act that asserts agency and implies that responsibility must be taken for the stories being narrated, particularly if they relate to membership of a collective. The value of 'voice' is grounded in relations of social co-operation and plurality and is therefore irreducible to the liberal individualism favoured by the Habermasian deliberative model.

Reflecting on these inquiries, this chapter will analyse Mipsterz social media forums, and particularly the Mipsterz email list,[4] as sites where engagement with creative projects and everyday online cultures opens up new repertoires of democratic participation, voice and community action—some of which emphasise forms of social co-operation which invoke deliberative models of participation, and others which are characterised by agonistic internal contestation. In keeping with the approach of the collection, we understand that the forms of intimacy, contest and struggle we analyse in the chapter have consequences for how members negotiate and perform digital citizenship.

## DIGITAL ETHNOGRAPHY: A CONTESTED METHOD AND SITE FOR DIGITAL CITIZENSHIP

A digital ethnography approach was chosen to address the question of whether Mipsterz exemplifies a kind of digital democracy and citizenship at work. The research design accommodated 'insider' and 'outsider' perspectives, made possible through a collaboration between 'Somewhere in America #MIPSTERZ' film co-creator, Mipsterz co-founder, email list moderator and second author, Abbas Rattani(AR), and lead researcher and first author, Amelia Johns (AJ). As digital ethnography always entails ethical challenges that implicate researchers—not as objective observers but as participants who affect the communities being researched and who therefore are implicated in negotiations around digital citizenship themselves—the approach and methods are outlined in some detail below.[5]

As a member and participant in the Mipsterz email list from July 2014, AJ had access to all conversations posted between the July 2014 and September 2015. In addition to this, one of the affordances of Google Groups is the ability to archive topic threads, making them a readily available resource for all members to access. This function was also utilised by AJ in accessing formative conversation threads that predated her own participation in the list. From her engagement with the community, it became evident that Mipsterz social media, and particularly the email list, was a rich site for exploring whether networked media and participatory digital cultures may offer marginalised groups an opportunity to articulate the diversity of their digital expressions, voices and identities and to contest unequal power relations. AJ considered the advantages and disadvantages in analysing these conversations and presenting the data in a domain which would give greater public visibility to these often 'intimate' interactions (Hine, 2015), particularly in terms of ethical issues concerning: ownership of data, privacy, obtaining informed consent and narrative appropriation (Knobel, 2003).

To address these issues, and particularly to include the voices and perspectives of Mipsterz participants and moderators in the analysis, AR was contacted and a collaborative research design proposed. AR agreed to assist with recruitment and design of research questions, and to have input to the analysis by providing context for discussions which referenced aspects of Mipsterz history, community formation and norms of moderation on the email list. AJ conducted interviews with five active participants in the threads analysed in the chapter. This option was taken to triangulate the systematic content and discourse analysis of exchanges taking place on the email list and give greater depth and insight into participants' interactions.

To seek permission to use data posted to the forum, and to recruit participants for follow up interviews, a web advertisement was posted to the group in November 2015. The first stage of recruitment involved an opt-out process, where members could email the researchers and decline to have their data considered for the research. This was followed by an opt-in recruitment and consent procedure whereby members whose data the researchers were interested in analysing and potentially publishing would be contacted via email and written consent requested for use of their conversations. At the suggestion of a member on the email list, a topic thread was created for the purpose of negotiating what ethical digital ethnographic research practice should entail, and these guidelines have been adhered to where possible throughout.

The email archive was narrowed down to two samples of posts and replies occurring on the email list, one random sample and one purposively selected. Neither sample is statistically representative but provides a cross-section of participation in the forum. The random sample comprises a collection of all posts on the forum between 18 June 2015, and 14 August 2015 (N=148). This enabled a robust, systematic analysis of individual modes of engagement in the forum and the types of topics discussed. Following this, a more in-depth discourse analysis of conversations occurring under three selected topic threads between the dates of 21 July 2014, and 21 September 2015, was undertaken. The threads were selected on recommendation of AR and interviewees who considered the exchanges on these topic lists to be formative to the Mipsterz narrative and relevant to the questions addressed by the research. This sample was analysed for the number of participants in each topic thread, types of engagement, for example, post/no reply and reply, sustained conversation between participants, political viewpoint expressed, and language and tone of the exchange (e.g. dialogue, agonistic contest, antagonism/trolling). Nine participants provided permission for selected posts to be included in this section of the analysis.

Owing to the contentious and sensitive nature of some of the interactions taking place on the email list, and in order to protect the anonymity of members as much as possible, pseudonyms have been applied except where participants expressed that they wanted to be named. In some cases, the names of threads have also been changed to lessen the public searchability of exchanges in question owing to sensitivities around representation (Hine, 2015).

## THE EMERGENCE OF THE MIPSTERZ DIGITAL COMMUNITY: OFFLINE AND ONLINE

The Mipsterz community formally emerged in 2012 as a platform for young US based Muslims to share interests, collaborate artistically, discuss ideas and plan in-person events. In particular, the group formed to present an alternative to other formal Muslim community spaces where some US-born Muslims felt that their identities and struggles were misunderstood. Mipsterz membership was originally formed through face-to-face friendship networks located in North-East US cities; however, with the expansion of the groups' social circle, restrictive schedules and distant living situations, the Mipsterz's Facebook page and email list were created to maintain social networks and ties. Friends of the group were added to the list, and as the 'Somewhere in America #MIPSTERZ' film increased in virality, the visibility of the community increased, for example, through mainstream media attention, leading membership to grow beyond these circles.

Arguably, although the community members we engaged with did not view structural inequalities as having a direct bearing on the community's formation, evidence of a feeling of marginalisation framed by dominant and hostile post-9-11 media representations in the United States and globally was persistently addressed, as well as a sense that the identity struggles and concerns of young 'Millennial' Muslims were not being addressed formally in Muslim community and religious spaces:

> **Layla Shaikley** (founding member, moderator): Muslims in the West, in America . . . we're in a particularly wounded state in the sense that we have been forced to be defensive as a result of the representation that is most dominant about us and who we are and what we believe.

This marginalisation has also made issues of representation, 'of who gets to speak for whom' a highly emotionally charged question, with some Mipsterz' cultural productions seeking to address this question by 'unapologetically' representing the everydayness of young Muslims lives. While there is limited space here to analyse responses to the 'Somewhere in America #MIPSTERZ' film, a number of critical comments were posted to YouTube and other social media forums by members of Muslim diaspora communities. These highlighted cultural, religious and class-based objections to the 'style' and 'swagger' of the women in the clip, which represented, to some, the lifestyles

**Figure 10.1   Photo still from the film, 'Somewhere in America #MIPSTERZ'.** *Source:* Sahar Jahani/Sheikh & Bake Productions, 2013.

of an educated, middle-class elite rather than being broadly representative of Muslim women and young people 'Somewhere in America'.

Notwithstanding these criticisms, the video did achieve wide visibility and provided a space for complex negotiations between religious tradition and the everyday lives and cultures of US-born young Muslims.

Explaining the importance of the video, moderator Layla (pictured riding skateboard in Figure 10.1) recalled a camp she attended with young Muslim girls of ages 18–20 years, who spoke of how the 'Somewhere in America' video had provided a 'representation of myself that I'm proud of, that I can circulate [through social media networks]':

> **Layla:** Having an image that circulates about yourself that is something you're proud of is pretty important, and the fact that these girls were maybe 18–20 years old and didn't have that, was kind of mind blowing.

The video also highlighted a generational disconnect between young 'Millennials' attracted to experimental 'third' cultures such as that offered by Mipsterz, and traditional religious and community groups—some of whom, in the face of Islamophobic media representations, had promoted withdrawal into a 'culture-less' and reductive expression of Islam (Hermansen, 2003). The Mipsterz community grew to offer an alternative for young Muslims who did not identify with these narrow frames of representation.

In trying to create a ground-up community capable of broadening and challenging narrow cultural and religious categories, everyday 'identity work' and creating a space for cultural exploration and experimentation were key activities:

> **Abbas Rattani:** Sometimes Mipsterz feels like an experiment in culture, or an experiment in creating a culture—what does it mean to be a part of a culture or a community which has a very fluid identity?

The flows of communication through Mipsterz social media fora—which include a dedicated Facebook page and email list[6]—highlight this cultural experimentation, aligning with theories of 'cultural citizenship', including those offered by Burgess et al. (2006), who perceive that 'communities of interest and practice, focused around hobbies, entertainment, and everyday creative practice', broaden opportunities for citizenship outside of normative markers grounded in the nation state and 'rational' deliberative modes of political participation. These online participatory cultures 'constitute sites of cultural citizenship' as they 'exist thanks only to the creative contributions, sharing, and active participation of their members' (Burgess et al., 2006, p. 148).

While the Facebook page is the current homepage for the Mipsterz community—through which a majority of interactions, submissions and content are posted—the email list is the primary space where members seek to understand themselves: through cultural production, dialogue and experimenting with ideas and thoughtful questions aimed at demystifying monolithic understandings of Islam. It is from this commitment in particular, to broaden Muslim youth identities and cultures beyond reductive characterisations, that another active member understood the appeal of Mipsterz to have grown: Whether people know it or not that has been dramatically coded into the attitude of Mipsterz.

These different types of engagement are also structured by the different affordances of Facebook and the Google Groups email list, with the Facebook page (a public rather than a closed page) offering a more public face and voice for the community, enabling broad visibility and shareability,[7] while the email list is negotiated as a more intimate space to share ideas and connect with like-minded people. It is also on the Mipsterz email list where agonistic contest and struggles over interpretations of religious theology and other forms of self-representation tend to play out in a more sustained fashion and where the Mipsterz project could be seen to be tested more thoroughly.

## TYPES AND MODES OF PARTICIPATION
## ON THE MIPSTERZ EMAIL LIST

A systematic analysis of topic threads, posts and exchanges found on the email list between July and September 2015, a time period that also coincided with increased global media attention to the spread of ISIS (or Daesh) in Iraq and Syria and increased surveillance and policing of Muslim communities in the United States, reveals that while engagement with political and social justice issues was not the most common activity for users of the email list, it did provide a space where members could retreat from a hostile political environment to be themselves, reflect, engage critically with ideas and share feelings. In particular, it provided a space where a diverse range of views and identities could be expressed, challenging reductive mainstream narratives.

This diversity is represented qualitatively and quantitatively in the first sample of interactions on the email list. Out of the 148 individual posts/replies, 40% of activity related to social and professional networking (e.g. members looking for apartments or roommates, professional networking, employment opportunities, organising social hangouts and dating/marriage), 20% related to political discussion and/or civic action and 16% related to engagement with Muslim diaspora culture and American popular culture (music sharing, promotion of members and other artists' creative work, open mic nights). Taking a broader view, this is representative of the topic threads archived on the Mipsterz forum (1612 topic threads to date).[8]

But despite the greater number of topic threads and posts being based around social connections and culture building, an analysis of the most popular topic threads in the time frame, *as measured by numbers of posts, participants, and replies* (indicating sustained dialogue between members; see van Zoonen et al., 2010) reveals greater *depth* of activity and interaction around topic threads covering issues related to inequality and social justice. For example, in this same time period, the 'Gender and Queer Stuff' thread, the 'Islamophobia' thread and other threads opened up a space of engagement with topics where hegemonic and reductive mainstream representation of Muslim communities were challenged, while topics not always spoken of or considered taboo within formal Muslim communities and religious spaces, for example, LGBTQ[9] issues, were also posed to the group, opening up rich and diverse forms of argumentation.

The next section will provide a richer descriptive account of the tone and content of interactions occurring on the email list under three selected topic threads, providing insight into the labour of maintaining an expressive culture of creativity, openness and inclusiveness, while seeking to hold members to account where they assert claims that limit, contain or belittle the agency and struggles of other members of the forum. In particular, these case studies highlight tensions between (1) *the value of pluralism*, or shaping a community open to a diverse range of positions and expressions, some of which, according to Mouffe will inevitably produce conflict, and (2) *the building of a 'safe space'* where 'minimal shared commitments' (Dahlgren, 2005), produced through developing rules and etiquettes for participation, encourage the emotional and social support considered vital to free expression. The analysis proposes that these tensions lay bare a central problem for thinking through obstacles and possibilities for conceptualising digital citizenship.

## DISCOURSE ANALYSIS OF THREE KEY TOPIC THREADS ON THE MIPSTERZ EMAIL LIST

### 99 Words

A number of threads on the Mipsterz email list are dedicated to building and sharing cultural affinities and promoting self-expression and creativity. While these communications are not necessarily politically oriented, they nonetheless serve to counter dominant narratives and myths that circulate about Muslim faith communities while providing a 'safe space' for young people to support one another in the face of persistent expressions of Islamophobia and other forms of social inequality that affect forum members.

An example of a conversation thread that engages in this kind of cultural and emotional work is '99 Words' (59 posts, 27 authors). The thread was created by Hussein to enable the community to connect, narrate stories and receive support, particularly after experiences of Islamophobic aggression. For Couldry, this type of 'narrative exchange' is vital to expressions of digital citizenship, in terms of fostering relations where 'imagining/empathising' and sharing/narrating stories with others build a supportive culture for thinking through issues that connect individual experiences to collective problems and issues (Couldry et al., 2014, p. 617).

The use of a cultural idiom in the title of the thread ('99 Words' is an allusion to the Islamic concept of the *99 names of God*)[10] is a common practice among forum members, who regularly make reference to cultural, religious and historical Islamic traditions and join these with contemporary cultural and creative practice. The short story was identified as a suitable format for harnessing the brief interactions and flows of communication that typify digital 'narrative exchanges' (Couldry et al., 2014) and channelling these towards creating intimate bonds of trust among members:

**Hussein:** We all have busy lives. So here's to a thread for the short vignettes and snapshots of our daily trials. Post ninety-nine words on anything and everything. Today I saw a man in the subway, dry blood caked all over his face and torn clothes, just sort of standing there. Nobody noticed or said a word until I smiled at him and he started talking about how the Walking Dead was his favorite show and his getup was this homage to a zombie show that never uses the word zombies. That's my day so far. Now it's your turn.

The thread was enthusiastically responded to, with members' daily experiences of racism, sexual harassment, health issues, loss of loved ones etc. being conveyed in a style that powerfully highlighted the micro-political struggles, joys and forms of connection of participants on the forum. In particular, this culture-building work was seen to be less intimidating than discussion taking place on more politically oriented threads, which tended to foster exchanges where passions sometimes spilled over into bullying. The thread '99 Words' enabled members to communicate feelings in equally impassioned and less destructive ways. While a humorous tone was often used in these exchanges, some vignettes demonstrated trust and vulnerability in the often raw feelings communicated:

**Amena Waseem:** weekend observations: Last night I watched as one of my friends cooed and fawned over her three month old son, as I handed him back to her. It has been the sweetest thing to witness. I remember four months ago, when the same friend was eight months pregnant and her sister lost her battle to cancer. I remember reminding her to eat and hydrate on the day of the funeral that she was missing, as I sat with her. Though nothing will replace her only sister, seeing her so full and resilient, sometimes feels beyond words

The importance of creative self-expression in fostering cultures of trust and support is central to many theories regarding citizenship of digital spaces. It is particularly central to theories of 'intimate citizenship' described by Plummer (2003), Dahlgren (2005) and Couldry et al. (2014), who identify the 'creation of social worlds and communities of support' where people can narrate their stories, empathise, find common ground and learn from others (Couldry et al., 2014, p. 617) as a key social context for the emergence of citizenship ethics and practices. Here, the citizen is imagined as a more affective and affected subject than the rational citizen of Habermasian public sphere traditions (Plummer, 2003).

Even when not directly political in orientation, these kinds of activities represent a form of political struggle according to Warner (2005), insofar as the cultural, personal and expressive forms of speech carried out in such spaces are maintained and structured by their relation to a larger hegemonic public sphere that stigmatises and excludes minority voices, and modes of speech not considered legitimate expressions of citizenship (Warner, 2005, p. 424).

The potential of these culture-building activities is further highlighted by Azam Zafar, who makes reference to the support provided by Mipsterz online and offline exchanges, allowing difficult negotiations around faith and identity to be navigated with confidence and humility:

> **Azam:** Birthday today. This year has brought moments I could not foresee and will not forget. Chai Parties. Rooftop iftars. Late-night espresso conversations. Housewarmings. Too many farewells. Concerts and comedians. Book clubs and Town halls. (Re)connected with faith—on my own terms. Prayed for the humility to see wisdom in tradition but also gained the confidence to trust my own fitrah and well-considered moral judgments over 'consensus'. First dates, usually at the Coffee Shop Bar. Felt less nervous there. Lots of new friends. Some so close, trust them with anything. Friendsgiving and a Surprise party. Grateful for it all.

The concept of the 'safe space', which was discussed in numerous Mipsterz topic threads, is here connected to forms of self-development vital to citizenship, for example, nurturing confidence to engage with diverse moral and political views to form one's own position. For Azam, his mention of finding trust in his *Fitrah*[11] directly speaks to the importance of cultures of support to self-actualising modes of citizenship and moral and political will formation. As Dahlgren stresses, the concept of 'civic culture' (2005), which he imagines as a kind of 'third space' between the rational, consensus-driven modes of speech demanded of deliberative democracy and the irreducible conflict dynamics in Mouffe's theory of 'agonistic pluralism', provides an important analytical tool for understanding these processes.

## Gender and Queer Stuff

Despite *99 Words* using creativity to subvert or augment rational modes of argumentation favoured in deliberative models of democracy, threads like 'Gender and Queer stuff' navigate a range of types of communication and argumentation, ranging from advocacy and support for LGBTQ identifying members of the community to more critical, interrogative modes of debate which challenge or question heteronormative and sexist aspects of religious orthodoxy, and which engage a larger number of interlocutors including perspectives that were described by members of the community as 'traditional'.

In particular, some of these exchanges highlight the challenge in seeking to maintain a 'safe space' that is welcoming of queer and gender diverse members of the Mipsterz community, while also remaining committed to inclusion and free expression of a range of views, some of which may reinforce structures of class, race and heteronormative exclusions performed in the name of 'tradition'.

The thread was created on 8 January 2014, by Ilana Alazzeh, the founder of the Muslims Against Homophobia and LGBT Hate Facebook page[12] and an active participant on the Mipsterz forum. When last accessed, the thread had 288 archived posts and active participation of 58 authors.[13] As the exchanges generated by this thread have been sustained well over a year, I will limit the analysis to the time frame outlined above (July to September 2015). On the one hand, posts and conversations during this time were directed towards sharing of information and resources to support LGBTQ identifying members of the email list. In particular members shared information about community/cultural events and invited other members to join them in shaping a space that was supportive and inclusive of queer voices and queer narratives:

> **Urooj Khan:** This seems like a pretty cool event: Coming Out Muslim is performing their show 'Radical Acts of Love' at the Rutgers Presbyterian Church on June 24 at 7pm: http://comingoutmuslim.com/new-york-show-june-24th/. It's free and there will be iftar afterwards—anyone interested in going?

Participants also posted articles which conveyed political and theological points of view on LGBTQ issues. These posts often generated replies and exchanges which were open, inclusive and critical of positions where LGBTQ and gender rights are not treated as equal to other rights (e.g. religious freedom), or where gender normative or heteronormative terms are used in misrecognition of someone's identity or sexual orientation.

Caitlyn Jenner's public coming out occurred during this time, generating a short rally of posts and replies on transgender recognition (or lack thereof) in formal Muslim religious community spaces. These discussions were framed by questions directed at how Muslim religious leaders were dealing with LGBTQ issues within their communities. Voices on the Mipsterz forum offered a range of critical positions, not just addressing the exclusion of transgender people from formal religious spaces, such as mosques, but also addressing symbolic/discursive forms of misrecognition by 'progressive' leaders, some of whom had pledged to create a 'safe space' to discuss LGBTQ issues following Caitlyn Jenner's transition, but did so while referring to her by her former name 'Bruce'. This triggered emotional and empathetic responses, with some participants understanding the erasure of Caitlyn's chosen gender and name as a form of transphobia and others sharing links to social theorists and activists to illustrate this:

**Azam:** Judith Butler on transophobia (old video but new interview below):

'No matter whether one feels one's gendered and sexed reality to be firmly fixed or less so, every person should have the right to determine the legal and linguistic terms of their embodied lives. So whether one wants to be free to live out a "hard-wired" sense of sex or a more fluid sense of gender, is less important than the right to be free to live it out, *without* discrimination, harassment, injury, pathologization or criminalization—and *with* full institutional and community support'.

However, the thread also generated internal contestation between normative Islamic theological positions regarding homosexuality and challenges to these positions by members drawing upon either contemporary Islamic scholarship or secular/post-secular legal definitions aligning with constitutional and human rights law.

One exchange was provoked by the publication of an open letter by Muslim religious scholar, Reza Azlan (Azlan & Minhaj, 2015), who, in light of the US Supreme Court Ruling legalising same-sex marriage in all US states, called upon Muslim community members to recognise themselves as beneficiaries of this law reform (in terms of equal application of human rights to all minority communities) even if it confronted their religious beliefs. The letter provoked an intriguing exchange on the Mipsterz email list with a range of moral positions, claims to identity, personhood and rights (including the constitutional right to hold certain religious beliefs) being thoughtfully voiced and tested.

For Ali, who was interviewed regarding his participation in the thread, the 'Gender and Queer stuff' thread had opened his own ideas and views (which he considered to be progressive) to be tested by more traditional or conservative voices. This allowed him to develop confidence in his own position:

**Ali:** On some of the more controversial issues on gender and sexuality. . . . I think you get a better sense of the way the forum allows you to express your opinions and test your ideas against people with more traditional viewpoints. Then if it doesn't make anyone uncomfortable in saying you know, yes, ok, I acknowledge that the historical or religious tradition says this but I disagree with that, it's fine because there is no definitive Mipsterz position.

And yet, while these discussions could be described as critical, they are still conducted in a deliberative mode insofar as passionate feelings do not threaten to derail or shut down dialogue, as they do in other forums, something highlighted by Ali:

**Ali:** I'm involved in some other private Facebook groups, and like they're often more social justice oriented, like explicitly. And sometimes the discussion triggers feelings for people that it is not a safe space, you know?

Nonetheless, in other topic threads on the Mipsterz email list, more agonistic, and even antagonistic, exchanges do occur, triggering feelings that erupt and spill over into forms of bullying and abuse. These incidents raised important questions for members of this digital community, and moderators, around how to maintain the email list as a space where freedom of expression is supported, but in a manner which does not threaten the well-being, safety and agency of other members of the forum.

One example of this is a thread (which will not be named here) that focused on women's rights to perform religious rituals that are usually the preserve of men. This led some, predominantly male, members of the forum to contest this practice as a distortion of orthodox religious practice. While some arguments were posed respectfully, others used normative theological positions as a basis to personally attack prominent female members of the forum.

While we will not provide examples of these provocative posts, they raised the ire of many female members of the forum, with the following responses serving to highlight the grievous nature of the provocation:

**Ilana:** Wow the sexism and hatred against women in this thread is absolutely appalling. Simply shocking.

Reminder, those male scholars you love so much are from women, ate from women, were first educated by women and while in the womb first started off as women. . . . People have no problem with women being early educators but sharing ideas at a Muslim Ted talk (*section omitted*) somehow disrespects the All Mighty Creator of the water cycle, cells, ecosystem, the world--our solar system--and billions of solar systems and galaxies. . . . REALLY???

**Noorjahan:**
*Traditionalist:* I know others are too oppressed to speak their mind on Mipsterz, they send me private emails expressing support when I share opinions that they're too afraid to say themselves.

*Me:* I'm sorry that in this tiny corner of the universe known as the Mipsterz list-serve where people like to have free-flowing discussion about contentious issues, that people don't feel comfortable enough to provide and defend their opinions publicly. In a recent thread, I was compared to the devil. It gave me pause, but I didn't cry about it. I don't know, I guess I have some serious balls.

Exchanges between one provocateur in particular, and a number of women and men who found his language offensive, continued over the course of a month, with the member also using certain Islamic sources and scholarship to discredit the legitimacy of LGBTQ identifying or supporting members of the community who discussed theological matters, leading other members to highlight this as a type of hate speech which should not be tolerated.

## Decorum

These discussions prompted the creation of the 'Decorum' thread in June 2015,[14] which responded to examples where confrontational speech carried out in 'hot' topic threads produced concerns that prioritising inclusion of a range of views and forms of argumentation on the email list might limit the voice and agency of other community members.

The thread, which was created by Noorjahan (Noor) Rahman, outlined the challenges and likely pitfalls of both regulating *and* failing to regulate speech which offends in digital interactions. Noor's initiating post posed a series of steps or themes that members could discuss, including the possibility of shaping a 'consensus' on modes of appropriate participation:

> **Noor:** This thread is not aimed to disparage by singling out an individual for criticism. Instead, I hope here we can outline a few community rules of conduct to help hold ourselves and others accountable to upright behaviour.

Noor specifically outlined three points of consideration. These related to the following: (1) tensions between free speech and censorship, where, for example, 'calling someone disrespectful in order to get them to be quiet or suppress their views' may potentially be construed as a form of harm; (2) she poses the question: 'How do we filter out anger-driven language to "principled" arguments that the speaker really believes should be said?' This addresses the problem of censorship limiting the legitimacy of members' right to voice their position. Finally, she asks as to how do members hold one another accountable, given that calling people out on their aggressive or offensive speech implies an imbalance of power and can lead to the silencing of dissenting or minority voices.

This list of concerns was responded to by 19 authors, all of whom were active participants in the debates outlined. While not attracting a large number of responses, the thread has been significant to evolving negotiations around appropriate participation in the forum. In particular, discussion addressed questions such as what are the basic requirements of shaping Mipsterz as a safe space? For LGBTQ identifying members and allies, but also women, and anyone who subscribes to views that challenge religious orthodoxy and other culturally or socially defined 'traditions':

**Hussein:** There are really oppressive, silencing dynamics in the wider society that we have to be conscious of when we engage. 'Tradition' matters, but so does the safety and comfort of queer folks here, so is the safety and comfort of people who live and think in a way that 'tradition' finds objectionable. . . .

Whoever and whatever you are, Mipsterz can be your home . . . just recognize that a dizzying array of people live here. Don't tear the place down.

In order to forge some shared rules and norms around how people can express their views, some members (and moderators) argued in favour of more deliberative modes of speech, particularly around contentious issues. The Mipsterz policy of minimal moderator intervention was also at stake in these discussions. For example, in some of the 'hot' topic threads, previously mentioned moderators postponed intervention, and have, to date, only locked one thread to prevent destructive posts continuing. Nonetheless, moderators do weigh in (as the example above shows) and seek to 'moderate' the speech of some members, address issues of cyberbullying and hate speech, etc.

However, beyond these minimal interventions, participants in the 'Decorum' thread tended to agree that a consensus on the question of acceptable speech was unlikely to hold, and that the value of engaging with diverse voices on the forum and the 'learning' that this enabled outweighed the harm of interactions occasionally crossing the line:

**Sarrah Shahawy:** for someone like me, who has been more of an observer than an active participant on Mipsterz threads so far, I still find a kind of magic in how Mipsterz works and much of that magic lies in its diversity. This forum is such a cool experiment, a forum for both conservatives and liberals and everything in between and around to discuss meaningful issues and to learn from each other--

**Danish Munir:** Co-sign. . . . I can't speak for others but can safely say that this listserv has been one of the biggest source of learning for me. I am truly appreciative of the diversity of thought here, even when I hear things that really make me uncomfortable and go against the fundamental principles and values I hold. In fact, especially when that happens.

I think this group is too broad to try and arrive at a set of "rules" by consensus. . . . But I'll go ahead and pledge that I will try my best going forward to be mindful of how I express my opinions. . . . I also pledge to ensure that I will not stand by and watch someone else get pummelled by a mob, even if they are in the wrong, because everyone should be free to express their ideas as long as they are doing so in a way that doesn't attack an individual's character or being. Attacks on ideas are and should be welcome—no matter how sacred they are.

## CONCLUSION

The findings, and particularly the emergence of internal contestation on the Mipsterz email list around questions of whether the community should operate normatively as a 'safe space' versus whether it should be maintained as a space of 'radical openness', demonstrate the challenges in trying to analyse fluid, contested and contingent digital interactions and deduce what types of citizenship are enacted through these exchanges, if any at all. Nonetheless the chapter reveals some interesting findings that may contribute to broader conceptualisations of digital citizenship, both in its normative and more radical expressions.

Firstly, the analysis revealed that a diverse spectrum of argument and voices are able to be maintained on Mipsterz social media, particularly on the email list, something that members felt was unique and not encountered in other more formal spaces of participation. Interviews with moderators and participants also strongly emphasised the importance of cultural negotiations and creative media to shaping an inclusive 'civic culture' (Dahlgren, 2005), as represented through the '99 Words' topic thread. This is driven by a commitment to create a space where the everyday cultures and diverse life experiences of young Muslims in the United States can be voiced and homogenous and stereotypical representations of Muslim communities challenged.

Some topic threads demonstrated a more critical dimension, as an array of religious, political, social and cultural beliefs and identities were more directly engaged and challenged through diverse styles of argumentation and speech, including agonistic confrontation. In thinking about what members gain from being involved in passionate disagreements that at times transgress boundaries of what is acceptable in other formal spaces of cultural religious or political representation, participants argued that they were able to reflect and make decisions on their own positionality, ethics, values, rights (e.g. to safety or privacy) and beliefs, while also considering their responsibilities to the broader community.

And yet, while scholars have drawn upon Mouffe's model to explain the way digital affordances shape democratic spaces—where irreducibly different and previously excluded voices are brought into a common public space to 'speak and act in plurality', well-founded criticisms of this theory are less often discussed. One of the more common criticisms of Mouffe's model is the challenge posed to her declaration that radical pluralism offers a model of democracy beyond consensus, and without exclusions. As most critics highlight, and as the findings of this chapter show, there can be no democracy without a degree of consensus, as all parties must agree on the symbolic and ethico-political ground that will enable open and free debate. As the eruption of forms of agonistic and antagonistic conflict on some Mipsterz topic threads demonstrates, this 'symbolic common ground' does not exist naturally but can only be arrived at through processes of deliberation, negotiation and the reaching of an agreement about 'rules' of participation, or even agreeing to disagree but laying out some guiding ethical principles.

Nonetheless the analysis did reveal that members learned most and were most engaged by topic threads involving passionate, agonistic negotiation of controversial issues and topics (e.g. relating to politics, global conflict, gender, sexuality and religion), even while expressing a desire to regulate and reign in affective speech acts if these threatened to alter the conditions that provided a safe space of interaction.

This moves understandings of digital citizenship beyond the tendency to identify digital communities as *either* spaces where radical democratic projects and citizenships are nurtured *or* as spaces where power manifests much the same way as in dominant public spheres. The findings of this chapter expresses a more complex reality typified by fluid negotiations of what constitutes 'good citizenship' of digital spaces, where the interdependence of deliberative and agonistic, normative and radical modes of participation and citizenship are a central part of these negotiations.

## NOTES

1. Amelia Johns would like to thank Fethi Mansouri and Michele Lobo, who supported this work as a side project of a larger Australian Research Council (ARC) Discovery Grant (grant number DP 130102601). The larger project explored Islamic rituals and faith-based practices and their contribution towards modes and practices of citizenship.

2. Abbas Rattani would like to thank Sarrah Shahawy, Hadi Kaakour and Jemel Derbali for their insights on navigating the intricacies and appreciating the complexities of faith communities online and offline.

3. 'Somewhere in America #MIPSTERZ': https://vimeo.com/140280212 . For media coverage, see Assefa (2015); Shakley (2014).

4. The Mipsterz email list was created using Google Groups: https://apps.google.com/learning-center/products/groups/get-started/.

5. Owing to space constraints, this provides only a very basic rationale for the methodology and approach chosen. It is hoped that future research collaboration will critically analyse and address challenges of digital ethnography both in the field and post-completion of research.

6. The mipster FB page had 16,163 likes as of August, 2016. The email list has a membership of 1,341 people as of August, 2016. Other members have also set up personal Instagram accounts, which are more focused on fashion. Articles, videos, etc. are also shared through use of hashtag #Mipsterz.

7. For example, it is on the Facebook page where the guiding principles of the community are publicised, with a Mipster being described as: 'an ironic identity,

one that serves more as a perpetual critique of oneself and of society. A Mipster has a social mind, and yearning for a more just order, a more inclusive community unbounded by stale categories' (Mipster, Facebook, 2012).

8. For example, 'Mipsterz4Mipsterz' is a thread created for members to help each other; the 'Shameless Plug' thread was organized for Mipsterz to promote their own projects and do so 'humbly'/through acknowledging a conflict of interest; 'Getting Married Young' and the various 'love' threads were created for members to share vulnerable stories and opinions around marriage and love.

9. This acronym has been applied as it is the most common terminology used by participants in the Gender and Queer Stuff thread.

10. It is believed that there are 99 names of God listed in the Quran and hadith to characterise God's diverse attributes and qualities.

11. Islamic concept related to the intrinsic, ontological, pre-determined self.

12. Mipsterz Facebook Page [created 2012], https://www.facebook.com/Muslims-Against-Homophobia-and-LGBT-Hate-430959760274485/.

13. 'Gender and Queer Stuff', Retrieved from Mipsterz archived conversation threads: https://groups.google.com/forum/#!topic/mipsterz/w1BA6orT6M8[276-300].

14. 'Decorum', Retrieved from Mipsterz archived conversation threads: https://groups.google.com/forum/?utm_medium=email&utm_source=footer#!msg/mipsterz/9SOE0hwX5tc/2i8BdgBlzJAJ.

# REFERENCES

Assefa, H. (2015, Jun 3). Mipsterz: a space for Muslim Hipsters CNN. URL: Editon. cnn.com/2015/06/03/living/mipsterz-muslim-hipsters.

Burgess, J., Foth, M., & Klaebe, H. (2006). Everyday creativity as civic engagement: A cultural citizenship view of new media. Presented at the Communications, Policy and Research Forum, Institute for Creative Industries and Innovation, Sydney.

Butler, J. (2005). *Giving an account of oneself*. New York: Fordham University Press.

Couldry, N. (2010). *Why voice matters: Culture and politics after neoliberalism*. London: Sage.

Couldry, N., Stephansen, H., Fotopoulou, A., Macdonald, R., Clark, W., & Dickens, L. (2014). Digital citizenship? Narrative exchange and the changing terms of civic culture. *Citizenship Studies, 18*(6–7), 615–629.

Dahlgren, P. (2004). Civic cultures and net activism: Modest hopes for the EU Public sphere (pp. 1–13). Presented at the One EU: Many Publics? University of Sterling. Retrieved from http://www.sv.uio.no/arena/english/research/projects/cidel/old/WorkshopStirling/PaperDahlgren.pdf.

Dahlgren, P. (2005). The internet, public spheres, and political communication: Dispersion and deliberation. *Political Communication, 22*(2) 147–162.

Fraser, N. (2007). Transnationalising the public sphere: On the legitimacy and efficacy of public opinion in a post-Westphalian world. *Media, Culture & Society, 24*(4), 7–30.

Georgiou, M. (2013). Diaspora in the digital era. *Journal on Ethnopolitics and Minority Issues in Europe, 12*(4), 80–99.

Habermas, J., & Cooke, M. (2000). *On the pragmatics of communication.* Cambridge, MA: MIT Press.

Hermansen, M. (2003). How to put the genie back in the bottle: "Identity", Islam and Muslim youth cultures in America. In Omid Safi (Ed.), *Progressive Muslims: On gender, justice and pluralism* (pp. 306–318). Oxford: Oneworld.

Hine, C. (2015). *Ethnography for the internet: Embedded, embodied and everyday,* London: Bloomsbury.

Isin, E. F., & Ruppert, E. (2015). *Being digital citizens.* London: Rowman & Littlefield.

Knobel, M. (2003). Rants, ratings and representation. *Education, Communication and Information, 3*(2), 187–210.

Leurs, K., & Ponzanesi, S. (2010). Mediated crossroads: Youthful digital diasporas. *M/C Journal, 14*(2). Retrieved from http://journal.media-culture.org.au/index.php/mcjournal/article/view/324.

Mouffe, C. (2000). *The democratic paradox.* London: Verso.

Mouffe, C. (2013). *Agonistics: Thinking the world politically.* London: Verso.

Papacharissi, Z. (2009). The virtual sphere 2.0: The internet, the public sphere, and beyond. In A. Chadwick & P. N. Howard (Eds.), *Routledge handbook of internet politics.* London: Routledge.

Plummer, K. (2003). *Intimate citizenship: Private decisions and public dialogues.* Seattle: University of Washington Press.

Shakley, L. (2014, Mar 13). The Surprising Lessons of the 'Muslim Hipsters' Backlash. The Atlantic. URL: www.theatlantic.com/entertainment/archive/2014/03/the-surprising-lessons-of-the-muslim-hipsterz-backlash/284298/.

Siapera, E. (2010). *Cultural diversity and global media: The mediation of difference.* Chichester, U.K.: Wiley-Blackwell.

van Zoonen, L., Vis, F., & Mihelj, S. (2010). Performing citizenship on YouTube: Activism, satire and online debate around the anti-Islam video Fitna. *Critical Discourse Studies, 7*(4), 249–262.

Warner, M. (2005). *Publics and counterpublics.* New York: Zone Books.

## Chapter 11

# 'Holding a Space' for Gender-Diverse and Queer Research Participants

Sonja Vivienne, Brady Robards and Sian Lincoln

Choosing how to represent one's self in digital social spaces might seem banal and everyday for some, but for others this process can be fraught and highly political. Consider a YouTube video detailing the physical changes associated with gender transition, or a selfie with a same-sex lover shared in a country where homosexuality is illegal. Sites like Facebook, Instagram and YouTube, and apps like Snapchat, Tinder and Grindr are centred in many ways around identity politics: who the user is, who they are not, what they stand for, who they are connected to, who they want to fuck, what their families look like and how their everyday lives play out. While it could be argued that all representations and performances of self are inherently political, the stakes for young gender-diverse and queer people who undertake 'performative self-making' are amplified. Despite progress in Western nations around gay rights, the visibility of (some) transpeople and a general move towards 'tolerance', people who do not conform to a dominant set of cisgender, heteronormative ideals continue to be at risk of stigmatisation and exclusion. As a result, this cohort of people with diverse genders and sexualities (DGS[1]) are still overrepresented in statistics on suicide, depression, homelessness and drug abuse (Hillier et al., 2010). On top of these very real potential harms, there is a less tangible risk that these complex and somewhat fluid identities be judged inconsistent, deceitful or 'incoherent'. The process of performative self-making on an ongoing basis—especially the ways these are enacted and archived in digital social spaces—can be deeply personal and political vehicles for digital citizenship.

In this chapter, we consider two distinct research projects in which we work alongside young people to analyse their digital self-representations. Building upon the introduction of this book and, more particularly, the themes of this section on *cultures* that evoke digital citizenship, we see both 'citizenship' and 'digital engagement' as a broad suite of practices and processes that underpin meaningful belonging in modern networked society. For young people, sculpting a presence online is a rite of passage that takes place well before they are entitled to vote, drive a car or live independently, and it entails complex negotiations with family, friends, authority figures and institutions, as well as unknown individuals and communities. Being a digital citizen summons young people (and indeed all of us) to manage the contradictory expectations of different groups: peers, family, partners, prospective employers and others. Further, digital citizenship summons researchers to consider the complex lives of our research participants and the consequences of re-contextualising their digital traces, relocated far from their embedded social context to scholarly publications and discussions.

We canvas digital citizenship from two perspectives. On the one hand, we explore the various acts of digital citizenship practised by our research participants and, on the other, we reflect upon research methodologies that are affirming of their status as digital citizens. As our discussion below reveals, the 'digital traces' (Bowker, 2007) that constitute performative self-making through social media (status updates, images, likes etc.) are deeply embedded in and reflections of life experience. We argue that engaging our participants as co-analysts and co-curators of their own digital traces helps us to 'check-in' with them and uncover personal insights and allows us to 'check-back' on how we have interpreted them.

Coupled with more traditional techniques such as the qualitative interview, we can collaborate in uncovering the rich meanings and narratives associated with disclosures in digital spaces. Co-analysis reveals the complexity of participant insights, in turn supporting researchers in making congruent arguments out of diverse perspectives for example one person's ideas that change over time and/or distinct ideas from 'similar' people. Here, we use 'congruent' (implying in agreement) rather than 'coherent' (implying a social judgement of consistency that can be normative and constrictive). In this respect, we argue that our methodological approaches are particularly suited to the multifarious and intricate complications that are so typical of networked publics, and life lived simultaneously across digital and physical spaces. In other words, in co-writing the *specific* and *particular*, we can reveal some common threads woven into the fabric of digital citizenship, while simultaneously sustaining the digital citizens existence. We call this 'holding a space' for our participants, in which to undertake co-analysis, co-curation, checking-in and checking-back.

Over the last five to ten years, a range of research methods have emerged that strive to better understand the ways in which young people inscribe and reflect on their lives through digital media. Traditional methods of inquiry like surveys (Madden et al., 2013; Xenos, Vromen & Loader, 2014), interviews (Lincoln, 2012; Marwick & boyd, 2011; Robards, 2014) and focus groups (Vromen, Xenos & Loader, 2015) continue to play a central role here. At the same time, new methods afforded by digital media have also emerged, including hashtag analytics (Highfield & Leaver, 2015) and analyses of digital media 'texts' including profiles on social network sites (Dobson, 2015) and YouTube videos (Werner, 2014) to name just a few. It is our intention here to extend upon traditional research methodologies by advocating for methods that privilege meanings made by participants. However, we acknowledge that not all research *should* necessarily involve co-analysis and 'checking-in' with or 'checking-back' with research participants, and there may be instances where this is impractical or even unethical. For example, when personal safety is dependent on a participant's anonymity, researchers may need to obscure or simplify identifiable details. Also, when researching people in positions of power and public importance, the capacity for critique and independent academic analysis is important. We acknowledge the critical role of researchers in analysing, critiquing, theorising, surfacing and foregrounding meaning that is not always apparent to participants.

In the particular case studies we describe here, our focus is on young people of DGS, who tend to be silenced, excluded and marginalised. For this reason, and because their actions and identities are complex, we have resolved to centre their stories and their voices. For queer and gender-diverse people, the internet can be used for coming to terms with a sense of self (Hillier et al., 2010; Hanckel & Morris, 2014; Taylor et al., 2014) connecting with like-minded others (Russell, 2002), finding sexual health information (Mustanski, Lyons & Garcia, 2010) and dating (Cushman et al., 2008; Roth, 2014). There are also risks associated with internet use for young queer and gender-diverse people, including bullying, privacy and predation. While both 'queer' and 'transgender' are nominalisations that can be used in a range of different ways, we build upon Susan Stryker's definition of 'trans' as a term that '[refers] to all identities or practices that cross over, cut across, move between, or otherwise queer socially constructed sex/gender boundaries' (Stryker, 2006, p. 254). Similarly, when referring to a cohort or community, we use 'DGS' (diverse gender and sexuality) as an umbrella term to describe a range of identities, in preference to the rather unwieldy and potentially exclusive acronym GLBTQIS (gay, lesbian, bisexual, transgender, queer, intersex, same-sex attracted). When referring to an individual, we default to the terms that each participant uses for themself.

In this chapter, we suggest that working with participants as co-analysts or as partners in the research process can be rewarding and productive, especially when it comes to discussions around performative self-making undertaken by young people with DGS in digital spaces. We have found that the distinct but intersecting methods we used in otherwise unique research projects highlight common strategies that a particularly vulnerable cohort of young people use to counter risky oversharing and breaches of privacy. First, *The Facebook Timelines* project (conducted by Robards & Lincoln) engages young people as co-analysts of their own 'digital traces' on Facebook. As Bowker (2007) explains, digital traces (photos, status updates, likes, reviews, profiles) come to stand in for us on the web, potentially persisting long after we make them. Second, in the *Stories Beyond Gender* project (facilitated by Vivienne), young people engage in collective community work to share stories of trans and gender-diverse identities on a variety of social media platforms. Facilitated workshops that explore and create digital self-representation centre participants as expert curators of their own online archives and as advocates for more accepting social environments. While acknowledging the ways in which we are all fodder for algorithms that serve advertising and surveillance (Gillespie, 2010), we spotlight some nuanced strategies for exerting control. These two projects highlight the selective self-representation strategies that young DGS people transfer from everyday physical encounters to their online spaces. We argue that these practices of 'social stenography', (boyd, 2014, pp. 65–69) in which identity is constituted as an ongoing negotiation with networked publics, are increasingly pertinent to all digital citizens. As such, our traditionally marginalised research collaborators are pioneers in an emergent performance of digital citizenship.

## PROJECT INTRODUCTIONS

Although these studies were conceived of and undertaken separately, with different groups of people in different locations and with different purposes, they both reveal insights into how simply being present in networked publics as a young gender-diverse or queer person can operate as a form of 'everyday activism'. Here, we follow Vivienne's (2016, p. 4) use of this term to describe a not-necessarily strategic or organised form of activism, but where young people are 'called upon in everyday life to use their personal stories in mundane environments to challenge social norms'. Taken together, the projects also reveal the importance of engaging participants as co-analysts who unveil these personal stories of 'everyday activism' through *in situ* analysis of their digital traces.

### Facebook Timelines

This study is ongoing, but it began in 2014 and currently includes 24 young people in both Australia (*n* = 13) and the United Kingdom (*n* = 11) using the same research design and method. We (Robards & Lincoln) sought out and recruited participants in their twenties who had been using Facebook for more than five years, in order to investigate the sustained use of Facebook. Our small qualitative sample includes two gay men, one gay woman and one transman. We are interested in the ways in which young people's disclosure practices (what they posted, who they friended, how they constructed their profiles) had changed over time, both as they 'grew up' and as Facebook itself evolved and developed over its first decade. We are also interested in the gaps and silences in their 'Timelines' (Facebook's most recent iteration of the profile or 'wall'). What kinds of things were not shared? What had been deleted or modified?

To address these questions, we devised an in-depth interview schedule that involves sitting with our participants on a computer, tablet, or smartphone, and 'scrolling back' through their Facebook timelines with them. We call this the 'scroll back' method (see Robards & Lincoln, forthcoming, for more details). Centrally, our participants were the 'drivers' in this phase of the interview scenario (which would sometimes last for an hour or more). They scrolled back through their old posts (status updates, photos, news stories, memes), encountered posts they were tagged in by others and reflected on the curious ways Facebook chose to highlight certain posts and certain social ties. The 'scroll back' method was at once a process of self-discovery, nostalgia, embarrassment and somber reflection. Even if more difficult periods in our participants' lives were not captured here (death, relationships ending, failure in education, domestic violence etc.), there would often be 'shadows' of those times: a haircut (spurred on by a breakup) or a trip to a city (for a funeral). Visible digital traces acted as references to less visible stories that were told only through sitting with our participants and 'holding space' for them to reflect, fill in blanks and layer more extensive spoken narratives on to the narratives that were mediated on (and by) Facebook.

Our participants were co-analysts *in situ*, using the interview scenario as an opportunity to talk in-depth about disclosures made (or not) on the site. While a 'one off' interview might seem limiting, the participants spoke about how rewarding they found this opportunity as it carved out the time and space for them to scroll back over years of disclosures. Scrolling back in the interview scenario enabled them to identify posts they wished to remove, share again or make private as well as occasionally confronting them with the digital traces of memories they were not so comfortable revisiting. It reminded them of events or instances that they had forgotten about, and in some cases made them nostalgic, embarrassed and amused.

## Stories Beyond Gender

The second project, *Stories Beyond Gender* is a community development initiative funded by a state government department for social inclusion. It builds on previous work in digital storytelling (Vivienne, 2016) to explore social media self-representation with a group of people who proclaim diverse gender and sexual identities (DGS). A series of weekend workshops were facilitated over a 12-month period, with loose objectives and outcomes largely framed by participants. Activities focused on creative self-representation as well as everyday activism and ranged from photo taichi[2] and face painting to drawing and creating memes. Workshop participants ($n$ = 40), ranging from 14 to 60 years in age, identified in many different ways but nevertheless had common interest in interrogating gender norms and stereotypes. Some participants ($n$ = 7) engaged in in-depth interviews with the researcher at a separate time and location.

During later stages of the initiative, a small group of participants in the urban workshops travelled to regional centres to facilitate workshops with trans and gender-diverse participants. This aspect of the project was intended to address geographic isolation and also concerns that the city-based cohort were not representative of experiences of DGS folk in the country. Once they had met in-person, it was easier for people to stay connected and mutually supportive online. Approximately half way through the project, the group undertook a facilitated World Cafe.[3] In this model, people from distinctly different walks of life are brought together in a safe space to share conversations 'across difference'. Many participants invited family members and colleagues, and there was a mix of anxiety (about potential discord) and pride (at exhibiting some of the creative content that had been produced). In the final stages of the project, the group decided to collaborate, while still generating their own individual content. They were keen to produce some short films that addressed common concerns (like 'most ridiculous things said to a transperson') as well as some physical resources (a booklet of their poems, stories, memes, art and photos) that could be distributed to social service providers, politicians, schools and employers.

For participants and researcher, this initiative evoked tensions between *research on* everyday practices and *interventions in* culture, framed as social change. While on the one hand personal interviews focused on capturing already-existing social media practices, on the other hand workshops aimed to develop creative skills and facilitate advocacy in a form more typical of community development/arts project. However, insights gained in one domain were found to be of benefit in the other and vice versa. By supporting participants as they negotiated their online and face-to-face networks, the research dimension of the project highlighted the simultaneous risks and rewards of nuanced digital self-representation. Digital traces are actively attenuated for distinct yet overlapping publics of friends, family, work colleagues and potentially antagonistic strangers. Participants shared these strategies in the workshop and then collaborated in disseminating their works and thinking online, as both creative endeavours and research outputs that, in turn, validate the framework of digital citizenship.

## WHY THESE TWO PROJECTS?

While the *methods* in each case study were quite different—single in-depth interviews looking back over years of Facebook use versus a series of workshops coupled with interviews—the *methodologies* were more closely aligned. Centrally, each project sought to 'hold' or 'put aside' space in which the researchers would spend time with participants, making sense of processes and practices around selective self-representation. In the *Facebook Timelines* project, this meant sitting with participants, sometimes for several hours, inviting them to craft narratives around digital traces and disclosures from years gone by. In the *Stories Beyond Gender* project, 'holding space' took the form of workshops that were driven by participants themselves. Initially the group analysed mainstream celebrity representations of trans and gender-diverse people, and creative experiments were chosen by each individual, with a view to sharing the outcomes with particular audiences on their own terms. Later, as the group decided to establish a stand-alone web presence (Facebook page, Tumblr), decisions regarding the site architecture and design were made collectively by those in attendance.

At the core of both of these research projects are similar research questions: How do complex people, with changing and/or contested identities, represent themselves in digital social media? In the *Facebook Timelines* project, the focus here was temporal: How have disclosure practices changed over time for people in their twenties who had effectively 'grown up' using the site? The *Stories Beyond Gender* project centred on gender-fluid identities at various stages of transition, and on collective representation where boundaries shift and are often contested. The research question was framed as follows: How can we represent ourselves creatively on social media and share our stories in ways that change public opinion? The wider methodological similarities ('holding space' and centring the participant—as co-analyst or co-curator) alongside the closely aligned overarching research questions render both projects suitable as case studies in this chapter, as we advance our argument for selective self-representation as a form of digital citizenship.

## VIGNETTES

In this section, we introduce five 'character vignettes', taken from our two projects, to provide examples of selective self-representation and meaningful belonging and to further develop our argument that these processes constitute a form of digital citizenship.

## Mark (22)—Facebook Timelines Project

Mark was a 22-year-old Australian, who had been using Facebook for six years at the time of the interview in 2014. Mark was a DJ, a criminology student and a passionate activist for DGS issues. He identified as trans (female to male), and was part of a collective of young transmen who documented their gender journeys on YouTube for other young transmen. When Mark 'came out' as trans, aside from his personal negotiations with family, friends, the health care system and the state, he also had to negotiate his digital trace:

> The main reason I deleted my old Facebook is because it didn't matter how many times I deleted old pictures or untagged pictures there was still all this history . . . like randomly things would pop up from old times, like somebody would be like, 'oh my god, remember this?' It would have my birth name, my tag and I'd be like, 'what? But I changed my name on Facebook'. How does that happen? But it would remember what it used to be . . . it wasn't so much that I was worried people would figure this out. It was more that for me I was trying to push away my birth name, an image that people had of me before so that people could better take on and understand the image that I had now. Like to go from pronouns to a new name and that sort of stuff . . . so I felt like that it would be more helpful to everybody and therefore more helpful to me to just delete that and just start again.

What Mark is drawing attention to here is both (1) the significance of Facebook in the performance of an identity (or the projection of an 'image') and (2) the complexity of undertaking this performance for a transperson. As Hogan (2010) explains, Facebook operates as a third party in Goffman's (1959) dramaturgical model, between performer and audience. Its algorithms and servers (designed by programmers) determine what is visible, what is possible and how digital traces of people's lives are configured.

## Robert (25)—Facebook Timelines Project

Robert was a 25-year-old, who was amongst the early adopters of Facebook in 2005, when it was still restricted to students in Northern America (with valid school email addresses) when he lived in Canada. Before Canada, Robert was in Hong Kong, where he was born; and after Canada, he came to Australia to undertake his training for and begin a career in medicine. Robert identified as gay. He came out to his conservative parents at the end of 2010, and in his own words, 'it went horribly'. Robert explained that the timing of his coming out to his parents immediately followed on from his first serious relationship, amidst 'a lot of pent up emotion'.

On Facebook, Robert's own disclosure practices had changed over time as he had grown up. Earlier on, he would post status updates quite frequently, but in his twenties he tended to post less even if he spent the same amount of time on the site, listening.[4] He did not disclose his sexuality on the site, and only ever came out to people in-person. He also periodically undertook his own 'scroll back' excursions to reflect on his earlier use of Facebook. Sometimes he would delete older posts:

*Robert:* You know how end of December [2010] was my big thing where shit happened [coming out to family and friends]?

*Brady:* Yeah.

*Robert:* I think I don't have any [posts here] because I went back and deleted them.

*Brady:* What sort of posts did you delete?

*Robert:* Just like whining posts and annoying people, whining posts.

These posts were not directly about coming out or his sexuality, but they prompted for him a recollection of this time. In other words, he was expressing his anxiety and the turbulence of coming out indirectly, and he revised these traces (by deleting them) in retrospect.

The other interesting dimension of Robert's Facebook use was the way in which he used the site as a kind of personal journal and an archive of memories. While Robert was mostly private when posting to his network, he also wrote some posts that were only visible to himself, including a post reflecting on some significant surgery. He explained: "Maybe [this is] just to read it myself. Sometimes I like to go back. . . . I still keep it there just to read and it does bring back some memories". In this sense, Robert was concerned not just with the semi-public performance of his own identity on Facebook but also with the ways in which these digital traces prompted his own memory-work. This resonates with Duguay's (2014) work that explores LGBTQ identities, impression management and 'context collapse' (Marwick & boyd, 2011; Vitak, 2012) on Facebook and the ways in which 'individuals intentionally redefine their sexual identity across audiences'. What we see Robert doing here is building up the boundaries of his sexual identity, to the point at which, at times, his disclosures on the site are completely private, only for him to read. This practice enables Robert to 'work through' and affirm his identity in the context of a social network site, even if there is no audience. The fact that it is disclosed on the site but only visible to him emphasises Facebook's significance in memory-work and self-archiving.

## Tash (30)—Stories Beyond Gender Project

Tash had a coming-out-as-trans story that included an interstate move and new workplace. Tash took considerable time and care to 'event manage' her transition across two separate Facebook profiles, with 'old' and 'new' overlapping for a one-month period. During this time, she used Facebook's direct message facility to individually contact old friends with invitations to chat about 'something important'. She then undertook these conversations via either Messenger or, for closer friends, Skype or Facebook video chat. The deactivating of the old profile was only undertaken after a substantial data dump, including many photographs that were only available for download in low resolution. Tash's new profile includes carefully considered differentiated groups of 'close friends' (four people), 'friends' (everyone else unless restricted), 't-group pages' (posts pertinent to transition and gender diversity) and 'restricted' (family, rarely seen acquaintances, new work colleagues who have yet to win trust). She noted that, while she doesn't have an active Google profile, she was inspired by the way Google circles work and translated the approach to Facebook. After establishing this new profile, Tash continued to use Facebook in a variety of off-label ways. She posted lengthy blog updates to her timeline and used her 'restricted audience' settings to share with her two closest interstate friends. Over time as she re-established trust with individuals, she added them back into her closer circles, eventually including 'even family members'. She used Facebook calendar to schedule and keep track of medical appointments and continues to find this useful as a means of keeping a range of info in one place. She copies some events back into her work calendar so she can look back on them and reflect on her personal development.

Tash used Facebook alongside other platforms, often with discrete publics. For example, she reserved Instagram for old interstate friends who were not aware of her transition, documenting localised experiences like giant crayfish and unique buildings. A pseudonymous profile on Tumblr, a platform largely unfamiliar to her old friends, allowed her to imbibe and share social values and perspectives on her new trans life. Her participation in special interest forums like susans.org were exclusively focused on transition, while on Twitter she deliberately avoided following anything or anyone gender related in order to keep up with news and current affairs. Tash was extremely aware of the nuances of her online self-representation and noted how some strategies have changed over time. As a young person, between the ages of 13 and 20, she hung out on Gaiaonline, where she was able to create a feminine avatar and identity that gave her greater freedom of expression to discover herself. As an adult, she described the challenges she faces on dating websites where intimate self-disclosure means either instantly outing yourself and perhaps ruining your chances or 'keeping it under wraps' and getting better 'hit rates'.

Disclosing later has attendant risks and can invoke disappointment or a sense of betrayal that can manifest in brutal rejection.

Tash's use of mobile apps like Endomondo Sports Tracker also reflected her awareness of physical trans-related safety concerns, a subject that is pertinent but may not have been discussed if our focus had been more platform specific. Tash appreciated the collaborative and competitive aspects of sharing fitness goals but would turn all locative features off before arriving home. She also chose not to use cloud data storage services and is acutely aware of the status of old identification cards that may be targets for identity theft.

## Lillith (22)—Stories Beyond Gender Project

Another trans-participant, Lillith, described how she shares selfies across different platforms for distinct purposes. She updates her Facebook profile with a similarly framed selfie each month for several reasons, partly for herself in order to observe subtle changes in soft tissue influenced by oestrogen and partly for her friends, so that 'they're kept in the loop' and are never unduly surprised by her changed appearance.

Lillith also posts these selfies to a subreddit called 'trans-passing' that she describes as being full of 'hypercritical transphobic haters'. She prefers these communities' criticism of physical appearance over the alternative: 'I'd rather they say "hey you look like a dude in a dress" rather than honey it up!' In the early days of transition, Lillith would post here to see if she passed as a boy, because at that stage she still needed to attend family functions in her male assignation.

Lillith's online engagement also extends beyond uses of social media to reveal sophisticated digital literacies pertinent to her embodied and tenuous status as a transgender citizen. In order to change the gender marker on official identification documents like birth certificate and driver's licence in Australia, a transperson must satisfy legal requirements in the form of the 'real life test' and/or have received medical interventions in the form of hormone therapy, gender reassignment surgery or a clinical diagnosis of 'gender dysphoria'. For many young people, these processes are prohibitively expensive and time consuming. Having to 'seek permission' from a (frequently white male) judge/medical specialist/authority figure in order to transition from what many see as an incorrect or false assignation of gender at birth can be deemed offensive. In some cases, young transpeople elect to take these intimate personal matters into their own hands by using digital trans-community forums to seek collective wisdom and the 'darknet' for ordering hormones from overseas where they are cheaper and more available. Lillith reflects on her choice to expose herself intimately in some forums, like reddit above, while maintaining vigilance against surveillance in other spaces:

> My online presence is very private when I want it to be. Like if I'm buying stuff online I'll use a VPN and go through Tor and I'll do it in a public library so my data's not really worth being tracked.

Lillith is in the liminal two-year period of the 'real life test' and has been thwarted in efforts to find employment because she has no documentation that aligns with her gender presentation. Prospective employers have been known to accuse young transpeople of fraud because certificates of qualification are in their former name. As a result of these difficulties, some young transpeople resort to sex work and 'camming'. In a shared interview space, several young transwomen were able to discuss the pros and cons of sex labour in private and public spaces, without necessarily needing to identify personally as sex workers. In terms of research process, the relative pseudonymity of generalised group discussion allowed them to discuss subjects they may otherwise find incriminating.

This group also reflected on how they use digital tools, devices and platforms to enhance their personal safety. For example, camming uses live streaming video chat and performance via webcam to platforms that not only connect performers and audiences but facilitate payment for requests. This labour, while less lucrative than embodied sex work, can allow transpeople to 'be themselves' (i.e. openly trans) in ways that are often physically dangerous offline. However, even in street sex work digital devices play their role. One young transperson described how she surreptitiously photographs client number plates and sends the image to a friend prior to getting in a car. She also sets up 'find my iPhone' with the friend, and, if she doesn't get back in touch in an agreed period of time, the friend has both car number plate and reasonably accurate geographic location. Depending on whether they have a level of faith in police response, they can then either report this information or use it themselves to attempt to locate their friend.

These uses of digital devices and platforms by young stigmatised transpeople constitute enactment of a kind of digital citizenship that effectively speaks back to more formal and contested legal frameworks. As well as enabling these very pragmatic performances, digital self-representation can facilitate philosophical and abstract explorations of gendered identity.

### Joslyn (25)—Stories Beyond Gender Project

Joslyn provides still further evidence of the complex interweaving of digital self-representation over time frames and multiple platforms and devices. Joslyn said she didn't like selfies and only includes them in chat on Facebook to occasionally 'save words' describing something like a new hat. While she acknowledged that this trace may still be searchable, she nevertheless regards it as more transient and disposable. During the *Stories Beyond Gender* initiative, Joslyn moved from finely wrought abstract illustrations with lead pencil and paper to using a tablet and stylus to produce manga-influenced colourful characters in graphic novel vignettes. She started posting these to DeviantArt because it hosts a queer-friendly art-focused community that she hoped would critique her work. When it became clear that each post garnered only a few broadly affirming comments, in the vein of 'nice work!' she started sharing her posts to Tumblr and Facebook as well. On Tumblr, her followers were trans or fandom related, while Facebook was constituted of mostly friends but not artists. Her awareness of how her work is interpreted (i.e. as 'artwork' or 'personal experience') in these different contexts is illustrative of everyday digital citizenship that assumes context collapse and challenges social injunctions to present coherence.

In a post on the *Stories Beyond Gender* website, Joslyn provides an illustration (Figure 11.1) and articulation of 'continuity':

**Figure 11.1    Joslyn's digital art and blog post on 'Stories Beyond Gender'.**

I sometimes wish that I had a time machine so that I could go back and tell that boy [her younger self] that he could grow into a woman instead, because he would love to hear that, because he didn't know that he 'qualified'. I have no trouble referring to my younger self as a boy, because that was how I identified, but I feel some discontinuity with that identity. . . .

Our memories are how we establish continuity with our younger selves, be they a couple of seconds, to a couple of years in the past. Eventually my memory of my early life will decay and be distorted by how I am now. Our brains don't store events like a video camera; when we remember things, their forms are reconstructed by our brains. Even now, I only really have a good near-term grasp of my life over the past decade, and the preceding decade fades into blackness.

I might eventually forget what I used to look like, because I don't keep many photos, although my mum will probably remember it till the day she dies.

Joslyn acknowledges the utility of photographs and/or video that document earlier incarnations of identity but also highlights their inadequacy in capturing the complexity of her whole story and self. This mirrors Robert's experience of going back to old posts on his Facebook timeline, some of which are visible only to himself, to reflect on key moments in his life. Even when jogged by visual evidence, memory decays.

## DISCUSSION

Our descriptive vignettes are offered here as examples of the kinds of selective self-representation that we argue are at the heart of digital citizenship. While our participants acknowledge and negotiate 'risk' in a social context that stigmatises non-normative presentations of gender and sexuality, they simultaneously challenge the designation of marginalisation. Our participants enact modes of *being* that are centred around agency. They determine what is visible and what is not and with whom their personal revelations are shared. Further, their adept navigation of ever-changing platforms and publics supports our argument for a methodological approach that affirms the depth of their preferred and complex identities. As we reframe and share their narratives in scholarly spaces, we draw attention to the strategies they employ, as they assert personal congruence in defiance of social pressure to adhere to a consistent or coherent narrative (i.e. live according to the gender they were assigned at birth and/or heterosexual norms). Further, by choosing methods (i.e. 'checking-in' and 'checking-back' over meaning making) that align with content (e.g. postmodern fragmentation of identity), we also bring our research participants and collaborators into being as digital citizens.

At the same time however, each form of social media orders and reorders disclosures according to a set of design logics that are beyond the control of users.

The platforms become the mediating 'third party' (Hogan, 2010) between the user and their network (and vice versa). Facebook has been criticised for the ways in which its central News Feed selectively privileges some posts over others, as determined by a hidden algorithm (Bucher, 2012; Robards, 2014). In this scenario, individual agency and control is finite. While digital representations of self travel in unpredictable ways, and our participants acknowledge this lack of control, their ownership of multiplicity in their identity-projects demonstrates a core understanding of the postmodern self as non-linear, sometimes contradictory and often pieced together from a range of practices, tastes and 'tribes' (Bennett, 1999; Robards & Bennett 2011). In some cases, these understandings are explicitly articulated by research participants.

Joslyn's digital illustration captures the idea of 'distortion' with vertical technicolour glitches overlaying the older woman who embraces her younger boy self, representing a disrupted signal or disintegrating video tape. Her matter-of-fact account of memory applies to cisgender and heterosexual people just as it does to transgender or queer people. However, in a cultural context that privileges coherence as a measure of well-being and agency, the risks of appearing 'inconsistent' are great.

Like the *Stories Beyond Gender* project, the *Facebook Timelines* project worked to neatly capture the various ways in which participants had changed or grown over time, and how they made sense of the digital traces of that change. In participating in the project, both Mark and Robert, described in this chapter, were confronted by earlier 'versions' of themselves, that is, earlier iterations of their own reflexive projects of self. The mediating influence of the 'digital' in self-representation is thus layered upon the already-impossible task of rendering a complete understanding of self in any tangible form, or indeed for oneself. Butler draws on Foucault's account of self-constitution to highlight the impossibility of describing a singular self.

> If I try to give an account of myself, if I try to make myself recognizable and understandable, then I might begin with a narrative account of my life. But this narrative will be disoriented by what is not mine, or not mine alone. And I will, to some degree, have to make myself substitutable in order to make myself recognizable. The narrative authority of the 'I' must give way to the perspective and temporality of a set of norms that contest the singularity of my story. (Butler, 2005, p. 37)

Just as Joslyn highlights the impermanence and inaccuracy of memory, Butler considers a problematic 'regime of truth that decides what will and will not be a recognizable form of being' (ibid, p. 22). The regime of truth does not 'fully constrain'; however, it provides 'a framework for the scene of recognition, delineating who will qualify as a subject of recognition and offering available norms for the act of recognition' (ibid, p. 22). These theoretical insights go some way towards explaining the tensions between popular injunctions to represent a singular coherent identity (as iterated by Zuckerberg and, indeed, self-help books that frequently reference 'inner truth') and everyday actualities in which we behave differently with different people, and change over time, in the course of 'growing up'. The 'act of recognition' is framed by norms in which we can only stray incrementally from previous representations, and the subject of recognition is framed by binary norms of masculinity and femininity.

Turning back now to the question of how we, as researchers, can meaningfully invite participants to co-analyse and co-curate their self-representations, it seems we are faced by almost insurmountable postmodernist quandaries. While we can recognise and analyse the complex processes by which participants selectively represent themselves and, further, argue that the multiple texts, platforms and meanings inherent in fragmented social media affirm these possibilities, how can we render them in a coherent scholarly discussion?

Narrative theorists and researchers Hyvärinen et al. (2010) offer four principle reasons for problematising coherence. As researchers, we risk privileging some coherent narratives over others, and seeking coherence predisposes us to a biased reading of any given situation. Attempts to present complexity in distilled form are not only at odds with the realities of our participants (and here they reference trauma survivors as we reference gender diversity), it also pre-empts 'adequate' or normative interpretations:

> Coherence is not an objective feature of an individual narrative as a text, but rather is something that has always been produced interactionally, thus implicating the researcher as a coherence-creating or coherence-declining agent. (Brockmeier, 2004, p 11)

Rather than considering ourselves as researchers who are either coherence creating or coherence declining, we defer here to the notion of congruence. In the trans and gender-diverse community, this is a word that in some ways speaks back to the notion of gender dysphoria in that it refers to alignment between one's *own* understanding of self and the way one is interpreted or read by the world one inhabits. *The Oxford dictionary* defines congruence as 'harmony' or 'compatibility', while coherence means 'logical', 'consistent' or 'unified whole'.

When we enlist participants as co-analysts of their digital traces and co-curators of meaning, we are effectively holding space for multiple meanings and interpretations. These meanings are not mutually exclusive or hierarchical but nevertheless afford an intelligible argument. The resulting narrative is contextualised (and authorised) by the originator and does not belie the greater complexity that underpins it.

So, what does this look like in research practice? In the case of Robards and Lincoln's project, co-analysis of a digital trace allows research participants to choose which aspects of their Facebook timeline they discuss. It invites their reflection on how their texts sit beside their memories of critical turning points in their lives and, further, how the meaning of disjunctures and/or alignments change over time. In the case of Vivienne's project, co-curation of digital self-representation allows participants to determine how they will create a digital trace and who they will share this with. Further, it invites them to consider what effect they desire and how this rhetorical stance may proselytise gender diversity.

Our efforts to enlist our participants in the research process have nevertheless been constrained in some cases by pragmatic processes of academic publishing. It is not always possible to return to every participant to seek approval for the way we have rendered their stories. Deadlines can be prohibitive, and in some cases (although not ours) the sheer number of participants makes this difficult. In other perfectly valid research methodologies, multiple anecdotes may be conflated and rendered as one so as to make them unidentifiable. Even with the best of intentions, the language of representation (intended for scholarly readership) is also not always accessible and may alienate participants. In seeking to check back with participants, after the analysis and writing is done, we also risk their withdrawal altogether. Where to from there?

Despite the obstacles to the research process that we outline above, we argue that checking back in after data collection and prior to publication can be worthwhile. While Vivienne makes a point of this routinely, Robards and Lincoln do not, instead seeking further information or clarification where needed. For Vivienne, checking back has often shed light on additional complex dimensions that had not surfaced in the initial contact. For example, when Vivienne sent Tash the extract from this chapter that was most pertinent to her navigation of coming out to multiple publics online, Tash proffered additional analysis. She spoke of her use of another digital platform, the dating site and app 'OK Cupid', and described how she coded and veiled reference to her trans-identity by including it at the tail end of her personal bio. In response to 'Contact me if . . .', she writes 'if you're cool with trans people' and explains that this is only visible if a viewer has already clicked through 'more info'. In this way, their first response is determined by her photographs and preliminary words, rather than being framed by knowledge of her trans-identity. Tash went on to explain how difficult it is to negotiate safe dating because, while on one hand it is important that a prospective lover 'knows in advance', on the other, Tash does not wish to *only* attract people who 'are into trans' and/or exclude those who might be ambivalent but open-minded. None of this detail surfaced in our initial interview or during workshops, and yet it is clearly pertinent to issues of trans self-representation online, particularly in the domains of intimate relations.

Despite some obstacles, we argue that our approaches enable our participants to check-in or check-back over their digital traces. However, checking in with old data doesn't always guarantee a complete narrative. Inevitably, there are posts that participants have no recollection of making or that have been made by people they no longer know from their now-distant past, and thus, despite enrolling our participants as co-analysts of their own digital traces, memory also has its limits. Nevertheless, in the face of the emergent complexities inherent in the practices of digital citizenship, we argue that we are increasingly beholden to align our framing of these practices around the preferred meanings of our participants. Checking-back and checking-in have enhanced our understanding of complex identities and added depth or another dimension to our understandings of behaviours that are called forth by the demands of digital citizenship.

## CONCLUSION

In this chapter, we have sought to accomplish two goals. First, we have attempted to outline some of the ways in which our young participants have engaged in practices of selective self-representation in digital social spaces. This has included 're-loading' a Facebook profile to align with a revised identity-project, through to uploading selfies to a subreddit each month, documenting embodied changes and inviting critics to comment on how well (or not) posters 'pass' in their performance of gender. We have framed these forms of selective self-representation in this chapter as acts of digital citizenship. As we have explained above, simply being non-normative (non-cis or not-totally hetero) and owning the identity-project in a public way (both in networked and physical publics) can be framed as a simultaneously personal and political act.

Second, we have layered this central argument with our own reflections on the methodological complications we have encountered, through endeavouring to privilege the voices of our participants. In doing so, we have suggested a 'call to action' for researchers to engage their participants in the research process beyond simply answering questions in an interview or completing a survey. Increasingly, our work involves young people (at least in our Western contexts), who are 'living out' their lives across multiple platforms, both in digital and physical spaces, carefully negotiating context collapse. As a result, and because we in turn redistribute a version of their personal narratives in scholarly form, their role in analysing their digital texts is crucial. In both the *Facebook Timelines* project and the *Stories Beyond Gender* initiative, we have strongly benefited from enlisting our participants as co-analysts and co-curators of their own digital traces, serving to further centre their own interpretations. This has taken place at separate stages of research, firstly in the gathering and generation of data (for both Lincoln and Robards, and Vivienne) and, secondly, in the articulation and dissemination of research findings (for Vivienne), when possible. We add the caveat 'when possible' here in acknowledgement that this cannot always be the case.

The vignettes we chose to include here (from Mark, Robert, Tash, Lillith and Joslyn) are not comprehensive or representative, but provide windows into the kinds of practices of selective self-representation that we are describing as everyday digital citizenship. Rather than focus wholly on the strategies our research participants use as digital citizens, we have also considered research practice. How do we represent complexity in the life stories of our participants? Arguably, the analytical process seeks out patterns and through lines, effectively distilling mess into meaning. Further, some life transitions (e.g. from childhood to youth to adulthood) are dominant and normative, while others (e.g. gender transition, sexual ambiguity), in the face of social bigotry, are deemed transgressive and thus contested and political. Research, too, becomes political when centred on instances of everyday digital citizenship, and we advocate that, whenever possible, we should not shy away from this, but incorporate it into our practice.

## ACKNOWLEDGEMENT

We would like to thank our participants—our co-analysts, and our co-curators—for their time, energy and consent. Without them, these projects would not be possible.

## NOTES

1. DGS is an acronym that addresses some of the exclusions implicit in LGBTQI (lesbian, gay, bisexual, transgender, queer, intersex) as finite and permanent identity categories. Diverse gender and sexualities also accommodate the 'in-between' and fluid self-representations that are so often dismissed as 'just a phase' or 'incoherence'.

2. Devas, B. (2015, May 22). Photographic Tai Chi [Digital Art Project]. Retrieved 29 from http://photomediationsmachine.net/2015/05/22/photographic-tai-chi/.

3. See www.worldcafe.com for more details.

4. We follow here Crawford's (2009) theorisation of 'listening' on social media rather than 'lurking'.

## REFERENCES

Bennett, A. (1999). Subcultures or Neo-Tribes? Rethinking the relationship between youth, style and musical taste. *Sociology*, *33*(3), 599–617.

Bowker, G. C. (2007). The past and the internet. *Structures of participation in digital culture*, 20–36.

boyd, danah. (2014). *It's complicated: The social lives of networked teens.* New York: Yale University Press.

Brockmeier, J. (2004). What makes a story coherent? In A. U Branco & J. Valsiner (Eds.), Communication & Metacommunication in human development (pp. 285–306). Greewich, CT: Information Age Publishing.

Bucher, T. (2012). Want to be on the top? Algorithmic power and the threat of invisibility on Facebook. *New Media & Society*, *14*(7), 1164–1180.

Butler, J. (2005). *Giving an account of oneself* (1st ed.). New York: Fordham University Press.

Cushman, M., McLean, R., Light, B., Fletcher, G., & Adam, A. (2008). Gay men, Gaydar and the commodification of difference. *Information Technology & People*, *21*(3), 300–314.

Dobson, A. S. (2015). *Postfeminist digital cultures: Femininity, social media, and self-representation.* Palgrave Macmillan US.

Duguay, S. (2014). 'He has a way gayer Facebook than I do': Investigating sexual indentity disclosure and context collpase on a social networking site. *New Media & Society.*

Gillespie, T. (2010). The politics of 'platforms'. *New Media & Society*, *12*(3), 347–364.

Goffman, E. (1959). *The presentation of self in everyday life.* New York: Anchor Books.

Hanckel, B., & Morris, A. (2014). Finding community and contesting heteronormativity: queer young people's engagement in an Australian online community. *Journal of Youth Studies*, *17*(7), 872–886.

Highfield, T., & Leaver, T. (2015). A Methodology for mapping Instagram hashtags. *First Monday*, *20*(1). Retrieved from http://doi.org/http://dx.doi.org/10.5210/fm.v20i1.

Hillier, L., Jones, T., Monagle, M., Overton, N., Gahan, L., Blackman, J., & Mitchell, A. (2010). Writing themselves in 3: The third national study on the sexual health and wellbeing of same sex attracted and gender questioning young people. *Australian Research Centre in Sex, Health and Society*. La Trobe University. Retrieved from http://apo.org.au/resource/writing-themselves-3-third-national-study-sexual-health-and-wellbeing-same-sex-attracted.

Hogan, B. (2010). The Presentation of self in the age of social media: Distinguishing performances and exhibitions online. *Bulletin of Science, Technology & Society*, *30*(6), 377–386.

Hyvärinen, M., Hyden, L. C., Saarenheimo, M., & Tamboukou, M. (Eds.). (2010). Beyond Narrative Coherence. Amsterdam/Philadelphia: John Benjamins Publishing Company.

Lincoln, S. (2012). *Youth culture and private space.* Houndmills, UK.: Palgrave Macmillan.

Madden, M., Lenhart, A., Cortesi, S., Gasser, U., Duggan, M., Smith, A., & Beaton, M. (2013). Teens, social media, and privacy. *Pew Research Center*, *21*, 1–48.

Marwick, A. E., & boyd, d. (2011). Networked privacy: How teenagers negotiate context in social media. *New Media & Society, 16*(7), 1051–1067.

Mustanski, B., Lyons, T., & Garcia, S. C. (2011). Internet use and sexual health of young men who have sex with men: A mixed-methods study. *Archives of Sexual Behavior, 40*(2), 289–300.

Robards, B. (2014). Digital traces of the persona through ten years of Facebook. *M/C Journal, 17*(3). Retrieved from http://journal.media-culture.org.au/index.php/mcjournal/article/viewArticle/818.

Robards, B., & Bennett, A. (2011). MyTribe: Post-subcultural manifestations of belonging on social network sites. *Sociology, 45*(2), 303–317.

Roth, Y. (2014). Locating the 'scruff guy': Theorizing body and space in gay geosocial media. *International Journal of Communication, 8*, 2113–2133.

Russell, S. T. (2002). Queer in America: Citizenship for sexual minority youth. *Applied Developmental Science, 6*(4), 258–263.

Stryker, S., & Whittle, S. (2006). *The transgender studies reader.* New York: Routledge.

Taylor, Y., Falconer, E., & Snowdon, R. (2014). Queer youth, Facebook and faith: Facebook methodologies and online identities. *New Media & Society, 16*(7), 1138–1153.

Vitak, J. (2012). The impact of context collapse and privacy on social network site disclosures. *Journal of Broadcasting & Electronic Media, 56*(4), 451–470.

Vivenne, S. (2016). Digital Indentity and Everyday Activism: Sharing Private Stories with Networked Publics. London, New York: Palgrave Macmillan.

Vromen, A., Xenos, M. A., & Loader, B. (2015). Young people, social media and connective action: From organisational maintenance to everyday political talk. *Journal of Youth Studies, 18*, 80–100.

Werner, A. (2014). Getting Bodied with Beyonce on YouTube. In A. Bennett & B. Robards (Eds.), *Mediated Youth Cultures: The Internet, Belonging and New Cultural Configurations.* Palgrave Macmillan UK.

Xenos, M., Vromen, A., & Loader, B. D. (2014). The great equalizer? Patterns of social media use and youth political engagement in three advanced democracies. *Information, Communication & Society, 17*(2), 151–167.

*Chapter 12*

# Politics of Sexting Revisited

## Kath Albury

In late 2009, the New South Wales (NSW) Education Department released the *Safe Sexting: No Such Thing* fact sheet, targeting parents. The fact sheet observed that naked or semi-naked pictures 'become part of a young person's "digital footprint", lasting forever and potentially damaging future career prospects or relationships . . . with young girls most at risk', and recommended that parents should have access to their children's phones.[1] (NSW Government, 2009). Just as this fact sheet was released, my colleague Kate Crawford (who was then based at UNSW) and I began to have hallway conversations reflecting on media coverage of sexting—an interest that led to the development of the *Young People and Sexting in Australia* project (Albury et al., 2013). Initially, the term 'sexting' was generally applied to the sending of suggestive or explicit text-based messages. By mid-2009, however, it was primarily understood as 'the practice of using a camera cell phone to take and send nude (including semi-nude) photographs to other cell phones or Internet sites' (Chalfen, 2009, p. 258). As we (and other researchers) observed, while many adults participated in these practices, young people—particularly young women—played a central role in popular discourses of sexting, and soon came to be framed as the archetypally 'at risk' sexting subject (Albury et al., 2013, p. 3).

In 2010, I began to consider the implications that evolving popular and academic debates regarding sexting might have in relation to the (highly contested) notion of young people's sexual rights and sexual citizenship. My first foray into this field was published in the proceeding of the Australia and New Zealand Communications Association Annual Conference (Albury et al., 2010). This article explored the notion of 'sexual citizenship' in order to unpack what my co-authors and I termed the 'politics of sexting'. These politics operated on a number of levels, from the impact of gendered double standards within Australian educational policy outlined above to the legislative conflation of young people's consensual practices of producing or sharing sexually suggestive and/or explicit images and texts with 'child pornography'. Much has changed since then, in terms of both digital technologies and the fields of research that study them—yet the politics of sexting have not shifted very far.

This chapter offers a welcome opportunity to revisit (and expand) the intersection of digital and sexual citizenship as it applies to the 'at-risk' figure of the sexting teen. I begin by reflecting on the ongoing tendency to pathologise young people's digital practices, and then consider how a rights-based approach to the question of 'digital sexual citizenship' reframes the 'problem' of youth sexting. If the notion of digital citizenship implies recognition of one's rights and responsibilities in online and mobile-mediated spaces, how does the notion of sexual citizenship intersect with and extend these rights and responsibilities? As I discuss in this chapter, within Australian debates (and policy frameworks), young people's claims to citizenship are more likely to be recognised in terms of what Petchetsky (2000) has defined as 'exclusionary', or protective rights. Like Petchesky (2000), I see the space of 'sexual rights' as emergent. That is, I recognise that the enabling conditions that would allow all young people to fully express such rights are contingent on a range of factors, including not only gender and sexuality but also socio-economic status, ethnicity, culture, religion and the political stability of the region in which they live.

Finally, acknowledging the mediated sexual practices of both adults and young people, I engage with the limitations of sexual citizenship as a concept and recognise the necessity of both top-down and bottom-up approaches to the politics of sexting. Rights-focused top-down approaches might include law reform that excludes consensual exchange of sexual images between young people aged under 18 from the definitions of 'child pornography' and educational policies and curricula that promote ethical reflection, and recognise both collective and individual concepts of sexual rights and responsibilities. Bottom-up approaches can be seen to emerge from digital sexual cultures themselves, in the form of vernacular comic/erotic approaches to digital literacy education; collective codes of ethics for commenting on and for sharing selfies and sexual images; and associated queer and feminist projects seeking to rework the politics of embodied/sexual visibility in mediated spaces (see Duguay, 2014; Warfield et al., 2014).

## SELFIES, SEXTING AND CITIZENSHIP

It would be remiss to seek to explore the question of sexting (and digital self-representation in general) as an expression of sexual citizenship without first acknowledging broader popular discourses condemning or trivialising young people's digital practices. As Senft and Baym (2015) observe, 'It is almost impossible to encounter a discussion of selfies that doesn't dabble in discourses of pathology' (2015, p. 1589). Whether they are presented as expressions of concern or as accusations, even 'supportive' adult discourses of sexting can dismiss the practice as evidence of young people's 'ignorance', 'low self esteem', 'addiction' and/or 'narcissism'. These responses shame individual young people for participating in *collective* digital cultures, and shift the blame for non-consensual picture sharing from perpetrators to victims. Further, as Crofts et al. (2015) argue, adult refusal to listen to young people's accounts of their media practices can create barriers to developing practical and empathetic educational and legal responses to non-consensual picture sharing.

As I will expand below, in the first stage of the *Young People and Sexting in Australia* study, my colleague Paul Byron and I facilitated three focus group conversations with young people aged 16–17. Participants in the focus groups discussed sexting (and selfies) in terms that evoked complex political debates, contesting the limits they felt their peers, family and teachers placed on their practices of sexual and gendered self-representation. Here, they discussed a young male friend who had posted a naked picture on Facebook, but had avoided adult censure because his self-exposure was read as 'funny' rather than 'provocative':

*Female:* That's the whole thing with the gender . . .

*Female:* Yes, definitely.

*Female:* It's like if a girl does anything in her underwear, it's immediately she's trying to get someone. She's trying to look provocative and sexy and stuff.

*Female:* That's a gender equality issue.

*Female:* Yeah. But if a guy does it it's hilarious and it's so funny.

*Male:* Yeah, I'm sure if there was a girl in that photo, people [i.e. parents and teachers] would have been called up and stuff, but because it's just a guy . . .

*Male:* A guy, like no one cares, they're just . . .

*Male:* No one cared.

A group of young women criticised 'sext education' content that failed to acknowledge the possibility of their sexual desires, including a desire for self-representation. As one participant put it:

I think it also raises issues about, are you allowed to do what you want with your body? I mean, if you are that confident that you want to post a naked picture on Facebook, should you be allowed to do that? I mean, if it's yours, if you're autonomous.

This association of body autonomy with individual self-confidence could be dismissed for evoking the kind of 'sexual citizenship as choosing/consuming subject' critiqued by Evans, Krogh & Carmody (2009), and indeed a number of sexting and selfie researchers have linked aspects of selfie culture to post-feminist constructions of girls as ideal citizen-consumers (e.g. Harris, 2015; McRobbie, 2009).

Following Gill (2007), we can understand post-feminist approaches to young women's practices of self-representation as reflecting both feminist and anti-feminist sensibilities. Young women's selfies are subject to intense surveillance from both adult and peers, and may be either celebrated or condemned on the basis of the viewer's assessment of the most appropriate forms of embodied performance of 'empowerment' or 'choice' (Albury, 2015). Critics of mainstream media representation might define selfies as expressions of 'choice' and 'body confidence'. At the same time, critics of sexualisation might condemn *the same* young women's sexual-self-representations as inappropriately 'pornified', or provocative. As I have observed elsewhere (Albury, 2015), while young men also take and share 'sexy selfies', their images are seldom subject to the same level of scrutiny. These complex issues of double standards in relation to perceptions of gendered representation (and self-representation) and the contestation of rights to bodily autonomy and bodily display are not unique to young people (Albury, 2015). Further, while I have referred to 'young people' here, it is not the case that sexting and other forms of mediated sexual communication (with or without picture sharing) are unproblematic for those aged over 18.

Global debates around revenge porn, recent leaks of hacked 'celebrity nudes' and the *Ashley Madison* leak have demonstrated that adults are also vulnerable to punitive or humiliating sharing of self-representations, and that this vulnerability is gendered. For example, in 2014, a mass hack of celebrity selfies was leaked, first to the online forum 4chan, and then to more mainstream media channels. The incident, popularly known as Celebgate or The Fappening (a portmanteau word combining 'happening' with 'fapping', a slang term for masturbation), most famously included Jennifer Lawrence's selfies. While some commentators responded to the 2014 leak of hacked celebrity nudes by blaming the female victims of the hack, popular responses more commonly framed the event as an invasion of privacy (Isaac, 2014).

Similarly, there was an element of victim blaming (and moralising) in response to the leak of hacked user *Ashley Madison*'s details in August 2015. Some commentators certainly expressed a belief that *Ashley Madison*'s (largely male) clients 'deserved' exposure, since the site specifically promotes infidelity. However, victims of this hack were not represented as pathologically naïve for having trusted the website's assurances of security and discretion (Hill, 2015). I suggest that in both cases, the adult victims of the leaks were recognised as legitimate sexual citizens in a way that young people are not. That is, as adults they were (in the main) afforded implicit rights to self-representation (and sexual privacy) that are not extended to younger people—particularly in popular, educational or policy responses to sexting.

The *Young People and Sexting in Australia* study explicitly adopted a rights-based approach, drawing on Articles 12 and 13 of the United Nations Convention on the Rights of the Child (1989), of which Australia is a signatory. Article 13 states:

> The child [which is defined in the Convention as a person aged under 18] shall have the right to freedom of expression; this right shall include freedom to seek, receive and impart information and ideas of all kinds, regardless of frontiers, either orally, in writing or in print, in the form of art, or through any other media of the child's choice. (UNCROC, 1989)[2]

This article does not explicitly define children and young people's right to create and access information (in the form of written text or images) relating to their bodies and their sexualities. However, my colleagues and I interpreted this article to include such rights. Like other researchers addressing the question of children's rights (and responsibilities) in digital spaces, we were concerned that 'a narrow focus on risk and safety can negatively impact children's right to participation and undermine their ability to access the benefits of digital media' (Third et al., 2014, p. 15). We also observed that rights *cannot* be disconnected from responsibilities, according to the article. Freedom of expression (and access to information) is limited by 'necessary' local laws, and '(a) . . . respect of the rights or reputations of others; or (b) for the protection of national security or of public order (ordre public), or of public health or morals' (UNCROC, 1989).

These caveats might seem to suggest that the application of child pornography laws to young people's consensual practices of self-representation should not be questioned, since they have been created to protect young people from exploitation by adult predators. However, Article 12 explicitly states that children should be 'provided the opportunity to be heard in any judicial and administrative proceedings affecting the child', with 'the views of the child being given due weight in accordance with the age and maturity of the child' (UNCROC, 1989). Despite this clear direction to those who seek to protect children and young people via policy and legislation, when we conceived the *Young People and Sexting in Australia* project, we could find no evidence that those aged under 18 had ever been consulted in Australia in relation to the laws that restricted their digital self-representation. This seemed particularly surprising, given that 16- and 17-year-old Australians are recognised as having 'adult' capacity in a range of areas, from driving cars to sexual consent.

Consequently, we began our investigation by considering the notion of young people's sexual rights. If Australian law afforded young people the capacity to consent to physical sexual activities, could it be argued that it recognised their 'sexual citizenship'? How then might we understand young people's 'sexual rights'? We began our inquiry with an exploration of the history of this relatively new (and still contested) field of human rights discourse and activism. In her account of the UN's debates around the inclusion of what she terms 'positive sexual rights' (particularly, rights to sexual expression and sexual pleasure) under the broader umbrella of human rights, feminist scholar Rosalind Petchesky asks, 'Why is it so much easier to assert sexual freedom in a negative than in an affirmative, emancipatory sense; to gain consensus for the right not to be abused, exploited, raped, trafficked, or mutilated in one's body, but not the right to fully enjoy one's body?' (2000, p. 88). While fully acknowledging the need to define 'exclusionary rights' such as those outlined above (which might be understood as freedoms *from . . .*), she (and her fellow activists) asserts the necessity of positive sexual rights or freedoms *to*, which, she argues, are contingent on a number of (not yet defined) ' *ethical principles . . .* and *enabling conditions*' (Petchesky, 2000, pp. 91–92, original emphasis).

Almost 16 years after Petchesky published her provocation regarding the necessity of defining ethical principles and enabling conditions for the recognition of sexual rights (which explicitly included the possibility of 'positive rights' not only for adults but also for children and young people), it is worth reflecting on how much (or little) may have changed as young people have increasingly gained access to sexual information via digital technologies. While not all young people have the same capacity to access digital technologies, Livingstone and Mason (2015) have noted that 'online sources of information about sexual health are important to all young people, and especially to low income, lesbian, gay, bisexual and transgender (LGBT) and homeless youth' (p. 9). The authors note, however, that more research is needed to understand the ways in which young people engage with this information. Furthermore, these same authors observe a lack of detailed evidence about the role that 'parents, schools and web resources' *currently* play in supporting young people's search for relevant information and, importantly, the role that professionals *should* play in this context (2015, p. 9). That is, there is a lack of evidence and consensus regarding 'best practice' in terms of educational content and delivery. Reflecting on Petchesky's vision of positive sexual citizenship, it would seem that a combination of both access to information and self-representation *and* evidence-based support frameworks are key enabling conditions for the development and support of young people's (digital) sexual rights.

## EDUCATION, SEXTING AND CITIZENSHIP

In Australia, much of the early discourse around sexting focused on protecting young people from sexual misconduct. Along with my 2010 co-authors, Estelle Noonan and Nina Funnell, Kate Crawford and I were particularly interested in the liminal position of Australian youth aged 16 and 17. These young people are deemed over the age of consent for sexual encounters, but cannot consent to mediated sexual self-representation due to their position as 'children' under Commonwealth law. As we noted then, Australian 16- and 17-year-olds are vulnerable to being charged as 'sex offenders' due to laws that are intended to *protect* them from adult predators. As US commentator Judith Levine observes, these laws create a confused and confusing subject positon for the 'sexting teen' who is both victim *and* perpetrator of child pornography offences (Levine, 2009).

In late 2010, the Australian Federal Police's ThinkUKnow education programme released a 'sexting ed' public service announcement, entitled *Megan's Story*. The initial teaching resources accompanying the campaign warned young people that 'once something is created in a digital format and then shared, you lose control over who sees it and what they do with it' (ThinkUKnow, 2010). As we observed, the video and its supporting materials did not raise the issue of the ethics (or legal consequences) of sharing another person's selfie (Albury & Crawford, 2012). Rather, the focus is on Megan, the misguided sexting teen, and her subsequent humiliation and shame when an unnamed boy forwards her picture to her entire class (including their male teacher).

We argued that like rape prevention education that focuses exclusively on encouraging women to monitor and restrict their own behaviour (while overlooking the role of perpetrators of sexual violence) '*Megan's Story* seems to emphasise an individual incident of "bad choices" and loss of control, without looking at the broader context of the classroom or the law' (2012, p. 465). When viewed alongside cybersafety messages promoting 'exclusionary rights', but *not* rights to participation in digital spaces, educational texts such as *Megan's Story* do not so much promote an understanding of young people's digital (and sexual) rights and responsibilities, as endorse quotidian forms of gender policing such as gossip and public humiliation as deterrents for 'wayward' sexual experimentation.

This does not mean that Australian laws do not play a significant role in defining (and delimiting) young people's sexual rights. In 2010, my colleagues and I drew on the work of political scientist Judith Bessant (2004) to consider the ways that children's rights (and, by extension, citizenship) are expressed in contemporary Australian law and policy.

Like Petchesky, Bessant acknowledges a spectrum of human rights incorporating both positive and exclusionary rights. She notes that as a signatory to United Nations Convention on the Rights of the Child (UNCROC, 1989), Australia commits not only to protect children and young people from actual and potential harms but also to protect their access to certain positive rights, or freedoms *to*. With this in mind, Bessant critiques the Northern Territory government's imposition of curfews (or restrictions of freedom of movement) in the name of 'protecting' children and young people. Considering the ways that protection can be seen to conflict with the UNCROC commitments, Bessant observes, 'The discriminatory nature of curfews is apparent when considering the likely reaction if any other specific group were to be excluded from public space on the grounds they *may* commit crimes in the future, or because they *may* become victims of crime' (Bessant, 2004, p. 395).

It should be acknowledged that legal and educational frameworks that address young people's sexualities via a lens of rights (and consent) can be confronting for educators and other concerned adults, who may view their primary responsibility as preventing digital sexual experimentation (i.e. abstinence), rather than promoting safety or harm reduction. In Australia, as elsewhere, a growing number of government agencies, non-government organisations and private consultancies are beginning to develop face-to-face training and resource packages for professional educators, parents and young people (Johnson, 2012; Ollis et al., 2013; Walsh et al., 2016). However, many resources currently address mobile and online practices (including sexting) primarily from the perspective of bullying and/or technological 'risk to reputation' (Albury et al., 2013; Dobson & Ringrose, 2016).

This approach has been broadly critiqued by researchers in education, media and cultural studies, gender and sexuality studies and criminology in Australia, North America and the United Kingdom (Hasinoff, 2012; Ringrose et al., 2012; Albury et al., 2013; Crofts et al., 2015; Hasinoff, 2015; Dobson & Ringrose, 2016), for failing to reflect young people's own accounts of participation in mediated sexual cultures. As noted above, these researchers also raise concerns regarding the tendency of many sexting 'prevention' campaigns and resources to reinforce shaming and stigmatising approaches to young people's sexuality and gender expressions. Again, this response by (well-meaning) educators has parallels with the broader field of sexual violence prevention. In reflecting on the challenges in developing best-practice standards for Australian education aimed at the primary prevention of sexual violence (Carmody et al., 2009), Evans et al. (2009) observe that the 'pedagogical approach when educating young people about sexual relationships is contested terrain', in that many educators are not only unfamiliar with effective approaches to sexuality education, but actively oppose the notion of 'young people as being competent social actors capable of making sense of sexual and intimate relationships' (Evans et al., 2009, p. 15).

Beyond the classroom, there are many adults (including those involved in child welfare and law enforcement) who support the continued application of child pornography laws to young people who engage in consensual sexting, arguing that the harsh legal penalties serve as a deterrent to young people who might take or share pictures without consent (Albury et al., 2013). This approach demonstrates the same disconnect that Bessant (2004) observes in her account of the curfew laws, in that young people's sexual rights are restricted to protect them from (potential) future harm that may or may not eventuate.

## THE *YOUNG PEOPLE AND SEXTING IN AUSTRALIA* STUDY

While there was a great deal of media coverage of the legal and social implications of sexting from 2009 onwards, we saw no evidence that young people in Australia (or elsewhere) had been consulted regarding the impact of existing laws, and/or the desirability and substance of law reform. Consequently, in the initial stage of our study, we invited young people aged 16–17 years to directly reflect on (1) legal understandings of sexting, (2) penalties for sexting and (3) representations of 'teen sexting' practices in popular media and educational videos produced for use in schools (Albury et al., 2013).[3] Our participants rejected the word 'sexting' as a loaded term used primarily by teachers and journalists and preferred the more neutral terms 'pictures' and 'selfies', and I use these terms interchangeably with sexting throughout this chapter.

Our study generated a 'taxonomy of sexting' that not only distinguished between consensual and non-consensual picture sharing but also acknowledged 'joke' or 'prank' images and 'private selfies', which were intended for self-reflection rather than sharing (Albury et al., 2013; Albury, 2015). These distinctions could only be drawn because the participants in our study were invited to engage with adult discourses within a rights-based framework— that is, they were invited to reflect on adult perceptions (and misperceptions) of digital media practices, rather than disclose their own practices, or those of their friends or peers. This approach was initially adopted primarily to avoid circumstances in which young people might incriminate themselves in relation to their own sexting practices (Albury et al., 2013). However, it had the unintended effect of significantly extending the existing debate on sexting, and was subsequently hailed for adopting an innovative and ethical stance in relation to young people and risk in new media (Barbovschi et al., 2013).

Participants in Stage One emphasised the importance of considering consent when determining whether or not legal penalties should apply to any given incident of sexting. While our sample size was small (17 participants in all), our finding reflected those of a much larger mixed-methods study conducted by the National Children's and Youth Law Centre, and NSW Children's Legal Aid (Tallon et al., 2012). A majority of the 1000 young people surveyed by Tallon and colleagues also supported penalties for taking or sharing images without consent, but opposed the application of child pornography laws to under-18s (2013). Similarly, participants in Crofts et al.'s (2015) study, which included focus groups and a survey of 1400 Australian young people, found that participants drew distinctions between consensual picture sharing and abuse. These three studies specifically adopted a rights-based approach, inviting young people to reflect on the 'problem' of sexting in their own terms.

## THE USES AND LIMITATIONS OF DIGITAL SEXUAL CITIZENSHIP

My colleagues and I began our reflection on sexting and sexual citizenship by revisiting Stuart Hall's discussion of the term 'representation' (Hall, 1997). Our questions were as follows: Who has the 'right' to sexual self-representation? What responsibilities are implied? What kinds of political understandings of sex, gender and citizenship are implicit within 'anti-sexting' policy and educational content? As we observed, Hall's exploration of the double meaning of representation is significant here. Representation is political—our local member of parliament offers us representation, when they 'stand in' for us, their citizens. The term 'representation' is also used in a perjorative sense, implying that something 'real' has been corrupted or obscured. However, as we observed in 2010:

> Hall argues that even thoughts and feelings, which most of us consider entirely 'real', personal, and unmediated need to be represented (communicated through language, gesture or visual image) if they are to be understood by others. This process is not transparent. As Hall puts it, 'meaning is a dialogue—always only partially understood, always an unequal exchange' (Hall, 1997, p. 4). . . . The question for those who study visual representation is 'does visual language reflect a truth about the world which is already there or does it produce meanings about the world through representing it?' (Hall, 1997, p. 7). (Albury et al., 2010, p. 7)

Taking Hall's work as a point of departure, we asked what it means in terms of young people's citizenship (or subjectivity) when they are excluded from legitimate sexual self-representation? Participants in the *Young People and Sexting in Australia* study identified a range of circumstances in which such pictures might be produced and shared. Some pictures were intended for what Crofts et al. (2015) have termed erotic 'gift exchange' within intimate relationships. Others were intended to be shared with platonic friends, either as jokes, to display 'fitness' (both in terms of sexual attractiveness and muscle development), or to share images of new underwear or swimwear (see Albury, 2015). Some naked or semi-naked images (which participants termed 'private selfies') were only ever intended to be seen by their creator, for the purposes of self-reflection, or self-contemplation (Albury et al., 2013, Albury, 2015). While the creators of these pictures may well have struck 'pornified' poses in some of their selfies, the contexts surrounding the creation and sharing of this diverse range of images clearly transcend any simple definition of 'teen sexting'. In light of this diversity of context and meaning, what opportunities for education and practical support and engagement are lost when adults read young people's naked or semi-naked selfies not as acts of self-representation and sexual citizenship, but only as 'self-objectification'? (See Albury, 2015.)

In asking this question, it is important to acknowledge that sexual rights and sexual citizenship (or intimate citizenship) are not unproblematic concepts. For example, Correa et al. observe that while such rights may be acknowledged within legislative, medical and policy frameworks that privilege heterosexual reproduction and normative family structures, they often rely on the exclusion of bad 'others' (2008, p. 161). These others (who include 'promiscuous youth') may be dehumanised (and thus denied sexual rights) when they 'fail to conform to normative standards of sexual truth', thus 'justifying' legal, medical or moral interventions (2008, p. 159). Certainly, this kind of classification of claims to sexual citizenship can be seen in contemporary debates regarding same-sex marriage, in which the 'politics of respectability' are deployed in claims for legitimacy (Warner, 2000). Further, Evans (1993) links sexual rights and sexual citizenship not with self-representation, but commodification. As my co-authors and I observed in 2010, 'Evans proposes that in regimes of sexual citizenship, young people's rights "are directly linked to [their] proto-roles as consumer and earner"'. In these respects, he argues, children [and young people] are learning 'what there is to say "yes" to, and to recognise that both answers involve economic, political as well as sexual judgments' (1993, p. 239; Albury et al., 2010, p. 7).

How, then, might these limitations be addressed in relation to young people and sexting? One immediate (and highly desirable) response would be the decriminalisation of consensual, non-exploitative picture exchange between young people aged under 18. Another would be further scholarly and applied research of the kind called for by Livingstone and Mason (2015), which not only seeks to define 'best practice' for adults seeking to support young people's sexual learning, but foregrounds young people's participation, as emphasised in UNCROC frameworks. These responses might undo some of the hierarchy of 'good' and 'bad' sexual expression identified by Correa et al. (2008), but could justly be termed 'top down' approaches (even where young people are involved in framing research agendas and law reform).

It is important to recognise that participants in digital sexual cultures have developed their own 'bottom up' strategies for exercising and promoting sexual rights and sexual citizenship that resist some of the limitations identified above. As Plummer observes, 'Rights and responsibilities are not "natural" or "inalienable" but have to be invented through human activities, and built into notions of communities, citizenship and identities' (1995, p. 150). What Plummer terms 'intimate citizenship' (similar to my conception of sexual citizenship) 'is concerned with all those matters linked to our most intimate desires, pleasures and ways of being in the world. Some of this must feed back into traditional citizenship; but equally, much of it is concerned with new spheres, new debates, and new stories' (Plummer, 1995, p. 151). While some of these stories are being shaped in opposition to digital sexual cultures, others are being shaped *through* them.

## SELFIE CITIZENSHIP

Drawing on Plummer's definitions outlined above, the production and sharing of naked and semi-naked selfies can be seen as a new sphere of digital sexual citizenship. To be clear, I am not describing these practices in order to prescribe (or even recommend) them to young people aged under 18. Rather, I point to the range of ways in which images are being created and circulated by adults to challenge the notion that sexting is inevitably a site of gendered risk and shame, a view that has been used to legitimate surveillance, criminalisation and abstinence-focused educational responses to young people's consensual practices.

For example, recent queer and feminist scholarship in the emerging field of selfie research has called attention to ways that 'public' selfie cultures on social media platforms such as Tumblr and Instagram (which are not always explicitly erotic, but often intensely gendered) can be understood as highly politicised sites of sexual identity formation (e.g. Fink & Miller, 2014; Tiidenberg, 2014; Warfield, 2014). While such sites are far from utopian, they are far more open to embracing sexual and gender diversities than traditional (or legacy) forms of media. Both male and female same-sex-attracted participants in Stage Two of the *Young People and Sexting in Australia* project spoke of explicit and non-explicit picture exchange both on platforms such as Tumblr and privately within dating and hook-up apps, as an 'ordinary' process that was used to establish trust with potential sexual partners. For these groups, consensual sexting was seen as an un-remarkable relational practice. While participants expressed many everyday reasons why they (or others) might choose *not* to share pictures, the practice was only considered problematic when trust was breached, and pictures were produced or shared without consent (Albury & Byron, 2014).

As a range of researchers have observed, adult participants in Not Safe For Work (NSFW)[4] selfie cultures have developed collective standards of ethics and aesthetics. Far from being humiliated when their pictures are shared, many NSFW selfie producers *invite* feedback for their anonymised sexual self-representations on a range of public sites, from reddit's gonewild (see Van der Nagel, 2013) to the Tumblr site *Critique My Dickpic*, which offers dick pic contributors of all genders 'objective, honest' and 'body positive' feedback, rating their photo composition and aesthetics of self-presentation from A+ to D– (Holden, 2016; Sara, 2016). These sites, alongside other forms of popular pedagogy (such as the online comic *Oh Joy Sex Toy* promoting legally and ethically informed strategies for what might be termed 'safer sexting' (Moen & Nolan, 2014)) point to adult cultures of community building against the potentially shaming and shameful practice of sexual self-representation. Such 'bottom up' or vernacular practices of sexual citizenship are not always organised or public. Some are intimate and are private practices of support or solidarity. For example, popular accounts of young women's practices of picture sharing deploy terms such as 'frexting' (friend-sexting) to describe the private exchange of intimate selfies as a form of affirmation and bonding between platonic female friends (McKay, 2016).[5]

Finally, practices of picture sharing can be invoked to promote other forms of digital citizenship that can be seen to intersect with the formation of sexual citizenship. The online zine, *Safer Nudes: a sexy guide to digital security* (Felize & Varon, 2015), not only encourages safer sexting, but promotes digital security strategies such as the use of VPNs, encryption and image-scrambling apps as techniques to avoid both unwanted picture sharing and government surveillance. In this instance, the risks of unwanted picture sharing are not met with abstinence messages, but with instructions for increasing one's practical digital literacy skills. The resource includes contact information for feminist organisations that challenge online abuse and revenge porn (such as takebackthetech.net), and a first person account of the gendered and racialised politics of taking and sharing sexy selfies.

## CONCLUSION

As this chapter has outlined, for the past five years or so, popular and expert anxieties around young people's engagement with mediated sexual cultures have focused on the potential risks associated with practices of sexual self-representation and image exchange. While I do not seek to diminish legitimate concerns regarding mediated abuse and exploitation (including revenge porn and non-consensual sexting), I have drawn on a rights-based framework to suggest alternative understandings of young people's consensual practices. Further, I have expanded the inquiry into the political implications of the criminalisation of young people's practices of sexual citizenship that formed the stepping-off point of the *Young People and Sexting in Australia* project. At the same time, I have acknowledged the growing body of scholarship that foregrounds young people's own accounts of taking and sharing sexy selfies, and calls for both the decriminalisation of consensual picture sharing and for supportive policy and education approaches that acknowledge young people as sexual subjects.

Throughout, I have envisaged 'digital sexual citizenship' not only in terms of rights to freedom from sexed and gendered abuse and exploitation but also in terms of young people's positive entitlements. Following UNCROC Article 13, I suggest such entitlements include not only access to information about their own bodies and identities, but also platforms for mediated communication, and self-representation. Finally, I have drawn on the emerging field of selfie research to explore adult engagements with sexting that directly address issues of sexual and digital exploitation. These engagements not only present new models for ethical behaviour, but also promote new literacies that support diverse forms of sexual self-representation. These strategies can be seen to represent the foundations of a nascent (and still contested) space of digital sexual citizenship.

## NOTES

1. New South Wales Government (2009). *Safe Sexting: No Such Thing Information Sheet for Parents*. Retrieved from http://www.schools.nsw.edu.au/news/announcements/yr2009/may/sexting.php.

2. UNCROC (United Nations Convention on the Rights of the Child) (1989) Adopted by the General Assembly of the United Nations, 20 November. Retrieved from: http://www2.ohchr.org/english/law/crc.htm.

3. Recruitment and data collection procedures for Stages One and Two of the *Young People and Sexting in Australia* project were approved by the Human Research Ethics Committee at The University of New South Wales Australia (Reference: HC12050). In addition to conducting three focus groups with young people aged 16–17 years, we also invited a range of adult stakeholders (including academic researchers, adolescent healthcare providers, representatives from youth legal services, representatives of state and federal police, sexual assault service providers and a retired Family Court judge) to provide feedback on our draft findings and recommendations, and to

participate in an interdisciplinary roundtable discussion. In Stage Two, we collaborated with ACON (formerly the AIDS Council of NSW) to conduct three further focus groups with self-identified same-sex-attracted young people aged 18–26 years.

4. The acronym NSFW, or Not Safe For Work, is generally used to flag sexually explicit images on sites such as Tumblr.

5. The *Hello Giggles* website on which McKay's (2016) frexting story appears does not describe frexting as a high-school aged women's practice. However the site has a designated 'Teen' category, so clearly views under-18s as part of its target audience. Neilsen et al. (2015) study of young Finnish women (aged 11–18) also found that many participants understood sexual picture sharing and messaging among peers as a form of sexual play.

## REFERENCES

Albury, K. (2015). Selfies, sexts and sneaky hats: Young people's understandings of gendered practices of self-representation. *International Journal of Communication, 9,* 1734–1745

Albury, K., & Byron, P. (2014). Queering sexting and sexualisation. *Media International Australia,* (153), 138–147.

Albury, K., Byron, P., Crawford, K., & Mathews, B. (2013). *Young people and sexting in Australia: Ethics, representation and the law.* Sydney: The University of New South Wales.

Albury, K., & Crawford, K. (2012). Sexting, consent and young people's ethics: Beyond Megan's Story. *Continuum, 26*(3), 463–473.

Albury, K., Funnell, N., & Noonan, E. (2010). *The politics of sexting: Young people, self-representation and citizenship.* Paper presented at the Published in proceedings of the Australian and New Zealand Communication Association Conference: Media, Democracy and Change, Canberra.

Barbovschi, M., Green, L., & Vandoninck, S. (Eds.). (2013). *Innovative approaches for investigating how young children understand risk in new media: Dealing with methodological and ethical challenges.* LSE London: EU Kids Online, London School of Economics and Political Science.

Bessant, J. (2004). Mixed messages: Youth participation and democratic practice. *Australian journal of political science, 39*(2), 387–404.

Carmody, M., Evans, S., Krogh, C., Flood, M., Heenan, M., & Ovenden, G. (2009). *Framing best practice: National standards for the primary prevention of sexual assault through education.* Sydney: National Sexual Assault Prevention Education Project, University of Western Sydney and Melbourne, VicHealth.

Chalfen, R. (2009). "It's only a picture": Sexting, "smutty" snapshots and felony charges 1. *Visual Studies, 24*(3), 258–268.

Crofts, T., Lee, M., McGovern, A., & Milivojevic, S. (2015). *Sexting and young people.* Houndmills, UK: Palgrave Macmillan.

Dobson, A. S., & Ringrose, J. (2016). Sext education: pedagogies of sex, gender and shame in the schoolyards of Tagged and Exposed. *Sex Education, 16*(1), 8–21.

Evans, S. P., Krogh, C., & Carmody, M. (2009). *'Time to get cracking': The challenge of developing best practice in Australian sexual assault prevention education*: Australian Institute of Family Studies.

Felize, N., & Varon, J. (2015). Safer nudes: A sexy guide to digital security. Retrieved from http://www.codingrights.org/wp-content/uploads/2015/11/zine_ingles_lado2.pdf.

Fink, M., & Miller, Q. (2014). Trans media moments Tumblr, 2011–2013. *Television & New Media, 15*(7), 611–626.

Gill, R. (2007). Gender and the Media. Polity.

Hall, S. (1997). The work of representation. In S. Hall (Ed.), *Representation: Cultural representations and signifying practices* (pp. 13–74). London: Sage.

Harris, A. (2015). Discourses of desire as governmentality: Young women sexuality and the significance of safe spaces. *Feminism and Psychology, 15*(1), 39–43.

Hasinoff, A. A. (2012). Sexting as media production: Rethinking social media and sexuality. *New Media & Society, 15*(4), 449–465.

Hasinoff, A. A. (2015). *Sexting Panic: Rethinking criminalization, privacy, and consent*. Urbana: University of Illinois Press.

Hill, K. (2015). The Ashley Madison hack, and the value of averting your eyes. *Fussion*. Retrieved from http://fusion.net/story/185749/the-ashley-madison-hack-and-the-value-of-averting-your-eyes/.

Holden, M. (2016). Critique My Dick Pick, *Tumblr*. Retrieved from http://critique-mydickpic.tumblr.com/.

Isaac, M. (2014). Nude photos of Jennifer Lawrence are latest front in online privacy debate. *New York Times*. Retrieved from http://www.nytimes.com/2014/09/03/technology/trove-of-nude-photos-sparks-debate-over-online-behavior.html.

Johnson, B. (2012). *They need to know...: A report on teachers' use of the South Australian Relationships and Sexual Health Curriculum*. Adelaide.

Levine, J. (2009). Decent Exposure. May. Retrieved from http://judithlevine.com/.

Livingstone, S., & Mason, J. (2015). *Sexual rights and sexual risks among youth online: a review of existing knowledge regarding children and young people's developing sexuality in relation to new media environments*. London: European NGO Alliance for Child Safety Online.

McKay, A. (2016). How "frexting" taught me to love my body. Retrieved from http://hellogiggles.com/frexting-changed-body-image/.

McRobbie, A. (2009). *The aftermath of feminism: Gender, culture and social change*. London: Sage.

Moen, E., & Nolan, M. (2014). 'How to selfie like a boss'. Retrieved from http://www.ohjoysextoy.com/selfie/.

New South Wales Government (2009). Safe sexting: No such thing information sheet for parents. Retrieved from http://www.schools.nsw.edu.au/news/announcements/yr2009/may/sexting.php.

Ollis, D., Harrison, L., & Maharaj, C. (2013). Sexuality education matters: Preparing pre-service teachers to teach sexuality education. Burwood: Deakin University.

Petchesky, R. (2000). Sexual rights: Inventing a concept, mapping an international practice. In R. Parker, R. G. Barbosa, & P. Aggleton (Eds.), *Framing the sexual* subject: *The politics of gender, sexuality, and power* (pp. 81–103). Berkley: University of California Press.

Plummer, K. (2002). *Telling sexual stories: Power, change and social worlds*. London: Routledge.

Ringrose, J., Gill, R., Livingstone, S., & Harvey, L. (2012). *A qualitative study of children, young people and "sexting"*. London: NSPCC. Retrieved from http://www.lse.ac.uk/media%40lse/documents/MPP/Sexting-Report-NSPCC.pdf.

Sara, M. (2016). "Critique my dick pic" is a body positive approach to sexting: BUST interview (NSFW) *BUST*. Retrieved from http://bust.com/sex/16085-critique-my-dick-pic-interview.html.

Senft, T. M., & Baym, N. K. (2015). What does the selfie say? Investigating a global phenomenon, introduction. *International Journal of Communication, 9*, 1588–1606.

Tallon, K., Choi, A., Keeley, M., Elliott, J., & Maher, D. (2012). *New Voices/New Laws: School-age young people in New South Wales speak out about the criminal laws that apply to their online behaviour*. Sydney: National Children's and Youth Law Centre and Legal Aid NSW.

Third, A., Bellerose, D., Dawkins, U., Keltie, E., & Pihl, K. (2014). *Children's rights in the digital age: A download from children around the world*, Melbourne: Young and Well Cooperative Research Centre.

Tiidenberg, K. (2014). Bringing sexy back: Reclaiming the body aesthetic via self-shooting. *Cyberpsychology: Journal of Psychosocial Research on Cyberspace, 8*(1), 3.

Van der Nagel, E. (2013). Faceless bodies: Negotiating technological and cultural codes on Reddit Gonewild. *Scan: Journal of Media Arts Culture, 10*(2).

Walsh, J., Mitchell, A., & Hudson, M. (2015). The practical guide to love, sex and relationships for years 7–10. Retrieved from http://www.lovesexrelationships.edu.au/.

Warfield, K. (2014). *Making selfies/making self: Digital subjectivities in the selfie*. Paper presented at the Fifth International Conference on the Image and the Image Knowledge Community, Berlin, Oct 29–30.

Warner, M. (2000). *The trouble with normal: Sex, politics, and the ethics of queer life*. Boston: Harvard University Press.

*Chapter 13*

# Civic Practices, Design and Makerspaces

## Pip Shea

Makerspaces have helped frame processes of design, adaptation and the repair of things and systems—hardware, software, networks, tools, food, currencies, energy, bacteria—as social activities (Sleigh et al., 2015). Makerspaces have also been revealed as sites that encourage self-directed civic practices and the assembling of new civic identities, or *DIY citizenship* (Toombs et al., 2014; Nascimento, 2015; Kubitschko, 2015; Shea, 2015; Hunsinger and Schrock, 2016). This chapter offers an additional contextual review and further evidence of emergent civic practices linked to makerspaces, focusing attention on peace-building projects in Northern Ireland. It specifically examines the role of design and material engagement in the performance of these ethical and social interventions. The study elucidates how the propagation of alternative thinking and responsible action in Northern Ireland's makerspaces is challenging normative understandings of civic participation.

Digital and networked technologies have contributed to a major shift in the ways we understand ourselves as citizens and how we view and perform everyday activities. The accessibility of information, the ubiquity of wireless connectivity, and the development of software platforms that mediate interactivity have manifested in a participatory turn in contemporary culture. This paradigm of participation now permeates aspects of society that were once deemed off limits for the untrained, the uneducated or the unwelcome. Networks and communities of practice are forming around different themes that help people perform and form new identities. The maker movement is one such area: a globally connected movement of *makers* who share an interest in do-it-yourself (DIY) philosophies and practices.

Maker communities are connected across networked software platforms and are developing around physical places called makerspaces and hackerspaces. Creative making activities can range from programming environmental sensors to laser cutting furniture, or brewing beer. Maker-spaces in different geographic locations share commonalities (Sleigh et al., 2015)—such as governance guidelines, accounting software or machine operation manuals—but the events and projects that emerge from these spaces reflect the socio-economics and politics of place. For example, as part of its European Union–funded peace-building activities, Fab Labs Northern Ireland engages people who wouldn't ordinarily seek out a digital fabrication lab. While Roco Creative Co-op in Sheffield—funded by social lender investment and community shares—offers a maker shed as part of a wider creative hub made up of gallery spaces, co-working facilities, independent retail outlets, a book shop, deli and beer shop.

Makerspaces are emerging at the grass roots, as well as within more traditional institutions such as schools, universities and libraries. Some makerspaces have been positioned as sites that shape new *civic* identities through cultural practices. The interplay between cultural practices and civic engagement has a long history in the context of European culture. In the mid-nineteenth century, much of British scholar John Ruskin's work revolved around the primacy of human creativity and how emergent industrial creative practices were oppressive and had a negative impact on the collective (cited in Gauntlett, 2011, p. 29). William Morris built on Ruskin's work, emphasising the role of creativity in community contexts. Like Ruskin, Morris rejected industrial creative practices and offered counter-cultural alternatives through expanded conceptions of creative practices and their relationship to place (cited in Gauntlett, 2011, p. 36).

Developing individual creative practices in order to represent oneself *in culture* has also been promoted as a route to enfranchisement by community arts and media movements in many parts of the world including Australia, Europe and North America. More recently, scholars have situated everyday domestic, leisure and consumption practices as acts of *cultural* citizenship. These are seen as civic activities in and of themselves as opposed to an enabler of civic participation (Hartley, 1999; Burgess, et al., 2006). Contemporary cultural citizenship practices still struggle for validation due to traditional views that civic engagement equates to participation in rational, verbal interactions about politics and current affairs. Other forms of participation that stress material perspectives on public engagement—such as grass-roots environmental initiatives—are often still unacknowledged in institutional framings of citizenship practices.

In an attempt to bolster evidence of material civic engagement within the maker movement, my study offers accounts from three makerspaces in Northern Ireland. Empirical data was collected over a two-year period. My observations were gleaned as a member and director of Farset Labs and as a user of Fab Lab Belfast. My role as director of the charity has enabled an added ethnographic dimension to this study as I have been exposed to the inner workings of the organisation. Desk-based research focused on online traces of projects and practices of Northern Ireland's makerspaces and scholarly literature investigating the wider maker community. The study specifically examines the role of design in the performance of these ethical and social interventions.

Civic practices in Northern Ireland are often conflated with peace-building rhetoric,[1] and therefore must be contextualised in relation to the sectarian conflict that began in the late 1960s, which in turn affects the rights and responsibilities of the citizenry. Colloquially known as *the Troubles*, this period was shaped by military and paramilitary violence by groups contesting the political sovereignty of Northern Ireland. The two groups in opposition were those who fought for the reunification of Northern Ireland with the Republic of Ireland, and those loyal to Britain who fought to remain part of the United Kingdom. Efforts to build peace culminated in 1998 with the signing of the Good Friday Agreement by Northern Ireland's political parties and the Irish and British governments. Although violence has subsided, reconciliation is ongoing, and top-down peace-building initiatives are common, though commonly contested (Murtagh, 2011). This contestation of top-down initiatives builds from a history of local social movements that emerged in underserved areas during the Troubles (Richmond & Mitchell, 2011; Acheson & Milofsky, 2008).

This study discusses challenges and opportunities associated with material civic practices shaped by makerspaces. It advocates for the ongoing resourcing and support of collaborative, material engagement in order to reveal the politics of designed things in civic contexts. It concludes with recommendations for further research to help makerspaces support civic activity.

## THEORETICAL GROUNDING

This study draws on Noortje Marres's (2015) 'material participation' thesis, Matt Ratto's (2011) 'critical making' proposal, and the political theory of 'agonism' (DiSalvo, 2012; Mouffe, 2000, 2013) to investigate and frame both critical and non-critical civic activities emerging from makerspaces. I use the term *material engagement* throughout the chapter to describe this spectrum of activities. Marres's take on material participation provides sightlines for my argument that makerspaces are enabling the design of *things* that facilitate civic action. Meanwhile Ratto's critical making proposal is used to underscore critical practices emerging from the collective energies of makerspaces. Agonism is used as a theoretical marker to highlight the productive frictions of the democratic project, to support design processes that embrace these frictions and to elucidate the Northern Irish post-conflict context.

Ideas and practices of civic material engagement are far from new. At the turn of the twentieth century, John Dewey proposed that political and moral phenomena unfold on the 'plane of objects' (1915, cited in Marres, 2015, p. 15). Towards the end of the twentieth century, Langdon Winner (1980) famously argued that explicit attention should be paid to the idea that artefacts and infrastructure have politics. Susan Leigh Star's (1999) response to this call was the application of ethnographic methods to the study of infrastructures, revealing methods for 'unfreezing' features that reveal political entanglements. These philosophical positions remain relevant in scholarly debates about the politics of objects and systems, because methods for countering these dynamics are still contested. This adds weight to the foundational argument of this study: that material engagement, critical or otherwise, can interrupt entrenched power.

Coined by sociologist Noorje Marres (2015), the term *material participation* brings attention to the role of 'things' in political participation. She is specifically concerned with everyday ways of dealing with things and how such activities reconfigure civic arrangements. Her thesis focuses on the multivalent nature of things, and pushes against two important areas of anti-materialist scholarship: classical political theory that conflates material entanglement with the private sphere of domesticity and leisure and modern social theory that renders industrial scale material objects a barrier to public participation (Marres, 2015, p. 10). The term 'material participation' encompasses practical philosophy, philosophy of technology and philosophical ecology. It promotes objects, devices and settings that enable civic action without 'investing time, money, attention, or ideology in the problem' (Marres, 2015, p. 10). Marres argues that political participation through things is enacted differently depending on the setting, and that material publics can form without individual, critical lenses (through designed things that turn political work into pragmatist living). Marres's work emerges from the recent 'material' and 'participatory' turns of media studies, sociology, feminist studies and science and technology studies.

Popularised by Matt Ratto, critical making refers to 'reflecting on how we build ourselves, our cultures, and our institutions through processes of material engagement'.[2] It attempts to conjoin conceptually based critical thinking and goal-based physical making (Ratto, 2011, p. 253). Ratto's rationale for merging these two activities is to reconcile the gaps between the practice and theory of technologies. Critical making differs from other approaches to design and making in that it focuses on 'the constructive process as the site for analysis' and emphasises the 'praxis oriented' activities and energies of the collective (Ratto, 2011, p. 253). Ratto's project is influenced by Ingold's insights in the *Textility of Making* (2010) which promotes an ontology that favours processes of formation and improvisational practice among material flows.

Agonism (agonistic pluralism) is a theory and practice of democracy that emphasises *dissensus*. It aspires to provide arenas where differences can be confronted rather than sidelined in the name of consensus. Chantal Mouffe's work is of particular interest as she uses agonism to argue that conflict and strife must be placed at the heart of democracy (2000). Agonism helps us be upfront about the contested sectarian civic politics of Northern Ireland, while suggesting that frictions arising from oppositional forces can be productive. It also creates a link with relevant design practices, such as Carl DiSalvo's (2012) adversarial design proposal: the practice of agonism through design. Adversarial design helps us 'move beyond understanding hegemony as simply a single-point exertion of force' by providing 'a view into the constitution of hegemony as a flexible conglomeration of individuals, organisations, ideologies and actions' (2012, p. 52).

Grounding this study in theories of material participation and critical making offers a way for us to consider both critical and non-critical forms of engagement in the material politics of living. Both act as lenses over *things*, in relation to humans, allowing us to view nuances, site-specificity and entanglements with other things. The political theory of agonism works to frame civic activity in the post-conflict Northern Irish context, while offering sightlines for future designed things that aspire to do the work of civic engagement.

## CONTEXTUAL REVIEW: MAKERSPACES AND CIVICS

Historical vectors leading to the current-day maker movement reveal strong ties with civic practices. Adrian Smith (2014) highlighted how the philosophies of the 'Movement for Socially Useful Production' of 1981 bear a striking resemblance to the ideas and practices underscoring the current maker movement. They emphasised 'tacit knowledge, craft skill, and learning by doing, through face-to-face collaboration in material projects' (2014, p. 7). These practical engagements in technology development were an intrinsic aspect of their politics, which as Smith points out, symbolised a reconnection with production at a community scale. Fifty years earlier, social ecologist Murray Bookchin speculated that collectives would organise around 'liberatory technologies' (Bookchin, 1967).

The Chaos Computer Club is widely considered to be the first grass-roots organisation in Europe to call itself a hackerspace. Empirical research has revealed that this organisation has evolved to serve as a 'civil society organization' that pools knowledge and skills that are increasingly 'relevant for political cultures and democracy at large' (Kubitschko, 2015, p. 1). However, the potentialities of makerspaces have been tempered with the argument that they are 'fringe phenomena' (Maxigas & Troxler, 2014) and that they have a marginal wider societal impact.

In previous writing, I have situated the case of Farset Labs as an enabler of alternative civic activity (Shea, 2015). Contrary to notions of citizenship equating to enfranchisement, the civic activities of Farset Lab members are often born of disenfranchisement. The lab itself emerged from frustration that certain services and communities were not being supported.[3] In response to my aforementioned article, founding director Andrew Bolster commented:

> A significant majority of the (member) population falls under what you could describe as the 'disenfranchised'; otherwise well-educated and experienced people that have been soured against politics (mainstream or otherwise) which they see as largely ineffectual grandstanding for their own good rather than for the good of the populace. In a way that frustration is what brought the labs about; we had ideas for projects, programmes, and outreach events we wanted to do/run, and no one seemed equipped to support them, so we did it ourselves.

Makerspaces often provide services to the community that are not, or cannot be provided by the state. They join a long line of third-sector initiatives that provide physical space and informal education, but defy the logic of traditional organisations as they 'develop under a tension between individualistic, entrepreneurial projects and collective, community based activities' (Siefkes, 2009; cited in Smith et al., 2013, pp. 7–8). The maker ethic inscribed in makerspaces has also been paradoxically situated as a complex negotiation of both a neo-liberal libertarian ethos and a 'care ethos' (Toombs et al., 2015).

The promise of material civic engagement associated with makerspaces emerges from the potentialities of communities of practice and distributed design—what Peter Troxler describes as the 'commons-based peer-production of physical goods' (2010, p. 1). The structures and dynamics of makerspaces have even been situated as somewhat replicating those of online communities who use commons-based production methods (Kostakis et al., 2015). As Smith at al. point out, the fact that 'high-tech capabilities are spreading into grassroots movements' is a significant turning point in the context of social movements (2013, p. 3). Similar to the ways in which digital networks signalled a paradigm shift in media and communications, low-cost digital fabrication machines and powerful consumer electronics offer citizens radical new approaches to production and consumption.

Despite runaway claims of an emergent 'industrial revolution' (Gershenfeld, 2005; Anderson, 2012) evidence exists to suggest that maker culture disperses production capacity, diminishes scale efficiencies and intensifies consumption through the personalisation of manufacturing (Smith et al., 2013). Questions of labour exploitation have also been raised about open, distributed design flows (Scholz, 2013). Civic hackathons—events often associated with maker culture—have been situated as arenas for 'provisional citizenship' (Gregg & DiSalvo, 2013) that cannot be disentangled from the current context of fiscal austerity (Gregg, 2015). Equity challenges that affect the performance of civics in makerspaces include the privileging of historically masculinised practices (Powell, 2012; Alper, 2013). This is true of both histories of technology and DIY practice. Engineering, computer programming and amateur electronics are all codified with white maleness, as is the original DIY movement of the 1960s/1970s, with its championing of self-directed home improvement. As Christina Dunbar-Hester notes, 'DIY itself has traditionally not been for just anyone' (2014, p. 85).

The case studies that follow bolster existing scholarly investigations of civic activity in makerspaces. Geographically situated in Northern Ireland, they offer perspectives from a post-conflict context. Even within this specific realm, the three makerspaces boast activities that are grounded in different political concerns. The civics of makerspaces reflect the people and places that shape them.

## CASE STUDIES: A FOCUS ON MAKERSPACES IN NORTHERN IRELAND

There are three spaces in Northern Ireland whose making practices focus on digital technologies: Farset Labs, Fab Lab Belfast and, Fab Lab Nerve Centre in Derry. These organisations were identified alongside 97 other UK makerspaces by National Endowment for Science, Technology and the Arts (NESTA) in its Open Dataset of UK Makerspaces.[4] Farset Labs is a non-profit company and registered charity based in Belfast. It is volunteer run and relies on a membership model of fundraising. People pay monthly or daily fees to gain access to the space, its machines and network of people. In contrast, Fab Lab Belfast and Fab Lab Nerve Centre Derry—collectively known as Fab Labs NI—focus their energies on *peace-building* initiatives. Fab Labs NI are supported by the European Union's Peace III Programme, a fund targeting peace and reconciliation in Northern Ireland and the border region of The Republic of Ireland.

First we will turn our attention to Fab Labs NI. Both these organisations form part of MIT's Fab Lab network, supported by the non-profit Fab Foundation. Both Fab Labs have full-time staff, enabling them to host school and community groups on a regular basis. Their activities focus on digital fabrication, providing an entry point for people to consider the materialities of digital technologies. Fab Labs NI comfortably address the criteria outlined in the Fab Foundation's *Fab Charter*[5]: both venues are open to the public for free or in-kind each week; they share designs among the wider Fab Lab network; and they adhere to the recommended list of Fab Lab equipment[6]:

- A laser cutter for making 3D structures from 2D designs
- A large CNC mill for making furniture and housing
- An NC knife and smaller mini-mill for making circuits and moulds for casting
- 3D printers
- An electronic workbench
- A suite of tooling and materials

Projects emanating from Fab Labs NI are grounded in *good relations* practices: meaning they aspire to bridge social divides in contested local contexts. This situates both Fab Labs as civic centres that serve their local communities while contributing to wider practices and discourses that serve the wider peace-building project currently under way in Northern Ireland. The *Transitional Justice Jigsaw Puzzle* is one such contribution. This project engaged women from a contested cultural area of Belfast in digital fabrication processes at the Fab Lab. They each made a jigsaw piece to represent their 'lived experiences of the conflict as well as their hopes for the future'.[7] The pieces were symbolically joined together to create a work that now hangs in the offices of the Victims and Survivors Service in Belfast.

In another show of civic activity, Fab Lab Belfast collaborated with the Forum for Alternative Belfast—a non-profit organisation that campaigns for a better and a more equitable built environment—to create plywood architectural models representing a speculative design for the city of Belfast. This project led to conversations about using laser-cut architectural models for participatory planning. Various approaches could be used to materially engage citizens and projects could focus on the *making* of models as a means to understanding the entanglements of planning, architecture and building processes.

In 2014, Fab Lab Nerve Centre undertook an ambitious civic engagement project called *Temple*. This initiative aimed to re-contextualise contested bonfire rituals performed by both Protestant and Catholic communities in the city of Derry. The project commissioned the Burning Man Festival's David Best to lead the community development of a digitally fabricated, wooden temple. Measuring 72-ft high, the temple was filled with messages and mementos from local communities and people who visited the structure. On March 21, it was ceremoniously burnt, turning associations of public bonfires on their head. The project tag line, 'built to burn, designed to heal', describes an event grounded in the civic intent of peace building. The temple structure was also recreated in *Minecraft*, appropriating a physical structure that began as digital material. Temple was an example of adversarial design: it appropriated a contested ritual to confront dissensus, and then used it as a medium for healing.

The Fab Lab Nerve Centre's association with Refugee Open Ware has been a widely publicised example of civic activity. This is the story of 3D printing techniques being used to make prosthetic limbs for casualties of the Syrian conflict.[8] Refugee Open Ware is a growing network of makerspaces in 'conflict-affected areas that provide training to displaced persons and host communities, while building solutions to the hardest problems facing victims of conflict'.[9] This classic example of distributed design through critical making has made a significant impact on the lives of refugees and created ongoing connections between conflict-affected societies and post-conflict Northern Ireland.

Turning our attention to Farset Labs, we see a rather different way of operating as an enabler of civic activity in Northern Ireland. While Fab Labs NI is concerned with nurturing maker agents through community development projects, Farset Labs primarily facilitates the activities of self-directed maker agents (with the exception of its outreach programmes Raspberry Jam and Farset Dojo).[10] Structured programmes feature heavily in the Fab Labs, while individual action is the primary source of momentum at Farset Labs.

Farset Labs is a non-profit company and registered charity based in Belfast. It was established in 2012 to respond to a demonstrated need for an independent, non-profit, charitable community of technology innovators. Farset Labs provides this community with an open space and shared resources to experiment, explore and grow themselves, their projects and relationships locally and globally. Currently, Farset Labs stands as a valued part of Northern Ireland's technology, entrepreneurship and STEM outreach communities, with collaborations with academia, government and the private sector. It is entirely volunteer run, funded primarily by membership fees. There are currently around 50 members. I became a director of Farset Labs in November 2015, alongside Andrew Bolster, David Kane, Dylan Wylie and Conor Robinson.

Farset Labs facilitates hacking activities in an environment that questions assumptions about the political entanglements of people, technology and things. Critical making activities emerging from the space emphasise how Farset Labs members intervene in the politics of everyday life. These activities range from hacks in the space itself—such as repurposing bubble wrap as window insulation—to encouraging other members to make their own home carbonation machines in response to ethical concerns over the corporate practices of Sodastream.[11] Farset Labs' Extendible Hardware License is another critical approach that provides a productive framework for hardware donations: people can recycle their unwanted technology by donating it to the Labs.

Farset Labs also supports the critical practices of other organisations that use the space to perform their own participatory design practices. Farset hosted the first *policy hack* organised by the Northern Ireland Council for Voluntary Action (NICVA). Through its policy hack series, this agency is borrowing 'the techniques and ethos of the tech sector, (to) apply them to a number of social policy topics and come up with solutions to key social, economic and environmental problems'.[12]

The governance mechanisms of Farset Labs set the tone of active participation: monthly town hall[13] meetings allow members to participate in the management of the organisation. Certain associations also shape perceptions and practices of the organisation. Farset members are involved in Northern Ireland's Tech for Good advocacy group; the lab has been engaged by Open Gov NI to host open data workshops, and is organising Maker Assembly NI, a daylong gathering of makers to critically discuss maker culture, its meaning, politics, history and future. Farset Labs also provides *somewhere to go*, when public spaces for working—such as libraries—are closed.

These examples have shown how material participation and critical making are entangled and emerging from the makerspaces of Northern Ireland. As citizens acquire the means to take matters in to their own hands—whether these *things* are designed by someone else, or self-made—they are renegotiating relationships between individuals, communities and the state.

## DISCUSSION

This study has established how emergent civic practices are renegotiating ideas of political participation in Northern Ireland. This is not surprising considering that it is a society with a history of disenfranchisement materialising as violent conflict. Among the raft of peace-building activities currently in motion are various initiatives calling for the proliferation of *social innovation*, for example, community share offerings in renewable energy non-profit organisations. Attached to the idea of social innovation is *Digital Social Innovation* (DSI). This term is gaining traction in the United Kingdom and Europe, and refers to the support and development of new digital solutions to address social challenges.[14] NESTA describes four main technological trends of DSI: open hardware, open networks, open data and open knowledge. A relevant takeaway from this report is that, of these four areas, the open hardware movement is the most closely networked. This highlights an opportunity to strengthen the flows of distributed designs that enable material participation: objects and systems that support people to incorporate pragmatic civic interventions. In a similar way that Refugee Open Ware is nurturing a network of makerspaces to develop open-source-appropriate technology for humanitarian purposes, designs could be more explicitly promoted as *things* for civic participation.

The potential of critical making in makerspaces is contingent on members recognising that their activities are being framed as civic practices. Applying the ideas and practices of Per-Anders Hillgren et al. (2011) is another way that critical making could get more of a foothold in the makerspace as they promote the practice of using prototypes as agonistic objects to reveal civic opportunities and dilemmas. This approach takes the idea of problem-solving through physical prototyping, but instead of solving the problem by design, they deliberately create a contentious prototype to allow people to freely discuss pros and cons. With this method, participants have material buy-in through shared construction, but they are actively revealing the politics of designed things.

This study has established that the constitution of civic action is diversifying. This phenomenon is captured in Matt Ratto and Megan Boler's edited collection *DIY Citizenship* (2014) and by the *Civic Media Project* (Gordon & Milhadis, 2015), a repository of over 100 short case studies of emergent modes of civic participation. But just as the promises of online participatory cultures were widely critiqued (Carr, 2010; Morozov, 2011), so have the promises of the maker movement. Jeremy Hunsinger and Andrew Schrock's (2016) edited collection deals with the contradictions of the democratising potential of making, drawing attention to how makers are often complicit in the exploitative practices of neo-liberalism and globalisation. This flags a need for evolving understandings of the interplay between makerspaces and civic activity.

Christina Dunbar-Hester's (2014) study of technology activist group *Pandora* supports the position for evolving understandings of the politics of DIY technology projects. She problematises 'universalist' approaches to these projects, arguing that white male activists parachuting in to communities to *improve* them—with technology—is fundamentally contentious. Other investigations of grass-roots technology making projects, support her claims (Powell, 2008; Jungnickel, 2009). To counter universalist approaches, Dunbar-Hester draws on Lucy Suchman's (2003) idea of 'located accountability' to support a call for activists to critique the social politics of technology. Her desire to foster 'radical inclusion' emerges from Donna Haraway's (1991) reminder that claiming to view a situation comprehensively requires seeing from a privileged position. This raises further questions when situating makerspaces as sites of civic activity, as the histories of DIY practice and technology making are sometimes exclusionary.

Designed software enables and constrains what happens in makerspaces; or, in the words of Ryan Schmidt and Matt Ratto, 'maker hardware requires maker software' (2013, p. 1). Kitchin and Dodge's *code/space* (2011) is a useful lens in this instance as it helps reveal software as a 'vital source of social power' (2011, p. 246). The 3D modelling software such as vector graphics packages, code repositories, chat applications, accounting software and word-processing tools are all implicated in the shaping of makerspaces. The corporate enclosures of maker software by large multinationals include

Google's acquisition of Sketchup and Autodesk's purchase of Instructables.[15] The seemingly share-happy Thingiverse—oft cited in speeches about how anyone can make anything—has also been revealed to heavily shape what *things* are available to make (Moilanen, et al., 2015). As so many maker-spaces are awash with techno-pragmatism, the appropriateness of software is determined by price, interoperability and general usefulness. Tools for help-ing people negotiate the code/space of makerspaces are limited, obstructing the *real* potential of civic engagement. Further research in this area could help reveal underlying structures and dynamics, to help practitioners navigate these emergent organisational forms.

## CONCLUSION

The accounts of civic activity offered in this study illustrate material partici-pation (pragmatist living as political work) and critical making (the combin-ing of critical thinking and physical making) at makerspaces in Northern Ireland. They show the ways in which civics are conceptualised and how practice is changing, and situate makerspaces as an emergent institutional form facilitating new civic media rituals. Makerspaces in the post-conflict context of Northern Ireland set a scene that emphasises alternative think-ing and responsible civic action. The sociotechnical dynamics of these civic activities are site specific and nuanced; some are performed through critical lenses, and some are not.

There are difficulties associated with recommending better practices and resources for makerspaces as they serve diverse communities with different needs. Fab Labs NI and Farset Labs are cases in point. Here are two organ-isations, sympathetic to each other's practices and ethics, occupying different positions on the civic participation spectrum. This provides further evidence of a need to study individual makerspaces to avoid the conflation of these very site-specific facilities. This echoes Susana Nascimento's call for those making decisions about makerspaces to 'direct their attention to the possibilities of empowerment for citizens and groups through the pursuit of social topics and goals' (2014, p. 3).

Ongoing scholarly engagement with identity politics in the makerspace is critical to the grass-roots citizenship project. The frictions between the needs and desires of the individual and the collective offer salient points of interrogation. These could offer sightlines for investment in practices that nurture inclusion in material deliberation activities. Questions about what constitutes *belonging* are also crucial to studies of civics and makerspaces, as notions of citizenship imply inclusion, or being on the inside of a nation state or community.

## NOTES

1. Civic activity and peace-building activity are often situated as one and the same in Northern Ireland. This conflation emerges from the need to re-establish civic practices in the aftermath of civil conflict. It is a strategy that can be very helpful in redirecting civic energies and acquiring funding; but it can be overused to the point where activities become unnecessarily burdened with the goal of building peace. In *Doing IT for Themselves: Management versus Autonomy in Youth E-Citizenship*, Stephen Coleman describes how Northern Ireland's WIMPS project helps to engage young people in politics. This example—like any other Youth E-Citizenship project— must be considered in its geopolitical context, but labeling it a peace-building project might be perceived as misguided or opportunistic.

2. Ratto, Matt and Megan Boler. Critical Making, Social Media, and DIY Citizenship: An Interview with Matt Ratto and Megan Boler (Part One)—by Henry Jenkins, 2014, http://henryjenkins.org/2014/05/critical-making-social-media-and-diy-citizenship-an-interview-with-matt-ratto-and-megan-boler-part-one.html#sthash.hlHg8y5r.dpuf.

3. Andrew Bolster's comments on: http://civicmediaproject.org/works/civic-media-project/diycitizenshipinthenewnorthernireland.

4. 'Top findings from the open dataset of UK makerspaces', NESTA, accessed November 18, 2015, http://www.nesta.org.uk/blog/top-findings-open-dataset-uk-makerspaces.

5. Fab Charter http://fab.cba.mit.edu/about/charter/.

6. 'Fab Lab Inventory spreadsheet' accessed November 12, 2015, https://docs.google.com/spreadsheets/d/1U-jcBWOJEjBT5A0N84IUubtcHKMEMtndQPLCkZCkVsU/pub?single=true&gid=0&output=html.

7. Rooney, Eilish. Transitional Justice Toolkit: A User's Guide. Transitional Justice Institute, University of Ulster (2012).

8. '3D printers used for prosthetic limbs in Syria conflict', BBC News, March 10, 2015, http://www.bbc.co.uk/news/uk-northern-ireland-foyle-west-31812040.

9. Ibid.

10. Farset's Raspberry Jam program is a monthly workshop exploring Raspberry Pi single-board computers. Farset Dojo events invite young people to the space to learn software programming skills and entry-level electronics.

11. DIY home carbonation machine http://www.popsci.com/diy/article/2012-06/how-make-your-own-home-carbonation-system.

12. 'Hacking our way to better outcomes', January 29, 2015, NICVA http://www.nicva.org/article/hacking-our-way-better-outcomes.

13. Town hall meetings invite members to actively govern the space. Town hall participants discuss events, facilities, finances, marketing and communications, and are invited to contribute to meeting agendas in shared online documents.

14. 'Growing a Digital Social Innovation Ecosystem for Europe', accessed October 5, 2015, http://www.nesta.org.uk/sites/default/files/dsireport.pdf.

15. 'More than just digital quilting', Available at http://www.economist.com/node/21540392.

# REFERENCES

Acheson, N., & Milofsky, C. (2008). Peace building and participation in Northern Ireland: Local social movements and the policy process since the 'Good Friday' Agreement. *Ethnopolitics, 7*(1), 63–80.

Alper, M. (2013). Making space in the makerspace: Building a mixed-ability maker culture. *Humanities, Arts, Science, and Technology Alliance and Collaboratory.* Retrieved from http://www.hastac.org/blogs/merylalper/2013/03/18/making-space-makerspace-buildingmixed-ability-maker-culture.

Bookchin, M. (1968). Towards a liberatory technology. *Anarchos,* 2. Retrieved from http://dwardmac.pitzer.edu/Anarchist_Archives/bookchin/tolibtechpart2.html.

Burgess, J., Foth, M., & Klaebe, H. (2006). Everyday creativity as civic engagement: A cultural citizenship view of new media. *Communications Policy & Research Forum.* Institute for Creative Industries and Innovation, Sydney, Australia.

Carr, N. (2010). *The shallows: What the internet is doing to our brains.* New York: W. W. Norton and Company.

Coleman, S. (2008). Doing IT for themselves: management versus autonomy in youth e-citizenship. In W. L. Bennett (Ed.), *Civic life online* (pp. 189–205). Cambridge, MA: MIT Press.

DiSalvo, C. (2012). *Adversarial design.* Cambridge, MA: MIT Press.

Dunbar-Hester, C. (2014). Radical inclusion? Locating accountability in technical DIY. In M. Ratto and M. Boler (Eds) DIY citizenship: Critical making and social media (pp. 75–88). Cambridge, MA: MIT Press.

Gauntlett, D. (2011). *Making is connecting: The social meaning of creativity, from DIY and knitting to YouTube and web 2.0.* Cambridge, UK: Polity Press.

Gershenfeld, N. (2005). *FAB: The coming revolution on your desktop. From personal computers to personal fabrication.* Cambridge, MA: Basic Books.

Gordon, E., & Milhadis, P. (2015). *The civic media project.* Retrieved from http://civicmediaproject.org.

Gregg, M. (2015). Hack for good: Speculative labor, app development and the burden of austerity. *Fibreculture,* (25). Retrieved from http://twentyfive.fibreculturejournal.org/fcj-186-hack-for-good-speculative-labour-app-development-and-the-burden-of-austerity/.

Gregg, M., & DiSalvo, C. (2013). The trouble with white hats. *The New Inquiry.* October. Retrieved from http://thenewinquiry.com/essays/the-trouble-with-white-hats/.

Haraway, D. (1991). *Simians, cyborgs, and women.* New York: Routledge.

Hartley, J. (1999). *Uses of television.* London: Routledge.

Hillgren, P. A., Seravalli, A., & Emilson, A. (2011). Prototyping and infrastructuring in design for social innovation. *CoDesign: International Journal of CoCreation in Design and the Arts, 7*(3–4), 169–83.

Hunsinger, J., & Schrock, A. J. (2016). The democratization of hacking and making. *New Media & Society, 18*(4), 535–38.

Ingold, T. (2010). The textility of making. *Cambridge Journal of Economics, 34*(1), 91–102.

Jungnickel, K. (2009). *Making WiFi: A sociological study of backyard technologists in suburban Australia.* Goldsmiths College London: PhD Thesis.

Kitchin, R., & Dodge, M. (2011). *Code/space: Software and everyday life.* Cambridge, MA: MIT Press.

Kostakis, V., Niaros, V., & Giotitsas, C. (2015). Production and governance in hackerspaces: A manifestation of commons-based peer production in the physical realm? *International Journal of Cultural Studies, 18*(5), 555–73.

Kubitschko, S. (2015). Hackers' media practices: Demonstrating and articulating expertise as interlocking arrangements. *Convergence, 21*(3), 388–402

Marres, N. (2012). *Material participation: Technology, the environment and everyday publics.* New York: Palgrave Macmillan.

Maxigas, and Troxler, P. (2014). Shared machine shops: Editorial. *Journal of Peer Production, (5)*. Retrieved from http://peerproduction.net/issues/issue-5-shared-machine-shops/.

Moilanen, J., Daly, A., Lobato, R., & Allen, D. (2015). Cultures of sharing in 3d printing: What can we learn from the licence choices of thingiverse users? *Journal of Peer Production, (6)*. Retrieved from http://peerproduction.net/issues/issue-6-disruption-and-the-law/.

Morozov, E. (2011). *The net delusion: How not to liberate the world.* London: Penguin.

Mouffe, C. (2013). *Agonistics: Thinking the world politically.* London: Verso.

Mouffe, C. (2000). *The democratic paradox.* London: Verso.

Murtagh, B. (2011). Desegregation and place structuring in the new Belfast. *Urban Studies, 48*(8), 1119–1135.

Nascimento, S. (2015). Critical notions of technology and the promises of empowerment in shared machine shops. *Journal of Peer Production, (5)*. Retrieved from http://peerproduction.net/issues/issue-5-shared-machine-shops/.

Powell, A. (2012). Democratizing production through open source knowledge: From open software to open hardware. *Media, Culture, and Society, 34*(6), 691–708.

Powell, A. (2008). WiFi publics: Producing community and technology. *Information, Communication & Society, 11*(8), 1068–1088.

Ratto, M. (2011). Critical making: Conceptual and material studies in technology and social life. *The Information Society: An International Journal, 27*(4), 252–260.

Ratto, M., & Boler, M. (Eds.). (2014). *DIY citizenship: Critical making and social media.* Cambridge MA: MIT Press.

Richmond, O. P., & Mitchell, A. (2011). Peacebuilding and critical forms of agency: From resistance to subsistence. *Alternatives: Global, Local, Political, 36*(4), 326–344.

Schmidt, R., & Ratto, M. (2013). *Design-to-fabricate: Maker hardware requires maker software.* Autodesk Research. Retrieved from http://www.autodeskresearch.com/pdf/CGAFabricationSpecialIssue2013.pdf.

Scholz, T. (Ed.). (2013). *Digital labor: The internet as playground and factory.* New York: Routledge.

Shea, P. (2015). DIY citizenship in the "new Northern Ireland": The case of a Belfast makerspace. In E. Gordon & P. Milhadis (Eds.), *Civic media project.* An Initiative of the Engagement Lab at Emerson College and MIT Press. Retrieved from http://civicmediaproject.org/works/civic-media-project/diycitizenshipinthenewnorthernireland.

Siefkes, C. (2009). The commons of the future: Building blocks for a commons-based society. *The Commoner*, March. Retrieved from http://www.commoner.org.uk/wp-content/uploads/2009/03/siefkes_future-commons.pdf.

Sleigh, A., Stewart, H. and Stokes, K. (2015). Open dataset of UK makerpspaces: A user's guide." London: NESTA. Retrieved from https://www.nesta.org.uk/sites/default/files/open_dataset_of_uk_makerspaces_users_guide.pdf.

Smith, A., Hielscher, S., Dickel, S., Söderberg, J., & van Oost, E. (2013). *Grassroots digital fabrication and makerspaces: Reconfiguring, relocating, and recalibrating innovation?* Science and Technology Policy Research Unit: University of Sussex. Retrieved from https://www.sussex.ac.uk/webteam/gateway/file.php?name=2013-02-swps-aps-sh-gdf-working-paper.pdf&site=25.

Smith, A. (2014). Technology networks for socially useful production. *Journal of Peer Production* (5). Retrieved from http://peerproduction.net/issues/issue-5-shared-machine-shops/.

Suchman, L. (2003). *Located accountabilities in technology production*. Centre for Science Studies, Lancaster, UK: Lancaster University. Retrieved from http://www.lancaster.ac.uk/fass/resources/sociology-online-papers/papers/suchman-located-accountabilities.pdf.

Star, S. L. (1999). The ethnography of infrastructure. *American Behavioral Scientist*, *43*(3), 377–91.

Toombs, A., Bardzell, S., & Bardzell, J. (2015). Becoming makers: Hackerspace member habits, values, and identities. *Journal of Peer Production*, (5). Retrieved from http://peerproduction.net/issues/issue-5-shared-machine-shops/.

Troxler, P. (2010). Commons-based peer-production of physical goods. Is there room for a hybrid innovation ecology? In *3rd free culture research conference*. Berlin, Germany.

Winner, L. (1980). Do artifacts have politics? *Daedelus*, *109*(1), 121–36.

*Chapter 14*

# Collective Digital Citizenship through Local Memory Websites

## Mike de Kreek and Liesbet van Zoonen

In this chapter, we discuss a double case study of collective empowerment within local memory websites from the perspective of digital citizenship. Local memory websites offer local residents a platform where they collect and share memories about particular places or experiences in their neighbourhoods and districts. Such digital memories can consist of audio recordings and videos, but in our case studies they are mainly pictures and text. Researchers and professionals alike have noted the potential of such websites to contribute to the well-being of a neighbourhood and its individual residents. In their studies, they have mentioned a wide range of social effects that ultimately could foster a stronger local community (Burgess, 2006; Stillman & Johanson, 2007; Garde-Hansen, Hoskins & Reading, 2009; Klaebe, Adkins, Foth & Hearn, 2009). However, it is unclear in the available literature how exactly the particular online dynamics of these websites contribute to these social effects (de Kreek & van Zoonen, 2013b). Our field study of 80 local memory websites, moreover, suggests that these online dynamics are strongly related to the way the websites are initiated and organised (de Kreek & van Zoonen, 2013a). These two observations have led us to question how organisational characteristics are connected to online dynamics and what kind of social effects these connections produce. Looking for answers, we present a detailed double case study of two local memory websites in Amsterdam: the Memory of East and the Memory of West.

The two websites are able to facilitate collective empowerment by resisting dominant influences of memory institutions, commercial popular culture and local politics. These findings align with Dahlgren's claim that civic engagement and the acquisition of corresponding competencies can manifest themselves in many kinds of public settings (Dahlgren, 2006). In these 'circuits of civic culture' (Dahlgren, 2003), digital citizenship can develop in the context of interlocking processes around practices, identities, values, trust, space and knowledge (Couldry et al., 2014). However, in this literature, acts of citizenship are predominantly discussed in terms of individual behaviour and possibilities, whereas a collective running a local memory website is also likely to have a social effect on its surrounding community, whether positive or negative. For example, the Memory of East developed into a website with only a few dominant topics, therewith unintentionally excluding residents who could not identify with these topics. In this chapter, we offer insights into such collective acts of citizenship by comparing the emergent online properties and organisational driving forces of the Memories of East and West. In addition, we argue that insights such as these should not remain in the academic realm but should be fed back into collective community practices. This is illustrated by showing how the research findings helped the involved groups to acquire new literacies about emergent properties of their websites and reconnect the group interest to the public good.

## EMPOWERMENT MEETS NARRATIVE IN ONLINE DYNAMICS

The two cases under study were the Memory of East and the Memory of West, referring to particular neighbourhoods in Amsterdam. Both websites were made by the same community software developer, which makes their online appearance similar to a high degree. The need for a comprehensive study arose out of a close collaboration between researchers and students of our university, the two memory websites and the involved organisations.

In 2001, the Amsterdam Museum started with the preparations for its first neighbourhood exhibition, called 'East, an Amsterdam Neighbourhood' (Ernst, 2006). The East area had a highly diverse population demonstrating various lifestyles and social backgrounds. The Amsterdam Museum was also unknown in this neighbourhood, which is why it wanted to promote itself among the inhabitants. In collaboration with a social welfare institute, an outreach project for the neighbourhood was set up in 2003. It consisted of collecting and sharing local memories on a website called the 'Memory of East'. The aims with this project consisted of 'improving social cohesion and accessibility, increasing skills and helping people to become better acquainted with art and culture, as well as the history of Amsterdam' (Ernst, 2006, p. 110). The exhibition finished in 2004, but the participants are still actively collecting memories and commenting on them online to the present day.

Inspired by the Memory of East, the 'Memory of West' was initiated in 2004 by the local government of a city district in 'New West' who partnered with a local community centre. In 2000, some of the district's areas with high concentrations of a few ethno-cultural groups were identified for urban renewal. The aim of urban renewal programmes was to foster greater socio-economic diversity and resilience. These redevelopment projects were set up in order to produce social cohesion by differentiation of 'a larger variety of apartments and environments as well as inhabitants' (translated from Hellinga, 2005, p. 86). In this context, the Memory of West aimed at 'increasing social cohesion in Amsterdam West, preventing social isolation among the inhabitants, improving the memory skills of the elderly and creating more tolerance among young and old by means of knowledge and understanding about each other and each other's past' (translated from Bekker & Helbergen, 2010, p. 1). The website is still active today in terms of both new stories and comments in the comment fields.

In order to identify a theoretical framework for conceptualising the social effects of both websites, we conducted a systematic review of the existing literature about local memory websites, from which we developed an analytical model that identifies empowerment on individual, group and community levels (see Figure 14. 1). This model aligns directly with empowerment theory: 'a multilevel construct applicable to individual citizens as well as to organisations and neighbourhoods' (Rappaport, 1987, p. 121). Potentially, local memory websites thus offer 'a mechanism by which people, organisations, and communities gain mastery over their affairs' (Rappaport, 1987, p. 122).

Existing research has identified how individuals can be empowered through their participation in local memory websites, that is, through experiencing pleasure, acquiring self-confidence or digital skills (Burgess, 2006). Much less is clear, however, about how local memory websites empower specific participating groups and the wider community in which they operate. In studying the online memory websites of East and West, we thus focused on assessing empowerment at the collective levels, specifically on the concepts marked with a letter (A, B etc.) in Figure 14.1. Moreover, we were interested in how these aspects of empowerment depended on the particular ways the websites were organised. Six organisational dimensions were identified on the basis of a field study of 80 local memory websites: the context, the participating partners, their aims, the characteristics of the memories, the ways of collecting them and the website's affordances (de Kreek & van Zoonen, 2013a).

We used the analytical model and the field study to focus our research question on the influence of organisational characteristics of online local memory websites on the empowerment of participating groups and the wider local community. However, we still needed an approach to connect the online dynamics of the websites to collective empowerment. We tackled this by using a combination of two narrative approaches to study the websites. The first approach consists of Rappaport's 'empowerment meets narrative' model (1995, p. 795), according to which personal stories and collective narratives are important

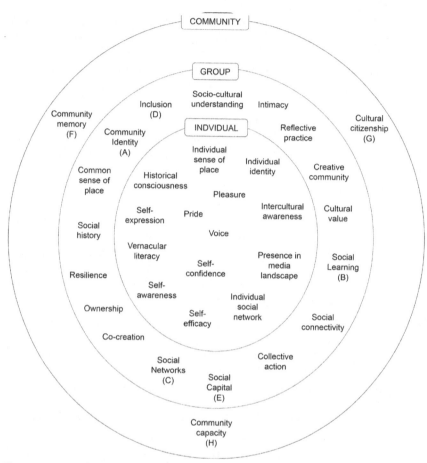

Figure 14.1  Analytical model for the social effects of a local memory website (de Kreek & van Zoonen, 2013b).

resources for empowerment. He argues, among other things, that inclusion in a collective identity is determined by 'what is allowed to be remembered' (Rappaport, 1998, p. 229). People who can relate to a collective narrative experience feel included in the collective identity, and those who do not have a connection feel excluded from it. In addition, Rappaport states that the mutual influence between personal, group and community narratives parallels the interdependencies across similar levels of empowerment (Rappaport, 1995; 2011).

The second approach was taken from Boje's work on organisational storytelling which provides a narrative method to identify collective aspects in large collections of stories (Boje, 2001). According to this approach, personal stories are not only part of someone's personal discourse but also part of a 'complex system of a collectively construed [discourse] of organisational "reality"' (Luhman & Boje, 2001, p. 163). This 'reality' as such can unintentionally or intentionally exclude or include people or groups, as with Rappaport's claims about collective narratives. Changes in organisational context and dominance of individual or group discourses can force one 'reality' into another. Assuming that organisational storytelling has similar dynamics as neighbourhood storytelling, the narrative methods applied in the former are applicable in the latter. Consequently, we have adopted 'story network analysis' as formulated by Boje (2001) to analyse the features of the online memories. This involved scraping the websites for the public features of the memories and complementing this with non-public elements from copies of both databases. The resulting data, covering more than ten years of activity, was subject to an exploratory data analysis (Tukey, 1977), for which the analytical model arrived at in Figure 14.1 provides the sensitising concepts, that is, 'directions along which to look' (Blumer, 1954, p. 7).

## COLLECTIVE EMPOWERMENT EXPRESSED IN ONLINE DYNAMICS

In order to arrive at meaningful elements in the online dynamics, we iteratively explored possible relations between patterns in the data and concepts from our analytical model. This resulted in three composite indicators of collective empowerment: online diversity, online activity and online participation. The developments of these indicators for each case are depicted in Figure 14.2, which gives a heuristic summary of the findings.

Over time, the online diversity in the Memory of West increases in terms of the keywords (topics, locations and periods), whereas this decreases in the Memory of East. On both websites, the online activity (number of stories and comments) and participation (number of different participants) fluctuates, but in the Memory of West these indicators develop more in parallel than in the Memory of East. This implies that the ratio between the numbers of contributions and participants delivering them remains stable. However, in the Memory of East, the online activity is relatively high and steeply rising in relation to the number of persons participating online, especially over the last five years. This means that the number of contributions per participant increases. For the Memory of West, both participation and online activity in 2013 drop to a level lower than the previous five years.

The analysis also related the patterns of three described indicators in Figure 14.2 to three concepts on the level of group empowerment in Figure 14.1, forming collective identities (A), social learning (B) and social networking (C). We assume that being part of a collective identity is

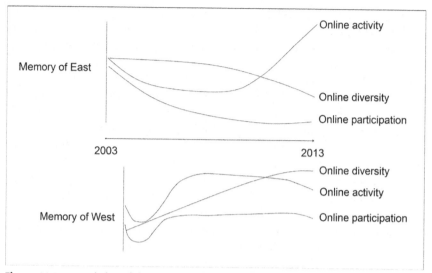

**Figure 14.2**  Heuristics of the development of three indicators in the online dynamics.

constrained by what that collective defines as worthwhile to remember (Rappaport, 1998). This implies that online diversity in terms of remembered topics and periods is directly related to the variation of identities different people can identify with. Consequently, focusing on its increasing online diversity, the Memory of West can be seen to be empowering in terms of available collective identities for its highly diverse population to connect with. Vice versa, the Memory of East disempowers certain groups, because the decrease in online diversity lowers the set of available collective identities for these groups to relate to.

If '[v]irtually all human knowledge is based on stories constructed around past experiences' (Schank & Abelson, 1995, p. 1), then the online activities of remembering constitute an important social learning process. This means that online activities, especially online comments on stories, reflect the degree to which participants exchange and discuss facts, experiences and beliefs, and learn from this. Although the total of online memories is nearly similar between the two cases, the activity in comments in the Memory of East (about 20,000) is much higher than in the Memory of West (about 9,000). This indicates that empowerment in terms of social learning is more fruitful on the website of East than on the one in West.

Gilchrist claims that in 'strong and sustainable communities' (2009, p. 12) the community network consists of a balanced variation in bonding capital (strong ties), bridging capital (weak ties) and linking capital (links beyond peer boundaries). In our study, we assume that online participation of many different residents, rather than a few, offers better preconditions for such a balance. The preconditions for network variation in the Memory of East lowered following the decrease in online participation. The Memory of West has been more stable, both in online participation and, thus, in the social networking preconditions. Consequently, looking solely at the developments of online participation, the heuristics imply that the social networking configuration is more empowering in the Memory of West than in the Memory of East.

A closer look at the interdependencies between the three discussed group concepts of collective empowerment sheds light on two more: inclusion and social capital (D and E in Figure 14.1). The presumably dense social networks, but with few participants, in the Memory of East, combined with its high level of social learning and dominant collective identities, imply stronger social capital than the Memory of West represents. This manifestation of social capital seems to be embedded in a self-affirming process, because the developments in the three other concepts are connected to each other. That is, a small, dense network with a strong collective identity and satisfying interactions between participants presumably has no immediate, intrinsic reason to change. On the other hand, the multiple collective identities in the Memory of West, carried by large, light networks with low levels of social learning, result in a more inclusive website than the Memory of East. The developments causing this inclusivity also keep each other in balance. That is, the multiple collective identities and light networks fuel each other's characteristics through incidental online activity in which new memories are added and new people briefly meet each other in comments.

## ORGANISATIONAL INFLUENCE ON COLLECTIVE EMPOWERMENT

In what follows, we explain how the differences in the organisational aspects between both cases can explain the differences in their collective empowerment. This leads to five organisational continuums, each with its own extremes, on which the cases can be positioned: context, partners, aims, digital memories and collecting memories. Both websites' affordances are left out based on their high degree of similarity.

### Context: From Preserving to Pioneering

In terms of context, the main differences between the Memory of East and Memory of West can be found in the age of their neighbourhoods and in the way they dealt with gentrification processes.

The main parts of Amsterdam East were developed in the 60 years before the Second World War. In this sense, this area has long been a traditional residential area of the city of Amsterdam. Once gentrification processes started in the 1970s, many residents rejected the city renewal and the government facilitating it. Around 1990, this led to the decision of the district administration to concentrate city renewal projects on preserving and restoring buildings. It seems likely that this wish to preserve was present among the participants who remained active after the exhibition finished in 2004. Collecting stories and pictures gave them a chance to focus on preserving the past, before it got lost. This has resulted in collective identities with which the residents who have childhood memories of the neighbourhood can identify. Other people, for young people or elderly who grew up somewhere else, cannot relate to these identities very well.

Amsterdam New West predominantly came into being in the 25 years following the war. People who moved there were considered, and considered themselves, as pioneers. Gentrification-driven city renewal started to play a role in the 1990s, offering a solution to two supposedly intertwined problems. There were so-called concentrations of ethnic groups that, according to the local media, threatened integration and lowered the image of their neighbourhoods. Restructuring certain neighbourhoods would dissolve the concentrations and would increase the market value. Although many projects were effected, this chain of arguments received a growing amount of criticism and, eventually, did not hold. What did hold, and probably got stimulated by these events, was the sentiment of being pioneers and newcomers in New West, be it 5 or 30 years ago. The people who participated in the Memory of West wanted to collect stories that celebrated this pioneering character by expressing the incentives and experiences of these adventurers. Instead of age and length of residence determining the validity of a person's memories, a person's first experiences after their arrival in New West offered the content for the online memories. This way, as opposed to the website in East, the highly diverse population in New West produced a variety of collective identities its residents could identify with.

## Partners: From 'Do It Yourself' to 'Do It Together'

The ways in which memory collecting has been organised differ between the two cases in terms of how projects are set up with partners and how the core teams are composed.

The Memory of East was supported by institutional professionals until 2007. Workshops were provided for target groups at organisations, without collaborating at an organisational level. The cultural entrepreneurs of the Memory of West, on the other hand, were able to set up subsidised collaborations and events into 2012. In these collaborations, win-win situations were created in which the aims of the Memory of West and those of a partner would overlap or complement each other. Consequently, the memory-collecting activities were strongly embedded in the partners' regular core business and in their physical environment. Methodological differences also had an impact, with the workshop-based approach in East and collaboration-steered process in New West both having their pros and cons. On the one hand, a workshop programme is easier to organise than collaboration in terms of alignment and negotiations. On the other hand, collaborations are likely to be more sustainable than a sequence of workshops if a steady stream of memories is the goal. More importantly, in New West, collaboration with partners in other locations contributed to diversity in the collective identities participants could identify with. This did not apply to the Memory of East.

The Memory of East had a mixed core team in terms of residents and professionals until the end of 2007. After that, a single cultural entrepreneur, hired by the museum since 2003, was both webmaster and the key figure in the story-collecting workshops. Despite her central role, her involvement was not funded during the year before the transfer of responsibility to the residents, which occurred in 2010. This resulted in disappointment among the people who were directly involved. From that moment, only residents who strongly identified with the more distant past of Amsterdam East and had time to invest made up the team that collected memories. The core team of the Memory of West always consisted of a tight group of cultural entrepreneurs, volunteering professionals and active residents. The entrepreneurs were closely connected to the core processes of collecting memories and organising the conditions necessary for it. The Memory of West also had a number of volunteering professionals. One person, for example, was professionally linked to the local newspaper but also wrote reportages for the Memory of West and sometimes the same stories for both. Another example was a copywriter, who also liked to write attractive, short stories about everyday topics for the Memory of West.

In summary, the Memory of East developed into a self-organising group of residents doing all the collecting activities themselves. The Memory of West, on the contrary, could be considered as a collaborative setting with a natural balance between various organisations, professionals and residents. It seems likely that this variation stimulated the presence of several perspectives in the organisation of the Memory of West and the creation of multiple collective identities people could relate to. Consequently, it evolved into a more inclusive community than the Memory of East, with less perspectives present in the core group.

## Aims: From Abstract to Concrete

Two important differences between the websites, in terms of communicated aims, are the attention to vulnerable citizens and the local embeddedness.

On a rather abstract level, both cases aim for social cohesion, social participation and belonging in the neighbourhood. Both cases also elaborate on their aims, such as stimulating contact across ages and backgrounds, sharing stories and emotions related to the neighbourhood and improving knowledge about the sociocultural history. The first difference is that the social participation aims of the Memory of West became more concrete and applicable than those of the Memory of East. In the context of participation of possibly vulnerable citizens, the Memory of West mentions improving self-esteem of youngsters, women and seniors, increasing computer skills and enhancing the memory function of the elderly. The Memory of East limits the concrete aims to computer skills. The second noteworthy difference is that in relation to social cohesion, the Memory of West wants to improve tolerance. Tolerance, according to the website, is the growth of reciprocal knowledge and understanding which is attributed to the sharing of memories. This elaboration of the way tolerance might be improved reflects the knowledge and experience of the multicultural centre in which the Memory of West has been embedded during its entire existence. In addition, it gives more urgency to the involvement of a variety of groups or neighbourhoods. Both the concrete attention for certain groups and connection with the multicultural centre have contributed to a continuous presence and inclusion of a variety of participants, as such ensuring multiple identities many people can relate to.

## Digital Memories: From Distant to Recent Past

The main difference in the characteristics of the memories between the two cases concerns news report items of the Memory of West.

These items have always been part of the category 'News' on the website, but they were also categorised for a number of years under the header 'Stories about the present'. Most of these contributions, as the name indicates, account for issues, experiences and events that are embedded in the present or the recent past. Some of them explicitly report on changes in certain neighbourhoods or openings and events of various sorts. Others concern more personal reports around a certain experience like a visit to a museum or a park. A third example consists of photo reports in which participants represent themselves or their neighbourhood. With 'Stories about the present', the Memory of West initiated projects with groups of participants ranging from young people to the elderly. Individual writers also contributed to this category on their own behalf. The resulting combination of content about the more distant past (around 2000 items) and the recent past (around 1000 items) relates to the high online diversity and multiple identities people in New West associate with. The Memory of East used to have a category 'News', but it was used only occasionally for announcements. Moreover, spreading announcements was not regarded as a core activity, which is why it ended up in disuse. Consequently, the Memory of East predominantly invited people to contribute memories about the distant past, which tended to attract people over the age of 60 who liked to share their childhood memories. This explains the general tendency of the Memory of East to primarily contain memories about the distant past that many of the present residents cannot easily identify with.

## Collecting Memories: From Numbers to Variety

Two final differences between the cases can be found in the actual collecting of memories and publicising them.

The Memory of East remained under the wings of the museum until 2010, although the role of professionals in supporting the project decreased after 2006. In 2010, the responsibility of the website was handed over to a small group of volunteer enthusiasts, who, owing to available time, wanted to take up that challenge. The independence was partial, however, because the hosting of the website was still financed by the museum. The core group of participants developed the idea that success in terms of high numbers of published stories and website visitors would convince the museum to continue financing the hosting. Moreover, success in these terms was feasible, because there were some specialists in a limited set of topics, who also had easy access to content. In addition, spreading new memories through Twitter and Facebook also reached a rather steady group of visitors and elicited comments. In terms of social learning based on high online activity, these developments were promising, with the network becoming smaller and denser and gathering around dominant topics. These topics fitted the sentiment of preserving the distant past since they covered, among others, the Jewish past, former neighbourhood shops and former soccer clubs.

After the Memory of West became an independent association, three years after the beginning of the project, entrepreneurial heritage professionals became involved. These professionals were able to translate the adventurous character of the community to other organisations in New West. They not only applied successfully for subsidies but also organised the networks and collaborations explicitly with partners from other districts' neighbourhoods. In these projects, digital memories about various other locations in New West were collected and intentionally produced by different participants. This kept the variety of the social network configuration high in terms of strong and weak ties, and also enabled boundary crossing. More importantly, it increased the number of identities inhabitants of the various neighbourhoods felt they could relate to. To summarise, the positioning of each of the websites on the continuums results in Figure 14.3.

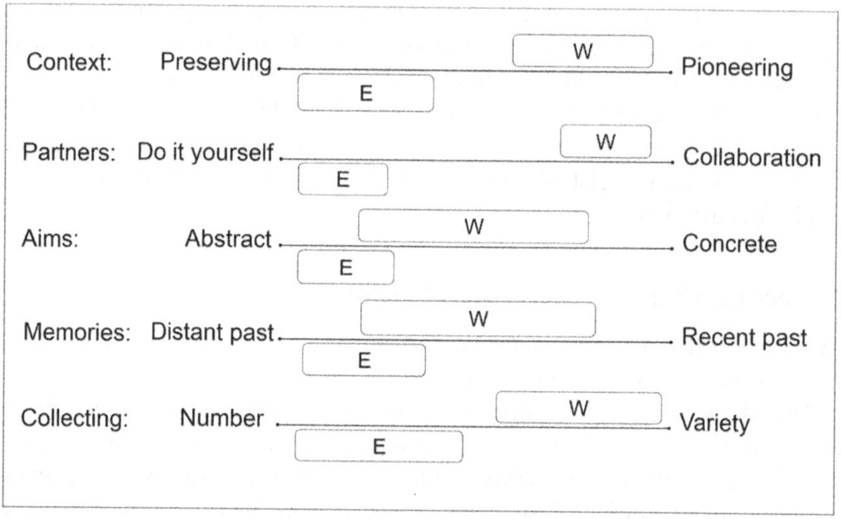

Figure 14.3   Five continuums based on the organisational dimensions.

## COLLECTIVE ACTS OF DIGITAL CITIZENSHIP

In the previous two sections, we have shown that the way each of the local memory websites is organised has specific influences on group levels of empowerment through emergent properties in its online dynamics. With respect to the study of such digital infrastructures, Couldry et al. states we should be 'open both to new "acts of citizenship" . . . *and* to a wider set of processes that constitute civic culture's starting-points' (2014, p. 615). Acts of citizenship are acts based on orientations, strategies and technologies through which the actors become 'claim-making' subjects, either intentional, based on rationality, or unintentional, based on affection (Isin, 2008). Exploring digital citizenship in narrative settings, Couldry et al. (2014) focus on the processes fostering a civic culture and less on the actual acts that are performed, whereas we focus on both. In addition, contrary to the mentioned studies of citizenship that focus on the individual subject, in this chapter we put more emphasis on collectives performing acts of digital citizenship.

Since the organisation underlying our cases could also be done differently, we argue that the influence of the website on its surrounding community is an 'act of digital citizenship' undertaken by the core group participants. Uncovering the specific acts of each case requires further zooming in on the relation between the group and the community levels of empowerment (see Figure 14.1). Our literature review about local memory websites shows that, in terms of community memory (F), residents are able to create a shared view of how their neighbourhood should be presented online for future use (de Kreek & van

Zoonen, 2013b). With respect to cultural citizenship (G), the existing literature claims that these online environments offer a public sphere where meanings and cultural values are negotiated. Finally, community capacity (H) is attributed to emerging online social networks, where members create discourses in favour of future collective action. Both websites can be claimed to foster the construction of community memory, the practice of cultural citizenship and the growth of community capacity, but they do so in fundamentally different ways.

The Memory of West has a weak online reputation consisting of an inclusive variation of collective identities representing sparsely knit networks which have a number of scattered online social learning places. This corresponds with the argument that '[c]ommunity-level empowerment outcomes . . . include evidence of pluralism, and existence of organisational coalitions, and accessible community resources' (Perkins & Zimmerman, 1995, p. 570). The Memory of East has a strong online reputation in terms of an exclusive collective identity representing a few tightly knit groups of participants each having their own active social learning environment. This matches with collective empowerment comprising the 'capability to reward (or punish) causal agents, influence public debate and policy, and shape community ideology and consciousness' (Zimmerman, 2000, p. 57). With its stronger social capital, the Memory of East is more likely to resist official memory intuitions, commercial popular culture and local politics than the Memory of West. On the other hand, with its more inclusive character, the Memory of West is more representative for the broad cultural backgrounds of its inhabitants than the Memory of East. We regard these emergent properties of both websites—ultimately the capability to resist or to represent—as collective acts of digital citizenship. To take responsibility for or to change these properties requires new literacies with respect to the online dynamics and the organisational characteristics of these websites.

## NEW LITERACIES FOR COLLECTIVE DIGITAL CITIZENSHIP

We had, and still have, a close relation to the Memory of East and the Memory of West. Consequently, our approach is inspired by the thoughts about 'making social science matter', which is elaborated by Bent Flyvbjerg in his book of the same title (2001). In this context, 'phronetic social research' is described as being 'about producing knowledge that can challenge power not in theory but in ways that inform real efforts to produce change' (Schram, 2012, p. 20). This kind of research is not concerned with generalisable, predictive models but focuses on answering four questions related to enhancing practical wisdom in a certain context (Flyvbjerg, Landman & Schram, 2012, p. 5):

1. Where are we going (with this practice)?
2. Who gains and who loses and by which mechanisms of power?
3. Is this development desirable?
4. What, if anything, should we do about it?

Following these questions, the organisational continuums in Figure 14.3 and their relation to empowerment have made it possible to reconsider the developments of both websites with the relevant stakeholders. Ideas about how to redirect certain developments towards the future have emerged. This is an ongoing conversation that has already started on various occasions where preliminary insights of our research were discussed directly or indirectly. With 'directly' we mean dedicated events where we presented insights that were validated and discussed in terms of whether what they implied was desirable or not. More 'indirectly', we followed up on certain topics in conversations during less-orchestrated meetings, this way amplifying the opportunity to collectively shape our thoughts.

The best way to illustrate how the insights produced in our research partly fuelled the conversations and discussions about the above-mentioned four questions is to turn to an example of a recent development in one of the communities. In the Memory of East, there has been a longer discussion during the monthly meetings about the tension between success in terms of numbers and in variety. This proves to be hard to resolve, because the two perspectives differs reflect different priorities. One person may say how impressive it is that an online memory was visited 350 times during two days, because it was spread through Twitter and Facebook. Another person may say that a shy and vulnerable workshop participant has just published a very personal story online after working on it for months and being hesitant to share it. To ensure the future of the website, the number of visitors for many seems like a stronger argument than that one single memory.

During a focus group meeting, we used the metaphor of an anthill to explain that the website as a whole has emergent properties we are not always aware of. Following that, we showed how the online diversity had decreased since 2010 and that the increasing online activity corresponds to a decreasing group of participants. Interesting enough, this was recognised immediately and interpreted in terms of various organisational aspects. But, more importantly, it also fuelled the discussion about the different faces of success. The numerical character of the graphs visualising the decrease of diversity made the urgency for involving 'other' residents, topics and neighbourhoods as real as the importance of numbers of website visitors. The introduction of the visuals brought the two convictions about what constitutes success into conversation with each other on a more equal level. A result was that it fuelled the appreciation for efforts that involved new groups, new neighbourhoods and new collaborations. In the wake of this, more stories of the recent past were contributed to the website. Consequently, the zone covered by the Memory of East grows towards the 'Variety' side on the 'Collecting' continuum in Figure 14.3.

It is an important insight for both of the communities in New West and in East that such a quest is not an either-or choice, but both sides on the continuum can exist at the same time without the one affecting the other. The opposite of this is often called the 'zero-sum game' with the central idea that one's increase of power implies the other's decrease in power (Narayan, 2005). In most empowerment literature, sharing social power is not considered as such a 'win-lose' choice. On the contrary, it is a '"win-win" phenomenon whereby providers gain as well as recipients' (Staples, 2004, p. 214). Moreover, 'it can actually strengthen while being shared with others' (Hur, 2006, p. 524).

## CONCLUSIONS

Theories of empowerment and citizenship mention processes and outcomes. Dahlgren's 'civic culture' points to a set of interlocking processes that facilitate individual 'people's actual participation in the public sphere, in civil and political society' (Dahlgren, 2003, pp. 154–155). Empowerment theory covers similar interdependent processes but also includes collective processes and outcomes: 'a mechanism by which people, organisations, and communities gain mastery over their affairs' (Rappaport, 1987, p. 122). Following Couldry et al.'s suggestion to look for new acts of citizenship and underlying processes in digital environments (2014), we have related the two local memory websites' emergent empowerment properties to collective acts of citizenship. Ultimately, the first case was described as being better able to resist dominant local discourses and the second as being more representative for its neighbourhoods' residents. Moreover, we showed how these acts are embedded in the core groups' characteristics along five organisational continuums. Our findings show that it is important not only to study cultural dynamics in an online public sphere to learn about individual civic agency (Dahlgren, 2006) but also to examine the relation between the interests of the core group of participants and the common good of the community. Our close relationship with both cases urged us to feed back the research results to both core groups. This helped them to acquire new literacies about the emergent properties of their collective actions and the organisational aspects with which they could influence this. Based on this, we would like to advocate this participatory approach in order to make research in digital citizenship matter to the communities it makes claims about.

# REFERENCES

Bekker, L., & Helbergen, W. van. (2010). *Geheugen van West—Rapportageperiode juni 2009–december 2009 (Memory of West: Reporting period June 2009–December 2009).*

Blumer, H. (1954). What is wrong with social theory? *American Sociological Review,* *19*(1), 3–10.

Boje, D. M. (2001). *Narrative methods for organizational and communication research.* London: Sage Publications.

Boje, D. M. (2008). *Storytelling organizations.* London: Sage Publications.

Burgess, J. (2006). Hearing ordinary voices: Cultural studies, vernacular creativity and digital storytelling. *Continuum: Journal of Media and Cultural Studies, 20*(2), 201–214.

Couldry, N., Stephansen, H., Fotopoulou, A., MacDonald, R., Clark, W., & Dickens, L. (2014). Digital citizenship? Narrative exchange and the changing terms of civic culture. *Citizenship Studies, 18*(6–7), 615–629.

Dahlgren, P. (2003). Reconfiguring civic culture in the new media milieu. In J. Corner & D. Pels (Red.), *Media and political style: Essays on representation and civic culture* (pp. 151–170). London: Sage Publications.

Dahlgren, P. (2006). Doing citizenship: The cultural origins of civic agency in the public sphere. *European Journal of Cultural Studies, 9*(3), 267–286.

De Kreek, M., & Van Zoonen, L. (2013a). New directions in research on local memory websites. *Journal of Social Intervention: Theory and Practice, 22*(2), 113–130.

De Kreek, M., & Van Zoonen, L. (2013a). Mapping an emerging field: Local memory websites. In L. Stillman, A. Sabiescu, & N. Memarovic (Red.), *Nexus, confluence, and difference: Community archives meets community informatics–Prato CIRN Conference Oct 28–30 2013.* Prato Italy: Monash Uiversity. Geraadpleegd van http://cirn.infotech.monash.edu/assets/docs/prato2013_papers/de_kreek2.pdf.

Ernst, M. (2006). East Amsterdam, an outreach project. In R. Kistemaker (Red.), *City museums as centres of civic dialogue?–Proceedings of the fourth conference of the international association of city museums* (pp. 107–112). Amsterdam: Amsterdam Historical Museum.

Flyvbjerg, B. (2001). *Making social science matter.* New York: Cambridge University Press.

Flyvbjerg, B., Landman, T., & Schram, S. (Red.). (2012). *Real social science–Applied phronesis.* New York: Cambridge University Press.

Garde-Hansen, J., Hoskins, A., & Reading, A. (Red.). (2009). *Save as ... digital memories.* Basingstoke: Palgrave Macmillan.

Gilchrist, A. (2009). *The well-connected community.* Bristol: Policy Press.

Hellinga, H. (2005). *Onrust in park en stad–stedelijke vernieuwing in de Amsterdamse Westelijke Tuinsteden (Turbulance in park and city–urban renewal in the Western Garden Districts of Amsterdam).* Amsterdam: Het Spinhuis.

Hur, M. H. (2006). Empowerment in terms of theoretical perspectives: exploring a typology of the process and components. *Journal of Community Psychology, 34,* 523–540.

Isin, E. F. (2008). Theorizing acts of citizenship. In E. F. Isin & G. M. Nielsen (Red.), *Acts of citizenship* (pp. 15–43). London: Zed Books.

Klaebe, H., Adkins, B., Foth, M., & Hearn, G. (2009). Embedding an ecology notion in the social production of urban space. In M. Foth (Red.), *Handbook of research on urban informatics: The practice and promise of the real-time city* (pp. 179–194). Hershey, PA: Information Science Reference, IGI Global.

Luhman, J. T., & Boje, D. M. (2001). What is complexity science? A possible answer from narrative research. *Emergence, 3*(1), 158–169.

Narayan, D. (Red.). (2005). *Measuring empowerment: Cross-disciplinary perspectives.* Washington DC: The World Bank.

Perkins, D. D., & Zimmerman, M. A. (1995). Empowerment theory, research, and application. *American Journal of Community Psychology, 23*(5), 569–579.

Rappaport, J. (1987). Terms of empowerment - exemplars of prevention: Toward a theory for community psychology. *American Journal of Community Psychology, 15*(2), 121–148.

Rappaport, J. (1995). Empowerment meets narrative: Listening to stories and creating settings. *American Journal of Community Psychology, 23*(5), 795–807.

Rappaport, J. (1998). The art of social change: Community narratives as resources for individual and collective identity. In (Red.), *Addressing community problems: Psychosocial research and intervention* (pp. 225–245). Thousand Oaks: SAGE Publications.

Rappaport, J. (2011). Searching for Oz: Empowerment, crossing boundaries, and telling our story. In M. S. Aber, K. I. Maton, & E. Seidman (Red.), *Empowering settings and voices for social change* (pp. 232–237). New York: Oxford University Press.

Schank, R. C., & Abelson, R. P. (1995). Knowledge and memory: The real story. In R. S. Wyer (Red.), *Knowledge and memory: The real story* (pp. 1–85). Hillsdale, NJ: Lawrence Erlbaum Associates.

Schram, S. (2012). Phronetic social science: An idea whose time has come. In B. Flyvbjerg, T. Landman, & S. Schram (Red.), *The real social science* (pp. 15–26). New York: Cambridge University Press.

Staples, L. (2004). *Roots to Power–a manual for grassroots organizing.* Westport: Praeger.

Stillman, L., & Johanson, G. (Red.). (2007). *Constructing and Sharing memory: Community informatics, identity and empowerment.* Newcastle upon Tyne: Cambridge Scholars Publishing.

Tukey, J. W. (1977). *Exploratory data analysis.* Reading, MA: Addison-Wesley.

Zimmerman, M. A. (2000). Empowerment theory–psychological, organizational and community levels of analysis. In J. Rappaport & E. Seidman (Red.), *Handbook of community psychology* (pp. 43–63). Dordrecht: Kluwer Academic Publisher.

# Index

# About the Contributors

**Kath Albury** is an Associate Professor in the School of the Arts and Media, UNSW Australia. Her current research projects focus on young people's practices of digital self-representation, and the role of user-generated media (including social networking platforms) in young people's formal and informal sexual learning.

**Bronwyn Carlson** is an Associate Professor in Indigenous Studies at the University of Wollongong. She is the recipient of two Australian Research Council grants. The first explores Aboriginal identity and community online on social media and the second is an examination of Aboriginal help-seeking behaviours on social media.

**Philippa Collin** is a Senior Research Fellow at the Institute for Culture and Society at Western Sydney University. Philippa's research focuses on the social and political dimensions of children and young people's digital media practices, participation and citizenship, mental health and well-being as well as the role of participatory research and design approaches for rethinking key concepts in social science.

**Mike de Kreek** teaches qualitative research methods in the Social Work Master Program at the Amsterdam University of Applied Sciences. He is also part of a Cultural and Social Dynamics research group in the Amsterdam Research Institute for Societal Innovation. There, he focuses on collective processes in the nexus between Internet, memories and locality. http://www.amsterdamuas.com/arisi.

**Ryan Frazer** is a Research Fellow at the University of Wollongong, working on a project that explores Indigenous people's use of social media and its relation to identity, community and help seeking. He is also working on a PhD, unpacking the experiences of people who volunteer with refugees and the politics of care.

**Gerard Goggin** is a Professor of Media and Communications at the University of Sydney. He is also an Australian Research Council Future Fellow, working on disability, digital technology and human rights. Gerard's key books include *Disability and the Media* (2015), *Global Mobile Media* (2011), *Cell Phone Culture* (2006), *Disability in Australia* (2005) and *Digital Disability* (2003).

**Amelia Johns** is an Alfred Deakin Institute (Deakin University) Research Fellow. Her research engages with issues of youth identity, intercultural relations and digital modes of political participation. Her work has been published in a number of journals and more recently as a book, *Battle for the Flag* (2015).

**Sian Lincoln** is a Senior Lecturer in Media Studies at Liverpool John Moores University, UK. Her research interests are in contemporary youth culture, youth culture and private space, and young peoples' uses of social media. Her book *Youth Culture and Private Space* was published in 2012 (Palgrave Macmillan), and she has published in a number of journals and edited collections.

**Deborah Lupton** is a Centenary Research Professor in the News & Media Research Centre, Faculty of Arts & Design, University of Canberra. Her latest books are *The Quantified Self: A Sociology of Self-Tracking* (2016) and *Digital Sociology* (2015).

**Anthony McCosker** is a Senior Lecturer and researcher in Media and Communication at Swinburne University of Technology. His research explores new media technology, digital and visual cultures, social media publics and practices, digital citizenship and digital health. He is author of the book *Intensive Media: Aversive Affect and Visual Culture*. For more information, see swinburne.academia.edu/AnthonyMcCosker.

**Andrew Quodling** is a doctoral candidate in the Digital Media Research Centre at Queensland University of Technology. His research examines how users and operators of social media services negotiate social and political conflict and the influence these conflicts have on the governance of social platforms and other online spaces.

**Abbas Rattani** is more notably known as the co-founder of MIP-STERZ | Muslim Hipsters and as the co-creator and producer of the critically acclaimed short film *Somewhere In America #MIPSTERZ*. He is also known for his work in comedy, music, film, Islamic studies and ethics.

**Brady Robards** is a Lecturer in Sociology at the University of Tasmania. His research explores how young people use and thus produce social media, with a focus on reflexive identity work. Brady's work appears in journals such as *New Media & Society, Young, Continuum,* and *Sociology*. Recent books include *Youth Cultures & Subcultures: Australian Perspectives*, and *Mediated Youth Cultures*. For more, see bradyrobards.com.

**Pip Shea** is a digital media researcher, maker and educator. She investigates how digital cultures and new organisational forms are shaping creative, civic and activist practices. She is a director at Farset Labs makerspace and technology charity in Belfast, Northern Ireland.

**Eugenia Siapera** is the Deputy Director of the Institute for Future Media and Journalism and the Chair of the MA in Social Media Communications at Dublin City University in Ireland. She is the author of *Understanding New Media* (Sage 2011, second edition forthcoming) and the co-editor of the *Handbook of Global Online Journalism* (Wiley, 2012).

**Amanda Third** is the Principal Research Fellow in the Institute for Culture and Society at Western Sydney University and Research Program Leader in the Young and Well Cooperative Research Centre (2011–2016). Third's current research investigates the sociocultural dimensions of young people's engagements with technology and engages in research knowledge practices.

**Liesbet van Zoonen** is a Professor of Sociology at Erasmus University Rotterdam and Dean of the Graduate School of Social Sciences and Humanities. Her work focuses on the meanings of popular culture for social and political issues.

**Sonja Vivienne** is a Lecturer and Researcher of Digital Media at Flinders University of South Australia. Her work explores digital self-representation, online advocacy and privacy with particular attention to queer and gender-diverse identities. In 2016 she published *Digital Identity as Everyday Activism: Sharing Private Stories with Networked Publics* in the Palgrave Macmillan series for 'Communication for Social Change'.

Made in the USA
Las Vegas, NV
14 January 2022

41261761R00173